Also by Julie Lavender

Creative Sleepovers for Kids!:
Fun Activities, Themes, and Ideas for
Overnight Parties for Boys or Girls

February 28   Lent
February 29   Leap Year Day

 # March

March 1   National Pig Day
March 2   Children's Author and Illustrator Week
March 3   National Anthem Day
March 4   Dentists' Day
March 5   National Shoe Week
March 6   Purim
March 7   Art Week
March 8   March Winds Day
March 9   False Teeth Day
March 10   Jerusalem Temple Rebuilt
March 11   Paper Day
March 12   Girl Scout Birthday
March 13   National Procrastination Week
March 14   Earmuff Day
March 15   Escalator Day
March 16   National Craft Month
March 17   Saint Patrick's Day
March 18   Rubber Band Day
March 19   National Bubble Week
March 20   Spring
March 21   National Agriculture Week
March 22   International Day of the Seal
March 23   National Frozen Food Month
March 24   Pecan Day
March 25   Feast of the Annunciation
March 26   National Umbrella Month
March 27   National Noodle Month
March 28   No Homework Day
March 29   Let's-Go-Fly-a-Kite Month
March 30   Doctors' Day
March 31   Eiffel Tower Day

April

April 1   April Fools' Day

April 2   National Grilled Cheese Sandwich Month

April 3   Holy Humor Month

April 4   Golden Rule Week

April 5   National Library Month

April 6   Passover

April 7   Palm Sunday

April 8   Mathematics Education Month

April 9   National Garden Month

April 10   National D.A.R.E. Day

April 11   Maundy Thursday

April 12   Good Friday

April 13   Easter Even

April 14   Easter

April 15   Income Tax Day

April 16   Eraser Day

April 17   National Week of the Ocean

April 18   National Automobile Month

April 19   National Coin Week

April 20   National Poetry Month

April 21   National Wildlife Week

April 22   "In God We Trust" Anniversary

April 23   National Science and Technology Week

April 24   Feast of Unleavened Bread

April 25   Seeing Eye Dog Anniversary

April 26   Boston Marathon Day

April 27   Reading-Is-Fun Week

April 28   Feast of Firstfruits

April 29   Zipper Day

April 30   National Honesty Day

May

May 1   Cheerio Day

May 2   King James Bible Publication Anniversary

May 3   National Barbecue Month

May 4   National Day of Prayer

May 5   Older Americans Month

May 6   National Tourism Week

May 7   Be-Kind-to-Animals Week

May 8   National Raisin Week

May 9   World Red Cross Day

May 10   Astronomy Week

May 11   National Postcard Week

May 12   National Windmill Day

May 13   Mother's Day

May 14   Small Business Week

May 15   National Bike Month

May 16   National Nurses' Week

May 17   Police Week

May 18   National Strawberry Month

May 19   International Museum Day

May 20   International Pickle Week

May 21   National Salvation Army Week

May 22   National Waitresses-Waiters Day

May 23   Atlas Day

May 24   Ascension Day

May 25   National Photo Month

May 26   National Backyard Games Week

May 27   National Egg Month

May 28   Memorial Day

May 29   National Salad Month

May 30   National Book Month

May 31   National Moving Month

June

June 1   Donut Day
June 2   Feast of Weeks
June 3   Pentecost
June 4   National Iced Tea Month
June 5   National Fishing Week
June 6   National Fragrance Week
June 7   Boone Day (Honors Daniel Boone)
June 8   Vacuum Cleaner Day
June 9   Children's Sunday
June 10   Ball Point Pen Anniversary
June 11   National Little League Baseball Week
June 12   Dairy Month
June 13   American Rivers Month
June 14   Flag Day
June 15   Cracker Jacks Day
June 16   Father's Day
June 17   World Juggling Day
June 18   Aquarium Month
June 19   Juneteenth
June 20   Bald Eagle Day
June 21   Summer
June 22   National Rose Month
June 23   National Forgiveness Day
June 24   Insect Appreciation Day
June 25   Fork Day
June 26   Beautician's Day
June 27   National Recycling Month
June 28   Zoo Month
June 29   Fireworks Safety Month
June 30   Tightrope Walk Day

July

July 1   International Joke Day
July 2   Halfway Point of Year
July 3   I Forgot Day

365 Days of Celebration & Praise

Daily Devotions and Activities for Homeschooling Families

Julie Lavender

Foreword by
Maureen McCaffrey Williamson

JOSSEY-BASS
A Wiley Imprint
www.josseybass.com

The publisher and the author have made every reasonable effort to insure that the activities in the book are safe when conducted as instructed but assume no responsibility for any damage caused or sustained while performing the activities in this book. Parents, guardians, and/or teachers should supervise young people who undertake the activities in this book.

Jossey-Bass books and products are available through most bookstores. To contact Jossey-Bass directly call our Customer Care Department within the U.S. at 800–956–7739, outside the U.S. at 317–572–3986 or fax 317–572–4002.

Jossey-Bass also publishes its books in a variety of electronic formats. Some content that appears in print may not be available in electronic books.

Library of Congress Cataloging-in-Publication Data

Lavender, Julie.
   365 days of celebration and praise: daily devotions and activities for homeschooling families / Julie Lavender; foreword by Maureen McCaffrey Williamson.—1st ed.
      p. cm.
Includes index.
   ISBN 0-7879-6819-6 (alk. paper)
   1. Family—Prayer-books and devotions—English. 2. Home schooling—Prayer-books and devotions—English. 3. Devotional calendars. I. Title: Three hundred sixty-five days of celebration and praise. II. Title.
   BV255.L35 2003
   249—dc21   2003005199

FIRST EDITION
PB Printing   10 9 8 7 6 5 4 3 2 1

Contents

Foreword by Maureen McCaffrey Williamson   xvii
Acknowledgments   xix
Introduction   xxi

 January

January 1   New Year's Day
January 2   Religious Radio Anniversary
January 3   Drinking Straw Day
January 4   Louis Braille's Birthday
January 5   Trivia Day
January 6   Epiphany
January 7   Letter-Writing Week
January 8   National Ski Week
January 9   Plough Monday
January 10   Subway Day
January 11   International Thank-You Week
January 12   National Pharmacist Day
January 13   Stephen Foster Memorial Day
January 14   National Clean-Off-Your-Desk Day
January 15   Martin Luther King Jr. Day
January 16   Ratification Day
January 17   Hat Day
January 18   Hawaiian Islands Discovered
January 19   Golf Day
January 20   Inauguration Day
January 21   Frisbee Anniversary Month
January 22   National Hugging Day
January 23   National Handwriting Day
January 24   National Pie Day

January 25   National Soup Month
January 26   National Oatmeal Month
January 27   National Hobby Month
January 28   Football Season
January 29   Penguin Awareness Month
January 30   National Hot Tea Month
January 31   Scotch Tape Anniversary

 # February

February 1   National Freedom Day
February 2   Candlemas
February 3   Halfway Point of Winter
February 4   Armored Car Birthday
February 5   Weather Forecasters' Day
February 6   National Wild Bird Feeding Month
February 7   Ballet Day
February 8   Boy Scout Birthday
February 9   Pay-a-Compliment Day
February 10   Anniversary of First Published Magazine
February 11   Wedding Month
February 12   Grapefruit Month
February 13   American Heart Month
February 14   Valentine's Day
February 15   Ferris Wheel Day
February 16   Canned Food Month
February 17   Random-Acts-of-Kindness Day
February 18   Presidents' Day
February 19   Pluto Discovery Anniversary
February 20   Toothpick Day
February 21   Brotherhood-Sisterhood Month
February 22   National Cherry Month
February 23   Tootsie Roll Day
February 24   Potato Lovers' Month
February 25   National Music Month
February 26   Mardi Gras
February 27   Ash Wednesday

September 8   National Rice Month

September 9   Labor Day

September 10   Sew-Be-It Day

September 11   9/11 Day

September 12   National Biscuit Month

September 13   National Honey Month

September 14   Soccer Season

September 15   Grandparents' Day

September 16   Mayflower Day

September 17   National Tie Week

September 18   National Housekeepers' Week

September 19   National Student Day

September 20   National Laundry Workers' Week

September 21   National Farm Awareness Week

September 22   Children's Good Manners Month

September 23   Autumn

September 24   Good Neighbor Day

September 25   Rabbit Day

September 26   Deaf Awareness Week

September 27   Answering Machine Anniversary

September 28   Dog Week

September 29   Festival of Trumpets

September 30   Day of Atonement

 # October

October 1   Computer Learning Month

October 2   National Go-on-a-Field-Trip Month

October 3   International Dinosaur Month

October 4   National Housing Week

October 5   Bank Teller Appreciation Week

October 6   World Communion Sunday

October 7   National Roller Skating Month

October 8   Fire Prevention Week

October 9   Feast of Tabernacles

October 10   National Spinning and Weaving Week

October 11   National Newspaper Week
October 12   National Dessert Month
October 13   Clergy Appreciation Day
October 14   Columbus Day
October 15   Mushroom Day
October 16   Dictionary Day
October 17   National Clock Month
October 18   National Popcorn Poppin' Month
October 19   Sweetest Day
October 20   Comic Strip Anniversary
October 21   Hunger Awareness Month
October 22   Reptile Awareness Day
October 23   World Rain Forest Week
October 24   Cookbook Month
October 25   National Cleaner Air Week
October 26   Make-a-Difference Day
October 27   NIV of the Bible Week
October 28   Statue of Liberty Day
October 29   National Caramel Month
October 30   National Pizza Month
October 31   Reformation Day

 # November

November 1   Prime Meridian Day
November 2   Sandwich Day
November 3   National Religious Books Week
November 4   National Chemistry Week
November 5   General Election Day
November 6   Saxophone Day
November 7   Cat Week
November 8   X-Ray Day
November 9   National Parents-as-Teachers Day
November 10   National Fig Week
November 11   Veterans' Day

November 12   Harvest Month
November 13   Accountants' Day
November 14   National Teddy Bear Day
November 15   National Geography Awareness Week
November 16   Doll Collection Month
November 17   Homemade Bread Day
November 18   Adding Machine Day
November 19   Gettysburg Anniversary
November 20   American Education Week
November 21   World Hello Day
November 22   Aviation History Month
November 23   Pencil Sharpener Week
November 24   National Bible Week
November 25   National Farm-City Week
November 26   National Game-and-Puzzle Week
November 27   Thanksgiving
November 28   National Philanthropy Day
November 29   Peanut Butter Lovers' Month
November 30   International Drum Month

 # December

December 1   Advent
December 2   Rosa Parks Day
December 3   Cookie-Cutter Week
December 4   Basketball Season
December 5   Harriet Tubman Day
December 6   St. Nicholas Day
December 7   Anniversary of First Symphony Orchestra
December 8   Cotton Gin Anniversary
December 9   Christmas Card Day
December 10   Nobel Prize Day
December 11   First Reindeer in United States
December 12   Poinsettia Day
December 13   One-Way Street Birthday

December 14   Aardvark Week
December 15   First Ping-Pong Tournament
December 16   Audubon's Bird Count Day
December 17   Boston Tea Party Anniversary
December 18   North Pole Day
December 19   Giant Panda Anniversary
December 20   Flashlight Day
December 21   Winter
December 22   Forefathers' Day
December 23   Bingo Month
December 24   Happy Birthday, Street Cleaning Machine
December 25   Christmas—Happy Birthday, Jesus
December 26   Boxing Day
December 27   Kwanzaa
December 28   Chewing Gum Day
December 29   Shepherds' Day
December 30   Make-Up-Your-Mind Day
December 31   New Year's Eve

Bible Story Index   367

Memory Verse Index   370

Curriculum Index   373

The Author   377

Foreword

When Julie Lavender asked me to write the Foreword to her new book *365 Days of Celebration and Praise: Daily Devotions and Activities for Homeschooling Families,* I was delighted. Julie was a fixture at *Homeschooling Today* when I took over as editor of the magazine in 1997. Her "12 Days of Christmas" was one of the most popular features the magazine ever ran. As a busy homeschool mom and Christian herself, Julie knows what works for other Christian parents who homeschool.

The Lord is not just for church on Sunday. The Lord is part of your life and homeschool. It is He who gives you the strength to go on when the baby is screaming, your five-year-old has just spilled milk over the kitchen floor, and, all the while, six-year-old Johnny is trying to grasp the concept of stringing letter sounds together to make words. You just know he'll never learn how to read—that your mother-in-law, who wants you to send the children to "real" school and tells you so each time she sees you, was right all along.

You need the Lord to succeed. Your children need to have the Lord become part of their lives for them to succeed. More importantly, you both need the Lord to attain salvation.

365 Days of Celebration and Praise is Julie Lavender at her best. What a blessing for homeschooling parents—or teachers of any kind—to be able to start each day with a ready-made devotion and lesson that uses the calendar to teach an appropriate theme while imparting God's wisdom and comfort to you.

Julie knows that the key word for homeschoolers, no matter what they are doing, is *hassle-free.* You'll find no hours of overwhelming preparation with Julie's homeschooling aids. You get simple but interesting ideas on how to use God's Word as a major component for your homeschool. Julie has a knack for taking the ordinary, tying it to the Bible, and helping homeschool parents use it. A visit to the beach, for example, is something Julie knows how to make part of your homeschool. Better yet, she knows how to put it down on paper to give you easy and *accessible* lesson plans to use when teaching your children.

What makes Julie's homeschooling aids and devotions here so accessible? Each one is organized *for you*. Julie starts out by telling you what makes the day special. For example, did you know that January 4 is Louis Braille's birthday? Or that March 2 celebrates children's authors and illustrators? Or that September is National Courtesy Month? Julie gives you a Bible verse that expands on each day's theme, followed by questions to discuss with your children and an activity. Then she suggests a curriculum tie-in, Bible verses to memorize, and a prayer theme.

I can't imagine a more useful tool for homeschoolers than *365 Days of Celebration and Praise.* Julie Lavender's enthusiasm and know-how make it easy for you to make the Lord part of your homeschool days.

Laramie, Wyoming   Maureen McCaffrey Williamson
June 2003

Acknowledgments

First and foremost, I would like to praise our marvelous Heavenly Father, for "He has been good to me." God planted the concept for this book in my head almost ten years ago. Over the years, He has watered and nurtured His idea through the love of my family, homeschooling friends, pastors, writing mentors, and the blessings of each day, until *365 Days of Celebration and Praise* came to fruition. Thank you, God, for everything!

I am especially grateful for the Northwest Christian Writers Association—a group I was privileged to be a member of while living in the beautiful Pacific Northwest. It was a blessing to present my proposal at NCWA's annual Christian Writers Conference.

I am forever indebted to my editor, Mark Kerr, for capturing the vision of *365 Days*. Thank you, Mark, for lending an ear at the conference, for pursuing my idea, and for working to make this book a reality. Thank you, Catherine Craddock, Joanne Clapp Fullagar, Mary O'Briant, Katherine Sychra, Sandy Siegle, and Jennifer Chang.

Thank you, Jossey-Bass, for publishing *365 Days of Celebration and Praise*. Thank you for supporting the Christian growth and education of all families, including homeschooling families, through this endeavor.

Finally, I want to thank my beautiful family, for without them this book would not be possible. Thank you for your patience, encouragement, and help during the writing process and for your love always. David, thank you for being the light of my life and for the adventurous path our lives have taken. Jeremy, Jenifer, Jeb Daniel, and Jessica, thank you for allowing me to be your teacher. I enjoy every precious minute we spend together!

Statesboro, Georgia   Julie Lavender
June 2003

This book is lovingly dedicated to my "school":
my "Principal," parenting partner,
and wonderful husband, David,
and our "students"—our four fabulous children,
Jeremy, Jenifer, Jeb Daniel, and Jessica.

Introduction

Around Christmas, we often see the message "Jesus is the reason for the season." But what it all boils down to, in reality, is "Jesus is the reason for *every* season." With that in mind, my children and I have found a "season" or "holiday" to celebrate every single day of the year. I hope that you will use this book to celebrate every day as a gift from God and will praise His name for the dawning of each new day.

You may use this book in many different ways. After all, you're probably a homeschooling family and, well, we are known for our creativity, right? But the pattern I've suggested for each day is the same. First, the topic of the celebration is introduced; following are these sections: Questions to Discuss, Related Activity, Curriculum Connection, Verse to Memorize, and Prayer Suggestion. You might use my suggestions to stimulate your own ideas, follow my suggestions word for word, or pick and choose from my activities and celebration to enrich your own monthly calendar.

To make this book perpetual in use, the days will not fall on the correct calendar day each year. I advise you, as you are working on lesson plans, to glance ahead in the book, shifting the days to meet your schedule or to line up with the calendar. For example, Veterans' Day is always celebrated on November 11, regardless of the day of the week on which it falls. But Memorial Day is celebrated on the last Monday in May; therefore, the date changes yearly.

Many of the crafts described in the Related Activity sections will require brief preparations prior to the actual day of celebration, so I suggest you glance ahead at each devotion for those planning purposes as well.

Each day's suggestions for homeschoolers can be adapted to meet the developmental level of your children. For example, the Curriculum Connection for March 17 suggests finding the countries of Europe. Younger children can do that by following along with you on a map, whereas older children may be able to locate each country on a map, spell the name correctly, and state brief facts about each one.

Verses to Memorize may be treated in the same manner. Some verses are long but can be easily memorized by older children. Encourage younger children to memorize part of the passage, and even toddlers can quote the point of most verses.

All scripture, unless otherwise noted, is from the New International Version of the Bible.

I hope your family will enjoy these celebrations as much as my family does. Use the ideas as a starting point for a wonderful day with the Lord. How you choose to use my book is up to you, but it is my prayer that through daily celebrations and praise, your family will walk closer to God and celebrate His magnificent role in everyday activities. I will be praying for you!

January

January 1
New Year's Day

Today marks a brand new year—a time for new beginnings and changes. Read Ephesians 4:17-5:2. Paul tells the Ephesians to "put on the new self, created to be like God in true righteousness and holiness." Start this year by putting off the old, sinful self and putting on the new, holy self.

Questions to Discuss: What do you want to accomplish this year? What will you do to grow spiritually this year? Who do you want to tell about Jesus this year?

Related Activity: Using blank sheets of computer paper, let each person make a monthly calendar. Make each day's section large enough to write in prayer requests and answers to prayers. Include goals for each month, such as "read Genesis this month," "invite a friend to church," and so on.

Curriculum Connection: Study the calendar you made. How many days are in one year? How many months begin on Sunday? How many days are in each month? Is this a leap year?

Verse to Memorize: 1 Corinthians 5:7a—"Get rid of the old yeast that you may be a new batch without yeast—as you really are."

Prayer Suggestion: Spend a few minutes in silent prayer, praying for the upcoming year. Share your goals for the year with God, and ask for His blessings upon your year. After praying silently, join hands as a family, praying for the person to your right to meet his or her personal goals for the year.

January 2
Religious Radio Anniversary

Today is the anniversary of the first radio religious service.
Read Isaiah 52:7.

Questions to Discuss: How many ways can you think of to tell others about Jesus? What would it be like to be a radio broadcaster? Compare and contrast the following: hearing a service on the radio, watching a service on television, and sitting in church for a service.

Related Activity: As a family, listen to a show on your favorite Christian radio station. If time permits, make up your own radio show.

Curriculum Connection: Count the number of radios in the house, and determine to which channel the radio is tuned. Use an encyclopedia to find out who is credited with being the first person to send radio communication signals through the air and when this took place. Define these terms: *frequency, channel, call letters, live broadcast, pre-recorded.*

Verse to Memorize: Psalm 96:1–3—"Sing to the Lord a new song; sing to the Lord, all the earth. Sing to the Lord, praise his name; proclaim his salvation day after day. Declare his glory among the nations, his marvelous deeds among all peoples."

Prayer Suggestion: Pray for Christian radio broadcasters that they might share the gospel of Christ with others. Pray for those who might hear the word of God on the radio today and be touched by what they hear.

January 3
Drinking Straw Day

Celebrate the anniversary of this useful invention.
Read Judges 7:1-5 to find out how Gideon's men drank water.

Questions to Discuss: Why did God tell Gideon that ten thousand men were "too many" to take to battle? Why do you think God told Gideon to choose the three hundred men who cupped water in their hands and lapped while standing? Has God ever asked you to do a big job with just a few supplies?

Related Activity: Make a root-beer float (or any favorite soda), and drink it with a straw.

Curriculum Connection: Use a straw as a unit of measurement to measure various objects in your house. How tall, in straws, is your refrigerator? How long, in straws, is your table? How tall are you?

Verse to Memorize: John 4:13-14—"Jesus answered, 'Everyone who drinks this water will be thirsty again, but whoever drinks the water I give him will never thirst. Indeed, the water I give him will become in him a spring of water welling up to eternal life.'"

Prayer Suggestion: Pray for those who might receive Jesus' water.

January 4
Louis Braille's Birthday

Louis Braille, blind by the age of three, invented the raised alphabet for the blind in the early 1800s. Read about Saul, blinded temporarily, in Acts 9:1-31.

Questions to Discuss: Why do you think God caused Saul to be blind for three days? What sorts of things might be difficult for you if you were blind?

Related Activity: Have each person write on paper three things to do, such as "tie your shoes," "get a snack," or "read a book." Drop all the slips of paper in a basket. Take turns drawing out a slip. While blindfolded, try to accomplish that task.

Curriculum Connection: Discuss the five senses. In addition, read about Louis Braille and write a biography of his life. Where did he go at age ten? What very important code did he develop at age fifteen? What musical instrument did he play in church?

Verse to Memorize: 2 Corinthians 5:7—"We live by faith, not by sight." (Another is Luke 2:30-31—"For my eyes have seen your salvation, which you have prepared in the sight of all people.")

Prayer Suggestion: Thank God for the gift of sight. Pray for those who are blind.

January 5
Trivia Day

A dictionary defines trivia *as "insignificant or inessential matters."*
David, the psalmist, wonders how God, in all His majesty,
could consider man being anything but insignificant.
Read David's musings in Psalm 8:1-9.

Questions to Discuss: How big do you think God is?
Why are you important to God?

Related Activity: Make up a trivia game about
your family. Have each person write questions and
answers about himself or herself on index cards.
Mix up the cards, and take turns answering the
questions.

Curriculum Connection: Practice making analogies. Start
with "*trivial* is to *important* as *meaningless* is to [ ]."

Verse to Memorize: Matthew 10:30—"And even the very hairs of
your head are all numbered."

Prayer Suggestion: Say this prayer together, replacing the words
your name in the verse to make it personal: "When I consider your heavens, the work of your fingers, the moon and the stars, which you have set in
place, who is [your name] that you are mindful of me? Thank you, God, that
you are so mindful of me, that you know even the most trivial, insignificant
details of my life."

January 6
Epiphany

Often during Christmas, we celebrate the visit of the Magi as if their visit occurred soon after Jesus was born; actually, the visit occurred sometime during Jesus' first couple of years. Read Matthew 2:1-12 to find out more about this wonderful part of Jesus' infancy.

Questions to Discuss: Why did it take the wise men a long time to see Jesus? How did they know how to find Jesus? Why do you think the Magi brought gifts to baby Jesus? What gift can you give Jesus?

Related Activity: Make edible figures of wise men, using an inverted sugar cone as a base. Gently press a large marshmallow into the point of the cone for the head. Using frosting as glue, attach candies for facial features. Make crowns and robes from pressed fruit pieces, and press them into place. For extra fun, use different flavors of ice cream cones to show the varied ethnic backgrounds of the Magi.

Curriculum Connection: Find Jerusalem and Bethlehem on a map. What countries, to the East, do you think the wise men came from? Some believe the men may have come from Babylonia, Persia, and Arabia. Using a biblical map, decide which countries (they now have different names) these were.

Verse to Memorize: Micah 5:2—"But you, Bethlehem Ephrathah, though you are small among the clans of Judah, out of you will come for me one who will be ruler over Israel, whose origins are from of old, from ancient times."

Prayer Suggestion: Pray about your gift to Jesus. Ask God to keep you mindful of this gift in the days and weeks ahead.

January 7
Letter-Writing Week

*Paul wrote lots and lots of letters. Read part of one of
his letters in 2 Corinthians 3:1-3.*

Questions to Discuss: How can you show that you are a "letter
from Christ"? What is written on your heart?

Related Activity: Write a letter to someone, telling that person what
Jesus means to you.

Curriculum Connection: Using your letter, point to
these parts of a friendly letter: heading, salutation or
greeting, body, closing, and signature. In addition,
encourage older children to learn the two-letter
abbreviation for each of the fifty states.

Verse to Memorize: 2 Thessalonians 2:15-17—
"So then, brothers, stand firm and hold to the teachings
we passed on to you, whether by word of mouth or by letter. May our
Lord Jesus Christ himself and God our Father, who loved us and by his
grace gave us eternal encouragement and good hope, encourage your
hearts and strengthen you in ever good deed and word."

Prayer Suggestion: Pray for the person to whom you wrote a letter.

January 8
National Ski Week

"…and the mountain peaks belong to him." Read Psalm 95:1-7.

Questions to Discuss: What do you think is God's most amazing creation? What is your favorite thing to do in the mountains? (If you've never visited mountains, think of something you'd like to do there.)

Related Activity: Make a pretend ski slope using detergent. Start with a shoebox. Remove the lid; cut off one short end and slope both long sides of the shoebox. Cut off the edges of the lid, leaving a flat rectangular piece. Tape the flat piece to the cut shoebox to form the slope. Stir water into the laundry detergent, forming a thick paste. Spread the detergent on the slanted shoebox slope, and let it harden overnight. Meanwhile, make a skier. Using a craft pipe cleaner, twist the top to form a head. Bend the bottom one-third for a leg. Twist another strip in place for a leg. Twist the arms into place. Bend up a small amount for feet, and glue them onto cut craft sticks for skies. Wrap the hands around pretzel sticks. When the slope has hardened, let your skiers go for a run.

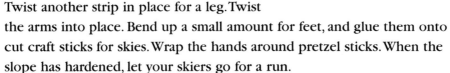

Curriculum Connection: Look on the Internet to find the real ski slope nearest you. Find it on a map.

Verse to Memorize: Job 37:6a, 7a—"He says to the snow, 'Fall on the Earth,' so that all men he has made may know his work."

Prayer Suggestion: Pray for those who work or play outdoors during the cold winter.

January 9
Plough Monday

(The word *plough* is the British version of our word *plow*.)

*In England, farm ploughs are blessed in church on the Sunday
after Epiphany. Then on Monday, farmers resume their work.
Read what Elisha did when the prophet Elijah called him
to do the Lord's work; this is in 1 Kings 19:19-21.*

Questions to Discuss: Why did Elijah rebuff Elisha when Elisha wanted to return to his family to say good-bye? What was the significance of Elisha's slaughtering his oxen and burning his plow? When God calls you, when does He expect you to reply? Once you are saved, how does God feel about your looking back toward your old, sinful life?

Related Activity: Play this game with your family: using chalk or masking tape, make a straight line on the ground or floor. Walk on the line facing forward, then turn your head and look behind you. Continue walking while looking behind you. Can you walk in a straight line?

Curriculum Connection: Compare and contrast a farmer in Elisha's day with a farmer today.

Verse to Memorize: Luke 9:62—"Jesus replied, 'No one who puts his hand to the plow and looks back is fit for service in the kingdom of God.'"

Prayer Suggestion: Pray for farmers.

January 10
Subway Day

London opened the first underground subway on this day in 1863.
Have you ever ridden on a subway? Read 1 Samuel 25:1-35 to see
where Abigail met David. Use your imagination to visualize how
the mountain ravine might resemble the tunnel of a subway.

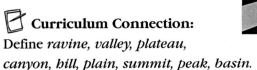 **Questions to Discuss:** How did David feel when Nabal refused to give him food and supplies? What did David plan to do to Nabal? How did Abigail help stem David's anger? What do you do when you are angry?

Related Activity: Use modeling dough to make a mountain range with a ravine and valley. Take a field trip on a subway, if you live near one.

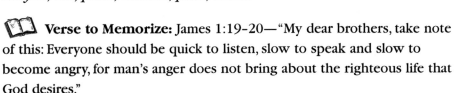

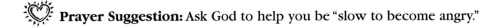

Curriculum Connection: Define *ravine, valley, plateau, canyon, hill, plain, summit, peak, basin.*

Verse to Memorize: James 1:19-20—"My dear brothers, take note of this: Everyone should be quick to listen, slow to speak and slow to become angry, for man's anger does not bring about the righteous life that God desires."

Prayer Suggestion: Ask God to help you be "slow to become angry."

January 11
International Thank-You Week

Although words could never truly express gratitude to the Heavenly Father for His magnificent gift—His Son Jesus Christ—one should be in a constant state of prayerful thanksgiving. Read Luke 17:11-19 to find out how many people remembered to thank Jesus.

Questions to Discuss: Why did only one healed man come back to thank Jesus? Do you forget to thank Jesus sometimes? What can help you remember to thank Jesus every day?

Related Activity: Write Jesus a thank-you note for something that happened recently.

Curriculum Connection: Learn the Roman numerals. What is the Roman numeral for 10?

Verse to Memorize: Psalm 107:1—"Give thanks to the Lord, for he is good; his love endures forever."

Prayer Suggestion: Make a list of the ways God has blessed you this year. Thank God for each one of those blessings.

January 12
National Pharmacist Day

Naaman, commander of the army of King Aram, was plagued with leprosy. According to God's plan, a captive young girl from Israel shared information with Naaman's wife that would forever change his life. Read 2 Kings 5:1-16 to find out what God's prophet, Elisha, prescribed for Naaman's cure.

Questions to Discuss: Why did Naaman get angry when Elisha told him to wash in the Jordan River? What happened when Naaman obeyed God by following Elisha's directions? Why should you obey God?

Related Activity: Take a field trip to a pharmacy or pharmacy section of a large department store. Thank your pharmacist. Look to see how the products are displayed on the shelves. How are the products grouped on each aisle? If you cannot take a field trip today, keep this in mind: cinnamon was sometimes used as a healing herb during biblical times. Make cinnamon toast and thank God for His healing powers.

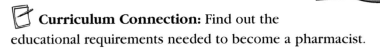

Curriculum Connection: Find out the educational requirements needed to become a pharmacist.

Verse to Memorize: Proverbs 17:22a—"A cheerful heart is good medicine."

Prayer Suggestion: Pray for pharmacists. Thank God that He has provided medicines to heal our afflictions.

January 13
Stephen Foster Memorial Day

Stephen Foster was one of America's best-loved songwriters. During his songwriting days, many of his popular tunes were sung, with different lyrics, in Sunday school classes. Read 1 Samuel 16:14-23 to find out about David's musical abilities.

Questions to Discuss: How did David's music help Saul feel? Does music soothe you? What else calms and soothes you?

Related Activity: Sing one or more of Foster's songs: "Old Folks at Home," "Suwannee River," "Oh! Susanna," or "Camptown Races."

Curriculum Connection: Read about Foster and other famous musicians such as Beethoven or Mozart.

Verse to Memorize: Psalm 13:6—"I will sing to the Lord, for he has been good to me."

Prayer Suggestion: Pray for music ministers, choir directors, and choir members.

January 14
National Clean-Off-Your-Desk Day

Is your desk a wreck? Then today is set aside just for you.
Read in 1 Peter 2:1 what Peter says you should get rid of.

Questions to Discuss: How can your life become cluttered with sin, just like your room or desk becomes cluttered? What happens if you do not rid your life of sin on a daily basis?

Related Activity: Clean your desk (or perhaps your room or yard).

Curriculum Connection: Organize your files and papers. Practice putting words in alphabetical order.

Verse to Memorize:
Psalm 24:4a, 5a—"He who has clean hands and a pure heart . . . he will receive blessing from the Lord."

Prayer Suggestion: Ask God to help you have "clean hands and a pure heart."

January 15
Martin Luther King Jr. Day

Martin Luther King Jr., a Baptist minister, was the prominent leader of the civil rights movement during the fifties and sixties. His pleas for social justice and an end to discrimination won him many supporters, as well as the Nobel Peace Prize. Read Acts 10:21-48 to see how God feels about discrimination.

Questions to Discuss: Does God show favoritism among people of different skin colors? Do you?

Related Activity: Use a gingerbread-boy cookie cutter to make paper dolls. Fold a piece of paper, accordion-style, the width of the cookie cutter. Draw the shape such that the arms of the boy are on the fold. Cut out the dolls; do not cut through the fold where the hands are. Open up the string of children, holding hands. Color and decorate the dolls, using a variety of colors for different shades of skin.

Curriculum Connection: Read about Martin Luther King Jr. Write a report on his life.

Verse to Memorize: Romans 15:7—"Accept one another, then, just as Christ accepted you, in order to bring praise to God."

Prayer Suggestion: Pray for people of all races, especially those who feel unjustly discriminated against.

January 16
Ratification Day

In mid-January of 1784, the Continental Congress agreed on the Treaty of Paris, which officially ended the American Revolution. The United States became a country of its own. Read Exodus 6:2–12 to find about God's people, who were searching for a country of their own.

Questions to Discuss: What did God promise to do for His people? What did He want in return? How can you show God that He is "your God"?

Related Activity: Make a family treaty. Write "The Lord God Is My God," and have each person sign it.

Curriculum Connection: Read about the Revolutionary War in America. How many colonies fought Great Britain? Where did the war begin? How long did it last? Make an outline of the important dates during the war.

Verse to Memorize: Exodus 6:7a—"I will take you as my own people, and I will be your God."

Prayer Suggestion: Pray for nations who are not free to worship as they choose.

January 17
Hat Day

What do you wear on your head? Read why David didn't wear anything on his head in that much-talked-about battle with Goliath. Read 1 Samuel 17:1–50.

Questions to Discuss: Why didn't David wear Saul's armor? Why do you think David chose five stones instead of just one? Who did David credit for the slaying of Goliath?

Related Activity: Use fabric paint to decorate a cloth hat. Have a fashion show when the hats are dry.

Curriculum Connection: Discuss the consonant-vowel-consonant phonics pattern. Practice rhyming short vowel words; start with the word *hat*. Also see if you can find the vocabulary word that means "a person who makes women's hats."

Verse to Memorize: Proverbs 10:6a—"Blessings crown the head of the righteous."

Prayer Suggestion: Pray for hatmakers.

January 18
Hawaiian Islands Discovered

*Captain James Cook of the British navy is credited with discovering
the islands of Hawaii in 1778, though Polynesians had
inhabited the islands for years. Read about Jesus' excursion
to the island-area of Tyre in Matthew 15:21-28.*

Questions to Discuss: Why did Jesus first refuse the Canaanite woman? Why did he reward her? What does the word *persistent* mean?

Related Activity: Make a tissue paper lei. You'll need ten to twelve sheets of colored tissue paper, 12" x 18", dental floss, one bead, and a sewing needle. Cut a thirty-six-inch strip of dental floss. Tie the bead three inches from the end. Cut each sheet of tissue paper into four-inch squares. Stack three squares of tissue paper together. Fold the tissue paper together, accordion-style. Carefully push the threaded needle into the middle of your rectangle; slide the strip to  the bead. Carefully twist the rectangle once or twice in the middle, just to help the flower hold its shape. Now fan out the piece on both sides of the twist. (The flower may untwist some.) Add more flowers to the lei, alternating colors as you go. Tie the ends together, and proudly wear your lei.

Curriculum Connection: Read more about the islands of Hawaii. Find out about the native Hawaiians and the meaning of the lei. Also find these islands on a map: Bermuda, Barbados, Jamaica, Puerto Rico, Solomon Islands, Long Island, Manhattan Island, Martha's Vineyard, Vancouver Island.

Verse to Memorize: Romans 3:22-24—"This righteousness from God comes through faith in Jesus Christ to all who believe. There is no difference, for all have sinned and fallen short of the glory of God, and are justified freely by his grace through the redemption that came by Christ Jesus."

Prayer Suggestion: Pray for those who live on islands, especially remote islands, that they, too, might hear the gospel of Christ.

January 19
Golf Day

More than likely, no one during biblical days played anything remotely similar to golf. But you can find out what would have happened if someone built a house on a sand trap when you read Matthew 7:24-27.

Questions to Discuss: Is your house built on rock or sand? What are some examples of "rain," "streams," and "wind" in your life? Compare a golf ball in a sand trap to a house built on the sand.

Related Activity: Make a sand creation to remind you not to build your house on the sand. Purchase colored sand from a department or craft store. Use a spoon and a funnel to fill a plastic or glass jar with sand. To make patterns in the layers, slide a toothpick down the side of the jar after several layers, pressing against the jar. The sand will tumble into the crevice you make to form pretty patterns. Fill the jar completely, then tightly twist on the lid. For more fun, play a rousing game of putt-putt golf.

Curriculum Connection: Learn to play golf. Define these golf terms: *fore, putt, birdie, drive, club, pin, tee, slice, hook.* Classify each word into its correct part of speech.

Verse to Memorize: Isaiah 26:4—"Trust in the Lord forever, for the Lord, the Lord, is the Rock eternal."

Prayer Suggestion: Pray for professional golfers.

January 20
Inauguration Day

Every four years, the president of the United States is inaugurated on this day. Read about the "inauguration" that God's people requested in 1 Samuel 8:19-10:1.

Questions to Discuss: Why did the Israelites want a king? What can you do to support the leaders of our country?

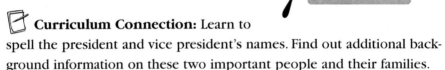

Related Activity: Make crowns from construction paper, and play an altered version of "Mother, May I?" Call your game "King, May I?" Wear your crowns while you play.

Curriculum Connection: Learn to spell the president and vice president's names. Find out additional background information on these two important people and their families.

Verse to Memorize: Proverbs 20:28—"Love and faithfulness keep a king safe; through love his throne is made secure."

Prayer Suggestion: Pray for the leaders of our country.

January 21
Frisbee Anniversary Month

*Have you ever played Frisbee on a really windy day? Unless you
are a professional player, catching a Frisbee on a windy day is
almost impossible. Read Ecclesiastes 2:9-11 to find out
how Solomon feels about running after the wind.*

Questions to Discuss: Solomon says that all of life is meaningless
without what? Why does Solomon compare a life without God to "chasing
after the wind?"

Related Activity: To celebrate the patent of this fun
invention, play a family Frisbee game.

Curriculum Connection: Discuss common (and not so common)
polygons. Why is a circle not classified as a polygon? What do these
terms mean: *triangle, quadrilateral, rectangle, square, pentagon,
hexagon, octagon, rhombus?* Encourage older children to determine the
circumference and diameter of the Frisbee you used during playtime.

Verse to Memorize: John 15:5b—"[Jesus said], 'Apart from
me, you can do nothing.'"

Prayer Suggestion: Pray that you can grow stronger in your knowledge of God.

January 22
National Hugging Day

What does embrace *mean? Is there a difference between the actions of embracing and hugging? Have you hugged anyone today? Read about a loving embrace in Genesis 29:1–14a.*

Questions to Discuss: Why was Jacob so happy to see Laban? How can you show your love to your family?

Related Activity: Give everyone in your family a hug, then treat yourself to chocolate candies.

Curriculum Connection: Estimate how many candies are in a bag. Count to see if your estimate was correct.

Verse to Memorize: 1 John 3:18—"Dear children, let us not love with words or tongue but with actions and in truth."

Prayer Suggestion: Pray for those who are lonely and have no one to hug today.

January 23
National Handwriting Day

This holiday was established on John Hancock's birthday to encourage more legible handwriting. Read Exodus 20:1-17 and Exodus 31:18 to find out about God's "handwriting." Also read Matthew 19:16-22.

Questions to Discuss: Why did God give Moses the Ten Commandments? Why did Jesus talk to the rich young ruler about the Ten Commandments? Do you think God intends for us to continue obeying the Ten Commandments?

Related Activity: Copy the Ten Commandments in your neatest handwriting on a large sheet of poster paper, cut to resemble a stone tablet.

Curriculum Connection: Compare the styles of writing on a computer. Type the Ten Commandments using at least five different fonts on your computer.

Verse to Memorize: Proverbs 7:1-3—"My son, keep my words and store up my commands within you. Keep my commands and you will live; guard my teachings as the apple of your eye. Bind them on your fingers; write them on the tablet of your heart."

Prayer Suggestion: Pray for children who are just learning to write.

January 24
National Pie Day

*What kind of pie is your favorite? Who can resist a delicious slice
of pie for dessert? Read Psalm 141:4 to find out what kind
of "delicacy" David says to avoid.*

Questions to Discuss: Why is evil called a delicacy in this verse? How can you avoid evil?

Related Activity: Make a pie with a homemade crust. Cut shapes with small cookie cutters or hand-form designs to decorate the edge of the piecrust.

Curriculum Connection: Learn these cooking measurements: three teaspoons = one tablespoon, four tablespoons = one-quarter cup, one tablespoon = one-half fluid ounce.

Verse to Memorize: Psalm 141:4a—"Let not my heart be drawn to what is evil."

Prayer Suggestion: Pray for professional bakers.

January 25
National Soup Month

Celebrate the cold days of winter with a warm bowl of soup.
Check out Genesis 25:27–34 to see who was ravenously hungry
for a bowl of warm stew.

Questions to Discuss: Why did Esau sell his birthright to Jacob? How did this exhibit Esau's lack of godliness? Is there something in your life that you need to take more seriously?

Related Activity: Remember those in your community who might be ravenously hungry for a nice warm meal. Volunteer in a soup kitchen.

Curriculum Connection: Explain these cooking terms: *dice, boil, simmer, broil, bake, pan-fry, thicken.*

Verse to Memorize: Job 20:5b—"The joy of the godless lasts but a moment."

Prayer Suggestion: Pray for those who volunteer in soup kitchens and for those who receive their nourishment at soup kitchens.

January 26
National Oatmeal Month

Oats are a cereal grain and belong to the same family of plants as barley, corn, rice, and wheat. However, oats have a higher food value than any other cereal grain. Celebrate the goodness of this grain during National Oatmeal Month by reading one of Jesus' parables about a farmer sowing wheat; the passage is found in Matthew 13:24-30 and explained in Matthew 13:36-43.

Questions to Discuss: What helps you remain a strong "seed" in a world full of "weeds"? How do you think you'll feel on "harvest" day?

Related Activity: Make oatmeal cookies. Share with those you love.

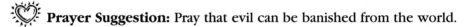

Curriculum Connection: Find five synonyms and five antonyms for the word *evil*.

Verse to Memorize: Matthew 3:11c-12—"He will baptize you with the Holy Spirit and with fire. His winnowing fork is in his hand, and he will clear his threshing floor, gathering his wheat into the barn and burning up the chaff with unquenchable fire."

Prayer Suggestion: Pray that evil can be banished from the world.

January 27
National Hobby Month

A list of hobbies is as varied as the people in the world. Do you have a hobby? Read 1 Chronicles 4:13-23. Hobbies and occupations were so important during biblical days that people were often identified according to their craft.

Questions to Discuss: What three occupations were mentioned in this group of people? What is your favorite hobby? How can you commit your hobby to the Lord?

Related Activity: Have a hobby hour when everyone works on their hobby at the same time. Share your work with family members. Have a hobby "show and tell."

Curriculum Connection: Name five adjectives that describe your hobby.

Verse to Memorize: 1 Corinthians 10:31b—
"Or whatever you do, do it all for the glory of God."

Prayer Suggestion: Ask God to show you how to use your hobby to His glory.

January 28
Football Season

Are you a football fan? Or would you rather "pass" on this sport?
Football players work hard to develop strong muscles. Shepherds in Jesus'
day were probably strong as well, often carrying hurt or injured sheep.
Read about one such shepherd in Luke 15:3-7.

 Questions to Discuss: Why was the shepherd so happy to find his lost sheep? Explain Jesus' parable. Compare the shepherd taking the sheep home to a football player carrying the football across the goal line.

Related Activity: Play a game of football, or watch a game (possibly on TV).

Curriculum Connection: What do these words mean: *punt, pass, kick, field goal, first down, tackle?* Learn the rules for professional or college football games.

Verse to Memorize: Luke 19:10— "For the Son of Man came to seek and to save what was lost."

Prayer Suggestion: Pray for football players and coaches.

January 29
Penguin Awareness Month

Penguins use their feet in remarkable ways. Their webbed feet make penguins marvelous swimmers and exceptional divers. They also use their feet as a resting-place for eggs and newly hatched chicks. Jesus wanted us to know something special about the feet of His disciples. Read His message in John 13:1–17.

Questions to Discuss: Why did Jesus wash His disciples' feet? How can you "wash the feet" of others?

Related Activity: Make a door hanger that looks like a penguin. Using black felt, cut two wings about four and one-half inches long. Cut a small pair of feet from yellow felt. Glue a one-inch, black pom-pom to the top of a white, wooden craft stick. Glue the wings in place, extending the felt over the edges of the stick to leave a white "chest" showing in the middle. Glue the feet at the bottom, placing the top of the felt behind the craft stick, allowing the feet to hang freely. Glue quarter-inch pom-poms in place for eyes and nose. When the glue is completely dry, glue a ribbon loop to the back.

Curriculum Connection: Learn more about the beautiful penguin. Where do penguins live? What do they eat? Write up and give an oral report on your findings. Be sure to include visuals.

Verse to Memorize: Luke 22:27—"For who is greater, the one who is at the table or the one who serves? Is it not the one who is at the table? But I am among you as one who serves."

Prayer Suggestion: Pray for those who take care of others.

January 30
National Hot Tea Month

Hot tea during the month of January may seem just as satisfying as a drink of cool water in the parching desert. In Genesis 21:8–21, Hagar and Ishmael were on the verge of dehydration and death because they could not find water to drink. Read this passage to find out who quenches their thirst.

Questions to Discuss: How did God take care of Hagar and Ishmael? How does God take care of you?

Related Activity: Brew a large pot of strong tea. Push cotton handkerchiefs into the tea with a wooden spoon, and let them soak for an hour or more. Drain the handkerchiefs, squeeze out the excess tea, and hang the handkerchiefs on a drying rack. When the cloths are completely dry, place several tea bags into each handkerchief, gather the edges and secure with a pretty ribbon. Give the gift to a neighbor or friend.

Curriculum Connection: Consult an encyclopedia to find out how tea is made.

Verse to Memorize: Isaiah 58:11—"The Lord will guide you always; he will satisfy your needs in a sun-scorched land and will strengthen your frame. You will be like a well-watered garden, like a spring whose waters never fail."

Prayer Suggestion: Pray for those who, for whatever reason, are separated from their families.

January 31
Scotch Tape Anniversary

What would you do if sticky tape had never been invented? How would you keep things attached, stuck together, or framed on your walls? God wanted His people to remember His commands. He tells them in Deuteronomy 6:1–25 to "tie [His commands] to their hands and bind them to their foreheads." Perhaps if tape had been invented, God's people could have taped the commands onto their bodies. Read to find out what God thought was important enough for them to remember at all times.

Questions to Discuss: Did God ask His people to love Him some of the time? How does God want us to love Him? What parts of your life do you need to give to God so that He has *all* of your heart?

Related Activity: Write the memory verse on paper and decorate it. Use tape to attach it to a construction paper frame; hang the reminder in your room.

Curriculum Connection: Find synonyms and antonyms for *all.*

Verse to Memorize: Deuteronomy 6:5—"Love the Lord your God with all your heart and with all your soul and with all your strength."

Prayer Suggestion: Ask God to help you give Him everything about your life: your work, your thoughts, your play, your actions.

 # February

February 1
National Freedom Day

On this date in 1865, President Abraham Lincoln approved the 13th Amendment, which abolished slavery. Read in Exodus 12:31-40 about God's people who had been treated as slaves in Egypt for quite some time.

Questions to Discuss: How do you think the Israeli people felt when they finally left Egypt? Is there a sin that *you* need to be freed from? Who can help you get free from that sin?

EGYPT

Related Activity: Play a game of tag. When you are tagged, you go to "Egypt" and have to wait until you are "let free" by one of your teammates.

Curriculum Connection: Find Egypt on a map. What sea is north of Egypt? Which sea is east of Egypt? What African countries border Egypt on the west and south? What country is on the eastern side of the Sinai Peninsula?

Verse to Memorize: Romans 6:17-18—"But thanks be to God that, though you used to be slaves to sin, you wholeheartedly obeyed the form of teaching to which you were entrusted. You have been set free from sin and have become slaves to righteousness."

Prayer Suggestion: Pray for those who are slaves to sin that they might be set free from sin through Christ Jesus.

February 2
Candlemas

Greek, Roman, and Anglican churches celebrate Candlemas on February 2—the day Mary visited the temple in Jerusalem for purification after the birth of Jesus. Read about this event in Luke 2:22.

Questions to Discuss: How do you think Mary felt about being the mother of God's Son? Why do you think God chose Mary to be Jesus' mother?

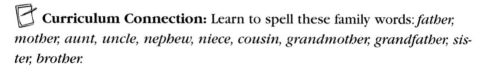

Related Activity: Boys, dress as Joseph and hold a baby doll representing Jesus. Girls, dress as Mary and also hold a baby Jesus. Say a prayer that you might have said to God, as Mary and Joseph, about baby Jesus.

Curriculum Connection: Learn to spell these family words: *father, mother, aunt, uncle, nephew, niece, cousin, grandmother, grandfather, sister, brother.*

Verse to Memorize: Matthew 18:11—"For the Son of Man has come to save that which was lost."

Prayer Suggestion: Remove the costumes you wore during the activity time, but continue holding "baby Jesus." Say a prayer of thanks to God about what Jesus means to you.

February 3
Halfway Point of Winter

Can you believe that you are in the middle of winter? Does it still feel like winter where you live, or is the weather beginning to warm? Read about the Maker of all seasons in Genesis 8:22.

Questions to Discuss: What is your favorite part of winter? What do you like least about winter?

Related Activity: Make a marshmallow snowman. Use frosting to stick two large marshmallows together, end-to-end. Add facial features with the frosting. To make a hat, warm a small chocolate log in the microwave for a few seconds until it is pliable. Roll it into a ball, flattening one side. Use frosting to stick the flat end onto a chocolate wafer cookie. Set the hat on top of the snowman's head.

Curriculum Connection: Look in the newspaper at a weather map. Find the coldest temperature and warmest temperature; check out the precipitation. What is the weather like in your state?

Verse to Memorize: Psalm 74:17—"It was you who set all the boundaries of the earth; you made both summer and winter."

Prayer Suggestion: Thank God for the beauty of the seasons.

February 4
Armored Car Birthday

The first armored car was used in this month in 1920.
Read about the Armor of God in Ephesians 6:10-18.

Questions to Discuss: Why does a car that carries lots of money need to be armored? Why did soldiers in battle wear protective armor in biblical days? Why do you need "armor" to resist the devil and sin in the world?

Related Activity: On a long strip of fabric, write the word *truth* with a permanent marker. Use this for a belt. To make a breastplate, turn a paper bag upside down. Cut a straight line on one side, starting at the open end. Cut all the way to the bottom flap. Cut a large circle for the head in that part of the bag. Cut circles for armholes in each side. Write "righteousness" across the front of the bag—the uncut side. Add other decorations, then wear the breastplate. Wear boots, cut a shield from posterboard, wear a helmet (or hat), and cut a sword from posterboard. Now you're ready! Talk about how each item protects you from evil.

Curriculum Connection: Look up the word *armor* in a Bible dictionary. Explain the literal and figurative meanings of the terms *helmet, shield, breastplate, sword, spear, bow and arrow,* and *sling.*

Verse to Memorize: Ephesians 6:10–11— "Finally, be strong in the Lord and in his mighty power. Put on the full armor of God so that you can take your stand against the devil's schemes."

Prayer Suggestion: While wearing your armor, ask God to help you stand strong, in full armor, against sin and temptation.

February 5
Weather Forecasters' Day

Read Jeremiah 10:12-13. Take a walk and observe today's weather. Is it breezy or calm? Is it cool or warm? Is the sky blue or filled with ominous rain-filled clouds? Lie on the grass and enjoy the weather—whatever it is. If there are clouds in the sky, take a few minutes to use your imagination and look for "pictures" in the sky. If there are no clouds, watch the trees dance in the wind. Enjoy the sunshine on your face or the splatter of rain on your body. Remember that "God made the earth by his power," which includes whatever weather conditions you are observing today.

Questions to Discuss: What is your favorite kind of weather? How do you feel during a storm? Who can comfort you in any type of weather?

Related Activity: Make a large calendar for the month, using poster paper. Fill in the days for February. Observe the weather for the rest of the month, using markers, crayons, or construction paper cutouts to signify each day's weather.

Curriculum Connection: Research the various kinds of clouds. Discuss these cloud types: cirrus, stratus, cumulus. What kinds of clouds did you see today?

Verse to Memorize: Daniel 2:20-21a—"Praise be to the name of God for ever and ever; wisdom and power are his. He changes times and seasons."

Prayer Suggestion: Thank God for the variety in weather conditions. Ask God to comfort you during weather that may seem frightening. Ask God to remind you that all weather comes from Him alone and request that He help you not to grumble if the weather does not always suit your fancy.

February 6
National Wild Bird Feeding Month

Did you know that the largest bird is the African ostrich and that it can grow as tall as eight feet? Were you aware that the smallest bird— the bee hummingbird—is only two inches long when it is fully grown? God's creativity and imagination are just awesome! Celebrate this bird month by reading in 1 Kings 17:1-6 about a time when God used wild birds to take care of His prophet Elijah.

Questions to Discuss: Did Elijah trust God to provide for his needs? Explain how God took care of Elijah. Do you trust God to take care of your needs? How would it feel to be fed by wild birds?

Related Activity: Punch holes in opposite sides of a plastic cup. Tie yarn in both holes to make a hanger. Spread peanut butter on the outside of the cup, then roll the cup in birdseed. Fill the inside of the cup with seed. Hang the feeder outside for the birds, and remember to refill the cup often.

Curriculum Connection: Learn the state bird for all fifty states.

Verse to Memorize: Philippians 4:19—"And my God will meet all your needs according to His glorious riches in Christ Jesus."

Prayer Suggestion: Tell God your needs—not your wants—and then ask God to help you trust Him to supply all those needs.

February 7
Ballet Day

The art of ballet was introduced to the United States on this day in 1827 at a theater in New York City. Read in 2 Samuel 6:1-15 to find out about David's dance.

Questions to Discuss: What made David so happy that he "danced before the Lord"? When God blesses you, how do you show your happiness?

Related Activity: Make a bell shaker to honor and praise God. Start with a sturdy paper plate. Punch holes about two inches apart around the rim of the plate. Tie colorful ribbons in each hole. Tie bells onto some of the ribbons. Rattle your bell shaker, give praises, and "dance before the Lord."

Curriculum Connection: Read about the history of ballet. To what country can the beginnings of ballet be traced?

Verse to Memorize: Psalm 149:3-4—"Let them praise his name with dancing and make music to him with tambourine and harp. For the Lord takes delight in his people; he crowns the humble with salvation."

Prayer Suggestion: Pray for dancers that they might use their dancing to praise and honor God.

February 8
Boy Scout Birthday

The Boy Scouts of America, founded in 1910, teaches young people to be good citizens and trains them to be good leaders. Scouts are taught to do their duty to God, to their country, and to other people. The Boy Scout motto is "Be prepared." In 1 Peter 1:13-16, Peter tells us how to "be prepared" for the return of Jesus.

Questions to Discuss: What can you do to be prepared for Jesus' return? How will you start the preparations today?

Related Activity: Make a typical Boy Scout scene. Use a paper plate for a base. Lean two halves of graham crackers together in a tent shape. Spread frosting across the top to stick the crackers together, spreading some frosting along the bottom edges, on the paper plate if necessary, to hold the tent in place. Spread frosting on the bottom of gingerbread-boy cookies, and stand them on the plate. Pile a few red cinnamon candies on the plate for the fire. Press a miniature marshmallow on one end of a pretzel stick. Use a dab of frosting to place a pretzel stick in each "scout's" hand.

Curriculum Connection: Read the Boy Scout oath. How can you apply that to your own life, even if you are not a scout?

Verse to Memorize: 1 Peter 1:15—"But just as he who called you is holy, so be holy in all you do."

Prayer Suggestion: Pray for Boy Scouts and their leaders.

February 9
Pay-a-Compliment Day

How many compliments have you given today? How many compliments have you received? Read Proverbs 12:25 to see what kind words can do.

Questions to Discuss: How do you feel when someone says kind words to you? How often do you give compliments to others?

Related Activity: On strips of paper, write seven compliments about each person in the family. Use different-colored strips for each family member. During the next week, pull out one strip of each color per day. Read aloud the written compliments, and brighten each person's day.

Curriculum Connection: Make a list of ten positive adjectives that you can use this week to compliment family members.

Verse to Memorize: Hebrews 3:13a—"But encourage one another daily."

Prayer Suggestion: Ask God to help you remember to compliment and say kind words to others on a daily basis.

You're a good helper!
How thoughtful you are!
You are very kind to others.

February 10
Anniversary of First Published Magazine

The first magazine in America was published during this week in 1741. Some of God's words were first "published" on an altar of stones. Read Deuteronomy 27:1-10 to find out more.

Questions to Discuss: What is your favorite magazine? Why did God want His commands written on stones?

Related Activity: Spend fifteen to thirty minutes looking at your favorite magazine. Then have each person share something he or she learned or found fascinating.

Curriculum Connection: Look at your magazine. Review the table of contents page, then look at the masthead, which usually follows the contents page. Find the editor's name. How many contributing authors are there? Where is your magazine published? How often is your magazine published?

Verse to Memorize: Deuteronomy 27:10a—"Obey the Lord your God and follow his commands."

Prayer Suggestion: Pray for magazine publishers and writers that they might tell the good news of Jesus Christ.

February 11
Wedding Month

February is the month for weddings. Jesus apparently thought weddings were very important, for it was at a wedding that He performed His first miracle. Read about this miracle in John 2:1–11.

Questions to Discuss: What was Jesus' first miracle? How do you think the people at the wedding must have felt when they witnessed this miracle? What miracle has Jesus performed in your life?

Related Activity: Mom and Dad, share with your children how the two of you met. As a family, look at wedding photos or videos. Share aloud how God has blessed your marriage.

Curriculum Connection: Find out what these vocabulary words mean: *groomsman, bridesmaid, maid of honor, matron of honor, flower girl, ring bearer, best man.*

Verse to Memorize: John 1:14—"The Word became flesh and made his dwelling among us. We have seen his glory, the glory of the One and Only, who came from the Father, full of grace and truth."

Prayer Suggestion: Pray for married couples that they will keep Christ in the center of their marriage. Pray specifically for your own marriage.

February 12
Grapefruit Month

The Florida Department of Citrus says that a serving of grapefruit provides more than 100 percent of the daily value of vitamin C. (Could that be what God had in mind when He created them?) Read about this day of creation in Genesis 1:11–13.

Questions to Discuss: What is your favorite fruit? Do you like to eat grapefruit?

Related Activity: Make a grapefruit person to decorate your table before breakfast. Wash a grapefruit with warm water and dry it. Use sturdy, wooden toothpicks to attach assorted food items for hair, eyes, nose, mouth, ears, and eyebrows. Try using lettuce, raisins, miniature marshmallows, shoestring licorice, gumdrops, jellybeans, and pressed fruit pieces or other soft candies. Let your "person" decorate your table, then carefully remove all picks, slice your grapefruit, and enjoy a healthy dose of vitamin C.

Curriculum Connection: See how many fruits you can name. Put them in alphabetical order. Is there a fruit for every letter of the alphabet?

Verse to Memorize: Genesis 1:12b—"And God saw that it was good."

Prayer Suggestion: Say this rhyming prayer, using your alphabetical list to fill in the blank: "Thank you, God, for [apples], so sweet. Thank you, God, for good fruit to eat!"

February 13
American Heart Month

Taking advantage of the "Heart Holiday" this month, the American Heart Association disseminates information about heart disease and stroke every year in February. Your heart needs physical attention as well as spiritual attention. Read 1 Samuel 16:1-13 to see how God feels about your heart.

Questions to Discuss: Explain the meaning of the memory verse. Are you guilty of looking at outward appearances instead of looking at one's heart?

Related Activity: Bake heart-shaped sugar cookies. Frost them with red or pink sprinkles or icing.

Curriculum Connection: Read about the heart; learn about the circulatory system.

Verse to Memorize: 1 Samuel 16:7b—"The Lord does not look at the things man looks at. Man looks at the outward appearance, but the Lord looks at the heart."

Prayer Suggestion: Ask God to help you look inside a person instead of outside.

February 14
Valentine's Day

Different authorities have differing views on how Valentine's Day actually began. Some trace this day to an ancient Roman festival; some credit the early Christian church and two saints named Valentine, and still others link this holiday to an English belief about birds and their mates. The current customs for Valentine's Day are probably a combination of all three ideas. No matter the origin of the day, Valentine's Day is set aside to express our love to special people. Read 1 John 4:7–21 to find out about the greatest Valentine's gift ever given.

Questions to Discuss: How did God show His love to us? How can we show our love to others?

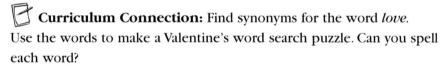

Related Activity: Make Valentine's cards for each member of your family. Write the memory verse on the front of the card, then personalize the inside.

Curriculum Connection: Find synonyms for the word *love*. Use the words to make a Valentine's word search puzzle. Can you spell each word?

Verse to Memorize: 1 John 4:19—"We love because he first loved us."

Prayer Suggestion: Ask God to help you show love to your family, your neighbors, and your friends. Thank God for His very special Valentine—Jesus Christ.

February 15
Ferris Wheel Day

This day celebrates the birthday of George Washington Ferris. Ferris, born in 1859, invented the Ferris wheel. One of the largest Ferris wheels was two hundred and fifty feet in diameter. Joshua led the Israelites around and around in circles outside the Jericho wall. Read Joshua 5:13–6:27 to find out about their "ride."

Questions to Discuss: What instructions did the Lord give Joshua about Jericho? Why do you think God's instructions were so specific? Do you have trouble obeying God?

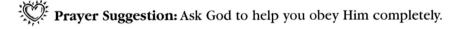

Related Activity: Build a wall, using blocks or boxes. March around six times, once for each day. Then march around seven times, blow pretend trumpets, shout "Praise the Lord," and knock down the walls.

Curriculum Connection: Practice measuring diameters of circles. How do you find the diameter when you only know the radius? What is a chord, in relation to a circle?

Verse to Memorize: Joshua 22:5—"But be very careful to keep the commandment and the law that Moses the servant of the Lord gave you: to love the Lord your God, to walk in all his ways, to obey his commands, to hold fast to him and to serve him with all your heart and all your soul."

Prayer Suggestion: Ask God to help you obey Him completely.

February 16
Canned Food Month

*What is your favorite food from a can? Read Acts 10:9-16
to find out about Peter's vision relating to food.*

Questions to Discuss: Read Matthew 15:1-20. Why do you think Jesus set aside the laws of clean and unclean food, as was written in Leviticus 11?

Related Activity: Collect canned goods; donate a collection to a local homeless shelter.

Curriculum Connection: Read the nutritional information on the labels of your cans. How many servings are in each can? How much is a serving? What vitamins and minerals are in each can? Which food seems to be the healthiest?

Verse to Memorize: 1 Timothy 4:4-5—"For everything God created is good, and nothing is to be rejected if it is received with thanksgiving because it is consecrated by the word of God and prayer."

Prayer Suggestion: Thank God for the things He has given you to eat. Pray that the food you donated will bless someone's life.

February 17
Random-Acts-of-Kindness Day

The Kindness Movement apparently got its start when a California writer coined the phrase, "practice random kindness and acts of senseless beauty." The phrase caught on quickly, appearing on bumper stickers and other novelty items. Although this particular phrase might have appeared in 1980, Jesus spoke about a "random act of kindness" in His parable of the Good Samaritan. Read Luke 10:25-37.

Questions to Discuss: Why do you think the first two men passed by the hurt man without stopping? Why was it significant that a Samaritan took such good care of the hurt man? What random act of kindness have you carried out today?

Related Activity: Make a list of ten kind things you can do this week. Keep the list in your room, and check off each act as you accomplish it.

Curriculum Connection: Find these places on a current map: Jerusalem and Jericho. Use a biblical map to find Samaria.

Verse to Memorize: Ephesians 4:31-32—"Get rid of all bitterness, rage and anger, brawling and slander, along with every form of malice. Be kind and compassionate to one another, forgiving each other, just as in Christ God forgave you."

Prayer Suggestion: Ask God to help you be kind to others.

February 18
Presidents' Day

Originally, the third Monday in February was set aside to observe the birthdays of two great presidents: George Washington, born on February 22, and Abraham Lincoln, born on February 12. Today, however, Presidents' Day honors all U.S. presidents' birthdays. Read about a particularly good leader during biblical days, in 1 Kings 3:1-28.

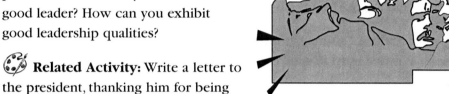

Questions to Discuss: What did Solomon ask for from God? Why did this please God? What do you think makes a good leader? How can you exhibit good leadership qualities?

Related Activity: Write a letter to the president, thanking him for being the leader of our country. Tell the president that you and your family are praying for him. Look for the president's address on the Internet.

Curriculum Connection: Write the names of the presidents in the order in which they served. Who was the youngest president? The oldest?

Verse to Memorize: James 1:5—"If any of you lacks wisdom, he should ask God, who gives generously to all without finding fault, and it will be given to him."

Prayer Suggestion: Pray for the president, that he would make wise decisions for your country.

February 19
Pluto Discovery Anniversary

Pluto is about thirty-nine times as far from the sun as the Earth is. Astronomers do not know much about Pluto because of its distance from Earth. However, God knows all about Pluto. Read Psalm 19:1–4.

Questions to Discuss: How many planets has man discovered? Who enabled man to discover the planets? What do you think it would be like to travel to another planet?

Related Activity: Make a model of the planets using balloons and string. Hang them from the ceiling in order.

Curriculum Connection: Learn the names of the planets in order; learn to spell each planet's name correctly.

Verse to Memorize: Psalm 33:6—"By the word of the Lord were the heavens made, their starry host by the breath of his mouth."

Prayer Suggestion: Thank God for His wonderful creation of the heavens—planets, stars, sun, moon—that which you can see and that which you know of by faith.

February 20
Toothpick Day

The equipment used to manufacture toothpicks was patented on this day in 1872. How often do you use toothpicks? Jesus talks about other pieces of wood in Matthew 7:1-5. Read about sawdust (wood particles much smaller than a toothpick) and a plank, which is much larger than a toothpick.

Questions to Discuss: What do the expressions "speck of sawdust" and "plank" mean in relation to the story Jesus told? Are you quick to judge others while ignoring your own faults?

Related Activity: Make a porcupine using toothpicks. Insert four screws in one side of a potato. Position the screws such that the potato will stand on the four legs. Push two screws into one end of the potato for eyes. Stick toothpicks in the top of the potato, forming quills. Place the potato in a kitchen window to remind you to watch your own "planks" rather than worry about other folks' "sawdust."

Curriculum Connection: Use toothpicks to make tally marks. Have someone call out a number and have another person make the correct tally marks for that number.

Verse to Memorize: Galatians 6:4-5—"Each one should test his own actions. Then he can take pride in himself, without comparing himself to somebody else, for each one should carry his own load."

Prayer Suggestion: Pray that God will reveal your faults so that you, with God's help, can remove them. Ask God to help you concentrate on your own faults rather than criticize another person.

February 21
Brotherhood-Sisterhood Month

This is a time set aside to work on the brotherhood and sisterhood of our nation. Jesus established this "celebration" years ago, though it was not recognized as such. Read Galatians 3:26-4:7 to see how Jesus set the precedent for this holiday.

Questions to Discuss: Do you have friends, family, and neighbors who look, speak, or act differently than you? Does God care what you look like on the outside?

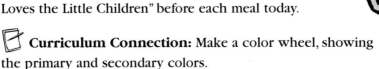

Related Activity: Make clothespin dolls in a variety of ethnic colors. Paint wooden clothespin dolls different shades of skin color. Add cloth robes and pipe cleaner arms. Stand the dolls in a bit of clay or dough for a base. Make a table centerpiece by placing a globe in the center of the table. Surround the globe with the brotherhood-sisterhood dolls. Sing "Jesus Loves the Little Children" before each meal today.

Curriculum Connection: Make a color wheel, showing the primary and secondary colors.

Verse to Memorize: Galatians 3:28—"There is neither Jew nor Greek, slave nor free, male nor female, for you are all one in Christ Jesus."

Prayer Suggestion: Pray that people of all races might live in harmony.

February 22
National Cherry Month

Michigan, Washington, Oregon, and California are the leading cherry-growing states. Does your state grow cherries? In Matthew 12:33–37, Jesus talks about fruit from "good" and "bad" trees. Read to find out what He says.

Questions to Discuss: Give examples of "good fruit." Compare those qualities with examples of "bad fruit" from a "bad tree."

Related Activity: Use this quick-and-easy recipe to make cherry cobbler: melt one stick of margarine in a casserole dish. Stir together one cup of self-rising flour, one cup of sugar, a dash of salt, and two-thirds cup of milk. Pour the mixture over melted butter; do not stir. Place two and one-half cups of sweetened, sliced, pitted cherries on top. Bake at 350 degrees for thirty to forty minutes.

Curriculum Connection: Learn to recognize a variety of trees.

Verse to Memorize: Psalm 7:8b— "Judge me, O Lord, according to my righteousness, according to my integrity, O Most High."

Prayer Suggestion: Ask God to help your words and actions show that Christ dwells within you.

February 23
Tootsie Roll Day

Do you like this chocolaty treat? The Tootsie Roll candy was introduced on this date in 1896. Many people enjoy the sweet taste of chocolate. God wants our words to be "sweet." Read Proverbs 16:24 to find out how your words can be like Tootsie Rolls to the soul.

Questions to Discuss: How do you feel when someone speaks to you in an unkind way? How do you feel when someone speaks to you in a kind way? What kind words have you spoken to someone today?

Related Activity: Snack on a Tootsie Roll. How does it taste? After you have enjoyed the sweet candy, take the time to share pleasant words to each member of your family.

Curriculum Connection: Use a thesaurus to find other words that mean the same as *pleasant.*

Verse to Memorize: Psalm 19:14—"May the words of my mouth and the meditation of my heart be pleasing in your sight, O Lord, my Rock and my Redeemer."

Prayer Suggestion: Ask God to help you speak only pleasant and kind words to others.

February 24
Potato Lovers' Month

Has your family ever had dinner together when one or more of the family members were angry with one another? How did the food taste? Do you remember what you ate? Proverbs 15:17 tells us that even the most expensive food on the menu would not taste good if those eating it had hatred in their hearts.

Questions to Discuss: How can you resolve a disagreement with a family member?

Related Activity: Prepare baked potatoes for dinner. While they are baking, play "Hot Potato" with an uncooked potato. Pass the potato quickly, while saying the books of the Bible in order.

Curriculum Connection: Write the plurals of some words that end in "o" (hint: potato-potatoes).

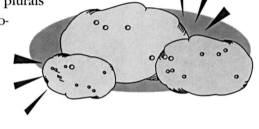

Verse to Memorize: John 13:34— "A new command I give you: Love one another. As I have loved you, so you must love one another."

Prayer Suggestion: Thank God for delicious vegetables to eat.

February 25
National Music Month

What is your favorite way to praise the Lord? Does it involve music and singing? If so, this is your month. Read Psalm 98:1–9.

Questions to Discuss: What is your favorite song or hymn? How can you use music to praise God? How do you think God feels when you praise Him?

Related Activity: Stretch rubber bands across a shoebox with no lid to make a harp. Sing a song of praise to God.

Curriculum Connection: Learn to read musical notes. What is a whole note, half note, quarter note, sixteenth note?

Verse to Memorize: Ephesians 5:19—"Speak to one another with psalms, hymns and spiritual songs. Sing and make music in your heart to the Lord, always giving thanks to God the Father for everything, in the name of our Lord Jesus Christ."

Prayer Suggestion: Pray for musicians.

February 26
Mardi Gras

Mardi Gras, meaning Fat Tuesday, is the Tuesday before the beginning of Lent. To prepare for the Lenten fast, eggs, milk, and fat were traditionally used up by this day because they were prohibited during Lent. Because pancakes became a traditional way to use up some of these products, the day also became known as Pancake Day. Read 1 Kings 17:7-24 to find out about a widow who did not have enough supplies to make pancakes in her home.

Questions to Discuss: Why did the woman tell Elijah that she and her son would die? Why did the widow do as Elijah asked, even though she had but a bit of flour left? How can you trust God to provide for your needs?

Related Activity: Make pancakes together.

Curriculum Connection: Learn about the basic food groups and the food pyramid. How many servings of each group should you have per day?

Verse to Memorize: Isaiah 50:10—"Who among you fears the Lord and obeys the word of his servant? Let him who walks in the dark, who has no light, trust in the name of the Lord and rely on his God."

Prayer Suggestion: Pray for widows, widowers, and single parents.

February 27
Ash Wednesday

The day after Mardi Gras is Ash Wednesday and the beginning of the Lenten season. Originally, only "public sinners" received the sign of the cross marked in ashes on their foreheads. The person who committed the sin had to make it public. Then he or she would undergo a lengthy penance before being able to return to the church. By the end of the eleventh century, other Christians began voluntarily receiving the ashes on this day as well. In John 8:1–11, Jesus comforts a public sinner and reminds others that they, too, are sinners.

Questions to Discuss: What do you think Jesus wrote on the ground? Is anyone without sin?

Related Activity: On paper, write the sins you committed this week.

Curriculum Connection: Learn to spell the days of the week and months of the year.

Verse to Memorize: Romans 3:10—"As it is written: There is no one righteous, not even one." (And 1 John 1:9—"If we confess our sins, he is faithful and just and will forgive us our sins and purify us from all unrighteousness.")

Prayer Suggestion: Ask God to forgive the specific sins you wrote on paper, then, carefully, with adult supervision, burn the papers.

February 28
Lent

Christians in Egypt established the Lenten season before A.D. 330. Today Christians observe the forty days before Easter, excluding Sundays, as Lent and remember Jesus' forty days in the wilderness. Because Jesus fasted and prayed, Christians traditionally use this time to fast and pray, preparing for Easter. Read about Jesus' time in the wilderness before He began His ministry in Matthew 4:1-11.

Questions to Discuss: Why did Jesus fast for forty days and nights? In verse 4, what does Jesus say is His spiritual "food"? Why do you think Satan tempts you when you are most vulnerable? Did Jesus succumb to temptation? What can help you fight temptation?

Related Activity: Choose one item to give up until Easter—a particular food, favorite toy, favorite television show. Each time you think about that item, use it as a reminder to talk to God.

Curriculum Connection: Count by tens.

Verse to Memorize: Hebrews 4:15—"For we do not have a high priest who is unable to sympathize with our weaknesses, but we have one who has been tempted in every way, just as we are—yet was without sin."

Prayer Suggestion: Ask God to help use the item you are giving up to prepare your heart for the Easter celebration.

February 29
Leap Year Day

February 29 is added to the calendar once every four years to keep the calendar year as close as possible to the solar year. Read in Acts 14:8–10 about a man who was able to "leap" for the first time after his encounter with Paul.

 **Questions to Discuss:** How long had the man in the story been crippled? Why did Paul heal him?

Related Activity: Play leap frog.

Curriculum Connection: Learn the number of days in each month. (Try using the knuckle method. Make two fists and hold your hands in front of you. Start with the left, pinkie knuckle. Point to it and say, "January." See how the bone is raised? That's thirty-one days. Touch the valley between the pinkie and the ring finger. That's February and has twenty-eight days. The raised knuckle at the base of the ring finger is March, with thirty-one days. Get it? The raised knuckles are always thirty-one days; the valleys, with the exception of February, are thirty days. Obviously, you'll run out of months before fingers. December stops on the ring finger, with the raised knuckle of the second hand.

Verse to Memorize: Galatians 3:9a—"So those who have faith are blessed."

Prayer Suggestion: Pray for a strong faith in Jesus Christ.

March

March 1
National Pig Day

Did you know that farmers in almost every country raise pigs? Celebrate this piggy day by reading about a son who wanted to eat the food intended for the pigs in his care because he was so hungry. Read Luke 15:11–32.

Questions to Discuss: Why do you think the younger son took "all he had" with him when he left for a distant country? What made the son decide to return home? Who forgave the young man? Who did not?

Related Activity: Make a pig book mark. Paint both sides of a large craft stick pink. Meanwhile, glue quarter-inch pom-poms for eyes to a pink, one-inch pom-pom head. Cut a small circle from pink felt for the snout; add black marker dots for the nostrils. Cut felt ears and a felt tail. Glue the ears and snout in place on the head; glue the head on the top of the dry craft stick. Glue the curly tail on the bottom, back of the craft stick.

Curriculum Connection: See how many baby animal names you know. What is the name for the babies of these animals: pig, cow, duck, goose, chicken, horse, lion, bear, penguin?

Verse to Memorize: Colossians 3:13—"Bear with each other and forgive whatever grievances you may have against one another. Forgive as the Lord forgave you."

Prayer Suggestion: Ask God to help you forgive others, just as He has forgiven you. Thank God for His forgiveness of sins.

March 2
Children's Author and
Illustrator Week

This day was established and set aside as a day to honor those who author and illustrate books for young people and to promote literacy. Much literature has been written over the years to guide and nurture young children. In Ecclesiastes 12:9–14, the author agrees that words of the wise guide and nurture.

Questions to Discuss: What is a goad? Why are the "words of the wise," directed by God, like goads? How can a children's author guide young people with the words of his or her books?

Related Activity: Write and illustrate a children's picture book. Make up a story or re-tell a story from the Bible. Make sure your words can be like goads.

Curriculum Connection: Read about the publishing process. What do these terms mean: *publisher, editor, illustrator, copyright, publicist?*

Verse to Memorize: Proverbs 9:10—"The fear of the Lord is the beginning of wisdom, and knowledge of the Holy One is understanding."

Prayer Suggestion: Pray for children's authors and illustrators.

March 3
National Anthem Day

Francis Scott Key, an American lawyer and amateur verse writer, wrote the words to The Star Spangled Banner *while being held prisoner by the British during the War of 1812. He was so inspired when he saw the American flag flying over Fort McHenry that he penned the words to the song. In March of 1931, Congress officially approved the song as the national anthem. Although most countries have their own personal national anthem, there is only one God who rules over all of the nations. Read Acts 8:1b-8, 11:19-30 to see how the persecution of the early church would eventually take the gospel of Christ to many other nations.*

Questions to Discuss: How did God use the persecution of the early church to spread His gospel to other places? How can you spread God's word?

Related Activity: Memorize the words to "The Star Spangled Banner," and sing it together as a family.

Curriculum Connection: Learn more about the history of "The Star Spangled Banner." Where is the flag held today that inspired Francis Scott Key? Did Mr. Key write the tune also?

Verse to Memorize: Matthew 28:19-20—"Therefore go and make disciples of all nations, baptizing them in the name of the Father and of the Son and of the Holy Spirit, and teaching them to obey everything I have commanded you. And surely I am with you always, to the very end of the age."

Prayer Suggestion: Ask God to help you spread His word in your own neighborhood, community, state, and nation.

March 4
Dentists' Day

Do you enjoy going to the dentist? Do you think your dentist would want to work on a lion's tooth? How sharp do you think the teeth of a lion are? Read Daniel 6:1–23 about a man who certainly did not want to find out just how sharp lions' teeth are.

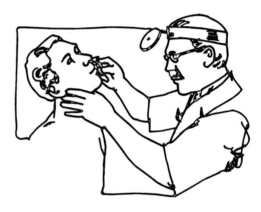

Questions to Discuss: Why was Daniel put in the lion's den? How did God prevent the lions from eating Daniel? Do you trust God to take care of you?

Related Activity: Make lion puppets and a Daniel puppet. Use white lunch-sized paper bags and yellow construction paper for the lions' head. Draw a face on the bag for Daniel. Re-enact the story from the Bible. Let the lions roar loudly at the beginning of the play, but hold their mouths tightly closed while Daniel is in the den.

Curriculum Connection: Find out the educational requirements needed to become a dentist or dental technician.

Verse to Memorize: Isaiah 12:2a—"Surely God is my salvation; I will trust and not be afraid."

Prayer Suggestion: Pray for dentists and their helpers.

March 5
National Shoe Week

The men of biblical days usually wore sandals that consisted mostly of soles strapped to the feet. Visitors to a home were usually treated to a foot washing by servants, because travelers' feet became dusty and sandy from walking along the unpaved roads. Read Luke 7:36-50 to find out about a special foot cleaning that a sinful woman performed.

Questions to Discuss: Why was the woman crying at Jesus' feet? Why did Jesus tell the woman to "go in peace"? Have you felt Jesus' peace?

Related Activity: Count how many pairs of shoes you have in your house. Do you feel blessed to own that many pairs of shoes? How many pairs of shoes do you think Jesus owned?

Curriculum Connection: What is a "pace"? Measure rooms in your house, using a shoe length. Will the measurements be different for each person?

Verse to Memorize: Romans 5:1— "Therefore, since we have been justified through faith, we have peace with God through our Lord Jesus Christ."

Prayer Suggestion: Give thanks to God for forgiving you of your sins that you might have peace through Jesus.

March 6
Purim

The book of Esther tells how God used a young Jewish girl to save the Jewish people from extermination. The Purim holiday was set aside in the Bible to remember this time in the life of God's chosen people. To understand the whole story, read Esther 2:19-9:32.

Questions to Discuss: How did God use Esther's position as queen to save His people? How can God use you to do a big job?

Related Activity: Haman used King Xerxes' signet ring, like a stamp, to attempt the extermination of all the Jews. Make stamps from potatoes and print pictures on drawing paper. Have older children carefully cut a potato in half. Then draw a simple outline or shape onto the potato. Carve away the outside of the outline, leaving the design raised. Let the younger children dip the stamps into paint and make pictures.

Curriculum Connection: Learn to recognize and spell these titles and their abbreviations, if they have one: King, Queen, Mister, Mistress, Miss, President, Doctor, Reverend, Professor.

Verse to Memorize: Exodus 29:46—"They will know that I am the Lord their God, who brought them out of Egypt so that I might dwell among them. I am the Lord their God."

Prayer Suggestion: Thank God for the stories in the Bible about His chosen people and for the lessons that we can learn from His word.

March 7
Art Week

In Exodus 31:1-11, God tells Moses about the special artistic talents He gave Bezalel and Oholiab. God had special jobs He wanted these men to do. Read the passage to see what plans God had in mind.

Questions to Discuss: What special skill or talent did God give you? How can you use that talent for God?

Related Activity: Create art pieces for an art show. Use any medium you like—painting, coloring, sculpting, gluing. Display your family art pieces, and have a show.

Curriculum Connection: Read about some of these art forms: architecture, ballet, dance, drama, drawing, graphic arts, jewelry, mosaic, painting, pottery, theater, weaving.

Verse to Memorize: Psalm 90:17—"May the favor of the Lord our God rest upon us; establish the work of our hands for us—yes, establish the work of our hands."

Prayer Suggestion: Ask God to help you use the gifts and talents He's given you for His glory and good.

March 8
March Winds Day

Is it windy today where you live? Celebrate this windy month by giving credit to the Creator of the wind. Read Ecclesiastes 8:8a.

Questions to Discuss: Can man control the wind? Who causes the winds to blow? Explain the old saying, "If March comes in like a lamb, it will go out like a lion."

Related Activity: Play with a pinwheel outside. If you do not have a pinwheel, use a streamer or long ribbon.

Curriculum Connection: Make a calendar for March. How many Tuesdays are in this month? What day does the month begin on? When does it end? Watch the Weather Channel on TV to see how windy each day in March is. Write the speed of the wind for each day.

Verse to Memorize: Psalm 147:5a—"Great is our Lord and mighty in power."

Prayer Suggestion: Sit in front of a fan while you say your prayers. Thank God for His awesome power—a power so awesome that He can control the wind. Ask God to remind you of His power each time you feel the wind blow across your face.

March 9
False Teeth Day

False teeth were patented on this day in 1822. If you are too lazy to take care of your teeth, you could wind up with false teeth one day. In Proverbs 10:26, God uses an illustration about teeth to warn against laziness.

Questions to Discuss: What is a sluggard? How would being a sluggard affect your message of Christ?

Related Activity: Use a Bible dictionary and concordance to find other proverbs about a sluggard. Pretend to be a slug on the ground for a couple of minutes. Make excuses about not working. How do you feel? Now get up and do some stretches and exercises for five minutes. How do you feel now?

Curriculum Connection: Learn more about your teeth. How many primary teeth are there? How many permanent teeth are there? What are incisors, canines, premolars, molars?

Verse to Memorize: Proverbs 10:4— "Lazy hands make a man poor, but diligent hands bring wealth."

Prayer Suggestion: Ask God to help you be diligent in all that you do.

March 10
Jerusalem Temple Rebuilt

God's temple, built by Solomon, was abused and plundered during the reigns of many kings after Solomon. When Nebuchadnezzar captured Jerusalem, he gathered all the treasures of the temple and carried them away. Eleven years later, Jerusalem was destroyed by the Chaldeans, who burned the temple after pillaging the remaining valuables. Not until the Jews returned from their exile in Babylon did God's house get rebuilt. Read Ezra 1:1-8, 3:7-13, 6:13-18 to find out about the Temple of Zerubbabel.

Questions to Discuss: Why did the temple need to be rebuilt? Why did God allow the first temple to fall? (Refresh your memory with 2 Kings 24:10-13, 25:9-17.) Is sin causing destruction in your life?

Related Activity: Build with blocks. How would you construct a house of worship for God?

Curriculum Connection: Study the meanings of words with these prefixes: *re, pre, pro, ex.*

Verse to Memorize: Isaiah 59:2—
"But your iniquities have separated you from your God; your sins have hidden his face from you, so that he will not hear."

Prayer Suggestion: Thank God for your house of worship.

March 11
Paper Day

The Chinese are credited with the invention of paper in A.D. 105. What would your life be like without paper? Read how John the Baptist's father used a writing tablet because he had no paper to write on.
Read Luke 1:5-25, 57-66.

Questions to Discuss: Why couldn't Zechariah speak? When have you had a hard time believing God?

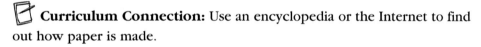

Related Activity: Make an interesting design with tissue paper. Tear colored tissue paper into shapes. Paint a sheet of white construction paper with vinegar. Place the tissue paper onto the vinegar-streaked paper while the vinegar is wet. Allow the paper to dry. Peel off the dry tissue paper, and your design will be revealed on your white paper.

Curriculum Connection: Use an encyclopedia or the Internet to find out how paper is made.

Verse to Memorize: Mark 9:23b—"Everything is possible for him who believes."

Prayer Suggestion: Ask God to help you believe in Him, even if God's words seem difficult to believe.

March 12
Girl Scout Birthday

The Girl Scout promise reads, "On my honor, I will try: to serve God and my country, to help people at all times, and to live by the Girl Scout Law." Read about a young girl in Exodus 2:1–10 who not only helped a special baby but, in turn, saved the lives of many, many others.

 Questions to Discuss: How many girls did you read about in this story? Have you ever had to be as brave as Miriam?

Related Activity: Play this game: place a baby doll in a basket, then have the family hold a sheet, preferably a blue one, to represent the waters of the river. Start the "Moses" baby on one end of the sheet. Hold up that end of the sheet and "send" the baby down the river. Try to get the basket to the other end, without the basket turning over.

Curriculum Connection: Learn about the history of Girl Scouts. Who was Juliette Gordon Low? Where was the very first troop meeting held?

Verse to Memorize: 2 Chronicles 15:7—"But as for you, be strong and do not give up, for your work will be rewarded."

Prayer Suggestion: Pray for Girl Scouts and their leaders.

March 13
National Procrastination Week

What does procrastinate *mean? Read about some
procrastinators in Luke 14:15–23.*

Questions to Discuss: In Jesus' parable, what does He mean by
"preparing a great banquet"? Why did the people in the story procrastinate
and make excuses for not coming to the banquet? Are you procrastinating
and not doing the will of God?

Related Activity: Make a list of things your family has been procrastinating about: visiting an elderly friend, cleaning your room, raking the yard.
Try to accomplish the things on your list this week. Mark off your accomplishments.

Curriculum Connection: Talk about clocks. Have younger
children discuss the hour and the half-hour; older children can learn to recognize time at five-minute intervals
and solve word problems involving time.

Verse to Memorize: 2 Corinthians 6:2b—
"I tell you, now is the time of God's favor, now is the
day of salvation."

Prayer Suggestion: Ask God to help you not to
procrastinate when doing His will.

*We never got around
to finding art for this page

March 14
Earmuff Day

Do you own a pair of earmuffs? If you do, then you can thank a Maine teenager for inventing them in the year 1877. How do you keep the rest of your body warm? Does each part of your body have the same function? Read 1 Corinthians 12:1–31 to find a discussion about the "body" working together spiritually.

Questions to Discuss: How does your family function and work together as one body? Which body part do you think is represented by each person? Is one person in the family a particularly good listener? Is another particularly good with his or her hands?

Related Activity: Draw an outline of one person in the family on a large sheet of drawing paper. (Rolled freezer paper, taped together for width, works well for this activity.) Label the gifts and talents of each person, something like this: "eyes"—good reader, "hands"—good helper, "feet"—fast runner, and so on. Put the person's name next to his or her gift. Talk about how God planned for your family to use their gifts collectively, as well as individually, to serve Him as one body.

Curriculum Connection: Encourage younger children to learn to spell the body parts as can be seen on the outside. Have older children label and spell the internal organs.

Verse to Memorize: 1 Corinthians 12:13—"For we were all baptized by one Spirit into one body—whether Jew or Greeks, slave or free—and we were all given the one Spirit to drink."

Prayer Suggestion: Thank God for the gifts and talents He has given your family. Ask God to help you use those gifts as a family to bless others.

March 15
Escalator Day

Do you like riding on escalators? The escalator was patented in 1892 in New York City. Read in Genesis 28:10-22 about Jacob's dream of something resembling an escalator.

Questions to Discuss: Explain the meaning of Jacob's dream about the stairway. How does it make you feel to know that God is always with you, wherever you go?

Related Activity: Use pretzel logs and pretzel sticks, along with frosting for glue, to make a ladder.

Curriculum Connection: Using the word *dream* as an example, practice finding rhyming words with long vowel sounds.

Verse to Memorize: Genesis 28:15a—"I am with you and will watch over you wherever you go."

Prayer Suggestion: Thank God that He is always with you.

March 16
National Craft Month

In Jeremiah 18:1-12 and 19:1-15, God sent Jeremiah to a craftsman's house. Find out what the craftsman's specialty was when you read today's passage.

Questions to Discuss: What does the word *mar* mean? How did the potter remove the imperfection in the pot? Tell about a time when God molded you and removed an imperfection.

Related Activity: Make something out of clay or dough.

Curriculum Connection: Write the words to the hymn, "Have Thine Own Way, Lord."

Verse to Memorize: Isaiah 64:8— "Yet, O Lord, you are our Father. We are the clay, you are the potter; we are all the work of your hand."

Prayer Suggestion: Ask God to help you be patient as He molds you and forms you into the precious craft that He intends for you to be.

March 17
Saint Patrick's Day

The man who came to be known as Saint Patrick, as purported in his own book, was taken captive by brigands and taken to Ireland to be sold into slavery. It was here that he became a Christian. Even though he later escaped, he soon returned to Ireland as a missionary to share the news of Christ with the people of Ireland. Many legends and stories are told about Saint Patrick. One particular story holds that Saint Patrick used the three-leafed clover to explain the Trinity to the Irish. Perhaps Saint Patrick used John 14:5–31 in some of his messages.

Questions to Discuss: Talk about God the Father, God the Son, and God, the Holy Spirit.

Related Activity: Make shamrock rolls. Roll the dough into three balls and place them on a cookie sheet very close together. Roll another piece of dough into the stem for the shamrock. As the rolls are baking, talk about the stem as the Godhead, joining all three "persons." Talk about the leaves as the Father, Son, and Holy Spirit.

Curriculum Connection: Locate the countries of Europe on a map or globe. Can you spell and identify each country?

Verse to Memorize: John 14:6—"Jesus answered, 'I am the way and the truth and the life. No one comes to the Father except through me.'"

Prayer Suggestion: Let each person read this benediction aloud, filling in the blank with a family member's name until each person has been prayed for: 2 Corinthians 13:14—"May the grace of the Lord Jesus Christ, and the love of God, and the fellowship of the Holy Spirit be with [person's name]."

March 18
Rubber Band Day

Guess what was invented on this day? How many times a week do you use rubber bands? What have you bound together recently? Read Revelation 20:1-10 to see who gets bound, without the use of rubber bands.

Questions to Discuss: How does the angel bind Satan? How long will Satan be bound? How long will Satan be in the lake of burning sulfur?

Related Activity: Make a rubber band ball. Crumple a sheet of computer paper and wad it into a tight ball. Cover with many layers of rubber bands. Keep the ball on your desk. The next time you need a rubber band, remove one from the outside.

Curriculum Connection: The word *band,* meaning a group of singers, and the word *band,* meaning a thin strip of material, are homonyms. Make a list of other homonyms and their meanings.

Verse to Memorize: Romans 16:20a—"The God of Peace will soon crush Satan under your feet."

Prayer Suggestion: Ask God to help you resist Satan's temptations.

March 19
National Bubble Week

Do you know why all bubbles are round? Read Isaiah 40:22
to find out who sits above the "bubble" we call Earth.

Questions to Discuss: Close your eyes and imagine God sitting on His throne, looking down at the round Earth. Describe the majesty of God's heavenly throne. Why does the verse in Isaiah compare people to grasshoppers?

Related Activity: Blow bubbles using various utensils found around the house, such as a slotted spoon, bug swatter, or pipe cleaner twisted into a circle. What shape are the bubbles?

Curriculum Connection: Read about surface tension to find out why bubbles are round.

Verse to Memorize: Psalm 47:7-8— "For God is the King of all the earth; sing to him a psalm of praise. God reigns over the nations; God is seated on his holy throne."

Prayer Suggestion: Praise the Lord for being the awesome, mighty King of the Earth.

March 20
Spring

Read Psalm 65:9-13. The psalmists declare that all creation—human and the inanimate elements of nature—celebrate the goodness of God. Springtime is a perfect time to praise God for the beauty of His creations.

Questions to Discuss: Are the trees beginning to bud where you live? Is the grass turning a brilliant shade of green in your yard? Are flowers beginning to burst forth with splendor? How can you "shout for joy and sing" of God's goodness?

Related Activity: Make place markers for your table as a reminder to thank God daily for the gift of spring. Use large craft sticks for stems, cupcake liners for blooms, construction paper for leaves, and glue to make flowers. Make one for each family member. Use puffy paints to decorate and write names on small flowerpots, one per family member. Fill the pot with soil, and stand the flower in the soil. Put the pots in the appropriate places at the dinner table.

Curriculum Connection: Write all the descriptive details of spring that you can think of. Use these details to write a poem about spring.

Verse to Memorize: Psalm 66:4—"All the earth bows down to you; they sing praise to you, they sing praise to your name."

Prayer Suggestion: Have each family member name his or her favorite parts of spring. Give thanks to God for these blessings and beautiful reminders of His goodness. End prayer time by singing, "For the Beauty of the Earth."

March 21
National Agriculture Week

Agriculture Week—a week of celebration to appreciate those in America who provide scrumptious food to eat—is held each year during the week containing the first day of spring. Read Galatians 6:7-10 to find out about God's agricultural methods and the wonderful harvest He has promised.

Questions to Discuss: How do you sow "sinfully"? How do you sow to please the Spirit? How does it make you feel to know that you have helped with God's harvest?

Related Activity: Play this memory game. Have the first person say, "I'm making vegetable soup to eat. Here's what I'm cooking in my yummy treat: squash." Then have the next person repeat that line and add another vegetable. Keep going until you can't remember all the vegetables in the list.

Curriculum Connection: Make a list of as many vegetables as you can name. Put the list in alphabetical order. Is there a vegetable for every letter of the alphabet?

Verse to Memorize: 2 Corinthians 9:6—"Remember this: Whoever sows sparingly will also reap sparingly, and whoever sows generously will also reap generously."

Prayer Suggestion: Pray for farmers.

March 22
International Day of the Seal

*Although seals spend much time in the water, many seals come on land to
bask in the sun or give birth to their young. The northern fur seal, however,
stays at sea for over eight months, migrating almost five thousand miles.
The fur seal travels from the Bering Sea to northern Mexico. What a trip!
Read Jeremiah's praises for the Lord in Jeremiah 31:35.*

Questions to Discuss: Why does Jeremiah refer to God as the
Almighty?

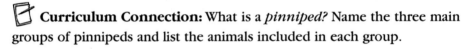

Related Activity: Have you
ever been to a marine animal park
and watched the trained seals and sea
lions? Crouch on your knees, fold your
hands backwards like flippers, and see if you
can balance a ball on your nose.

Curriculum Connection: What is a *pinniped?* Name the three main
groups of pinnipeds and list the animals included in each group.

Verse to Memorize: 1 Corinthians 10:26—"The Earth is the Lord's
and everything in it."

Prayer Suggestion: Thank God for pinnipeds.

March 23
National Frozen Food Month

Do you think you would ever turn down "food fit for a king?" Daniel did just that (see Daniel 1:1-21) and opted for a healthier diet. Read to see how he was blessed by doing so.

Questions to Discuss: Why didn't Daniel want to eat the royal food and drink the royal wine? What vegetables do you think Daniel liked to eat? Name the vegetables you like to eat. Do you prefer them fresh or frozen? Raw or cooked?

Related Activity: Use packages of frozen vegetables to make vegetable soup.

Curriculum Connection: Look at a chart of the vitamins needed for human health. Find the vegetable sources for each vitamin.

Verse to Memorize: Philippians 1:27a— "Whatever happens, conduct yourselves in a manner worthy of the gospel of Christ."

Prayer Suggestion: Ask God to help you be as courageous as Daniel.

March 24
Pecan Day

Did you know that the pecan tree is native to North America and that Georgia is the leading producer of pecans in a year? However, for the first five years, the pecan tree does not even produce nuts; only after about another five years do the trees produce a somewhat profitable return of nuts. Those who own pecan orchards have to be very patient. Read Genesis 43:11 to see which nuts Israel sent with his sons to buy food during a famine.

Questions to Discuss: What is your favorite nut to eat?

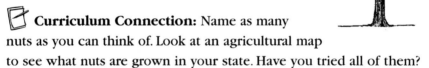

Related Activity: Using commercial slice-and-bake cookies, make kitty-cat cookies to eat. Slice the dough as directed on the package, and place a cookie on a baking sheet. Add two pecan halves for ears, candies for eyes, and pretzel sticks for whiskers. Bake according to package directions.

Curriculum Connection: Name as many nuts as you can think of. Look at an agricultural map to see what nuts are grown in your state. Have you tried all of them?

Verse to Memorize: Psalm 63:4–5—"I will praise you as long as I live, and in your name I will lift up my hands. My soul will be satisfied as with the richest of foods; with singing lips my mouth will praise you."

Prayer Suggestion: Thank God for good food to eat.

March 25
Feast of the Annunciation

Mary must have been stunned to hear the angel Gabriel's words in Luke 1:26-38. But what an awesome responsibility and privilege the Lord gave Mary. Read this passage to hear Mary's response to Gabriel—and to the Lord.

Questions to Discuss: Why do you think God chose Mary to be Jesus' mother? Did Mary obey God's words? How can you be obedient to God's word?

 Related Activity: Draw a picture of Mary. Make her face shine with happiness about being the mother of God's son.

Curriculum Connection: Define some words with the *tion* suffix and the *ness* suffix. Start with *Annunciation* and *happiness*.

Verse to Memorize: Luke 11:27-28—
"As Jesus was saying these things, a woman in
the crowd called out, 'Blessed is the mother
who gave you birth and nursed you.' He replied, 'Blessed
rather are those who hear the word of God and obey it.'"

Prayer Suggestion: Ask God to help you be obedient like Mary.

March 26
National Umbrella Month

Prior to the Great Flood, rain, as seen today, is not recorded in the Bible. Needed water for plants, animals, and humans came from underground springs and a vapor mist that covered the Earth. In other words, there was no need for an umbrella in those days. Can you just imagine the guffawing and laughter that occurred when Noah warned people of the imminent rainfall? They probably thought he was nuts. Read Genesis 6:1–7:24 to find out more.

Questions to Discuss: Why did God decide to send a flood? How do you think Noah felt as he was building the ark, without a dark cloud in sight? How do you think the people felt when the rains began to fall?

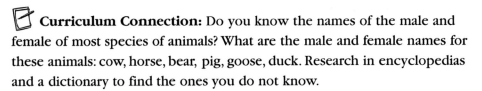

Related Activity: Paint an umbrella with Noah's ark and animal shapes. Use sponges for the animals, if you prefer. When your umbrella is completely dry, take a walk on a rainy day.

Curriculum Connection: Do you know the names of the male and female of most species of animals? What are the male and female names for these animals: cow, horse, bear, pig, goose, duck. Research in encyclopedias and a dictionary to find the ones you do not know.

Verse to Memorize: Hebrews 11:7—"By faith Noah, when warned about things not yet seen, in holy fear built an ark to save his family. By his faith he condemned the world and became heir of the righteousness that comes by faith."

Prayer Suggestion: Ask God to help you have faith like Noah.

March 27
National Noodle Month

Do you like your noodles plain, salted, buttered, or with cheese added?
Ruth and Naomi probably wouldn't have cared how their noodles
were prepared; they were hungry and had no one to care for them.
Read about God's hand in their situation in Ruth 2:1-23.

Questions to Discuss: How did God provide food for Ruth and Naomi? What has God provided for you today?

Related Activity: Make a collage of pasta. Glue a variety of shapes of pasta onto cardboard in an interesting design.

Curriculum Connection: Use uncooked pasta pieces to practice math facts.

Verse to Memorize: Psalm 111:5—"He provides food for those who fear him; he remembers his covenant forever."

Prayer Suggestion: Thank God for the food He provides your family.

March 28
No Homework Day

How about this for a holiday? Too bad there's only one per year. However, there is a permanent "rest" in Jesus' salvation. Read Hebrews 4:9-11.

Questions to Discuss: How do you "enter God's rest?" What can you think about today when you are resting?

Related Activity: No homework today! Instead, play a board game together as a family.

Curriculum Connection: Start with the word *homework*. Find other compound words.

Verse to Memorize:
1 Timothy 2:5-6a—"For there is one God and one mediator between God and men, the man Christ Jesus, who gave himself as a ransom for all men."

Prayer Suggestion: Thank God for your mediator—Jesus Christ.

March 29
Let's-Go-Fly-a-Kite Month

Have you flown a kite yet during this windy month? You'll miss an opportunity to enjoy an awesome display of God's majestic powers if you let the month slip away without enjoying the wind. Read Proverbs 30:4, and absorb God's greatness as Creator.

Questions to Discuss: Answer the question from the Bible passage. What are His name and the name of His Son? What makes God awesome to you? Give an example of His awesomeness as exhibited to you today.

Related Activity: This one's pretty obvious. Go fly a kite.

Curriculum Connection: Explain what *gravity* means.

Verse to Memorize: Psalm 47:2—"How awesome is the Lord Most High, the great King over all the earth!"

Prayer Suggestion: Praise the Lord for the awesome things He has done in your life, especially in the recent days.

March 30
Doctors' Day

In Mark 2:1-12, four friends loved and cared for their lame friend so much that they were willing to do almost anything to get him in the presence of Jesus. Read this passage to find out just what the friends did.

Questions to Discuss: For what kinds of illnesses do you need a doctor? Who is the greatest physician? How can Jesus heal you spiritually as well as physically?

Related Activity: Do this craft to remind you of Jesus' healing powers. On a large craft stick, draw facial features on one end. Glue scraps of material for clothing, and add pipe cleaner arms and legs. Cut and fold a piece of construction paper to resemble a mat. (If you have an empty check box, this would work well.) Punch four holes in the mat. Attach yarn to the holes. Tie the yarn to a pencil or dowel rod and pretend to lower the man to Jesus.

Curriculum Connection: Look in your phone book under "doctor" or "physician." Find out what physicians are in your area. Do you have a podiatrist? What about an endocrinologist? Identify each physician by his or her title.

Verse to Memorize: Matthew 9:35—"Jesus went through all the towns and villages, teaching in their synagogues, preaching the good news of the kingdom and healing every disease and sickness."

Prayer Suggestion: Pray for doctors.

March 31
Eiffel Tower Day

Paris's best-known landmark was completed on this day in 1889. Read 1 Kings 6:1–38 to find out about God's people's best-known "landmark."

Questions to Discuss: Why was the temple a special place for the Israelite people? Where and when do you feel closest to God?

Related Activity: Use graham crackers and frosting to build a sample of what you think the temple might have looked like.

Curriculum Connection: Find these famous landmarks on a map: Big Ben, Buckingham Palace, Empire State Building, Grand Canyon, Great Wall of China, Leaning Tower of Pisa, Niagara Falls, Seattle's Space Needle. How many are man-made? Is there a prominent landmark in your area?

Verse to Memorize: Psalm 73:28a—"But as for me, it is good to be near God."

Prayer Suggestion: Thank God for your place of worship.

 # April

April 1
April Fools' Day

A common theory on the origins of April Fools' Day suggests that the day started in France around 1564. Apparently, the calendar was changed so that January 1 was the beginning of a new year instead of April 1. The people who continued to give gifts and celebrate April 1 as a new year were called April Fools. The custom of playing jokes on family and friends became popular in France and spread to other countries. Have you fooled a family member for fun today? Read about five "foolish" women in Matthew 25:1–13.

 Questions to Discuss:
How were the five foolish bridesmaids like the five wise ones? How were they different? What is the lesson Jesus wants us to learn from this parable?

Related Activity: Find verses in Proverbs about "fools" and "wise men."

Curriculum Connection: Count by twos, fives, tens, twenty-fives, and hundreds.

Verse to Memorize: Matthew 25:13—"Therefore keep watch, because you do not know the day or the hour."

Prayer Suggestion: Ask God to help you "keep watch," preparing with great anticipation, for the day of the Lord's return.

April 2
National Grilled Cheese Sandwich Month

Did you know that the United States is the leading cheese-producing country and that Wisconsin is the leading cheese-producing state? Did you know that there are more than four hundred kinds of cheese? Have you sampled them all? When the disciples gathered the available food (read about it in Mark 6:30-44), no one had a cheese sandwich. Only bread and fish were found. Read about Jesus' miracle (minus the cheese) in this passage.

Questions to Discuss: How did Jesus provide for the needs—spiritual, physical, and emotional—of the crowd? How does God supply your needs? How can you thank God for taking care of your needs?

Related Activity: Prepare grilled cheese sandwiches for lunch. Slice each sandwich into five strips, and eat two large goldfish-shaped crackers with your five "loaves."

Curriculum Connection: Talk about place value. Cut paper into strips to represent one hundred people. How many will you need to make five thousand? Can you believe Jesus fed that many people?

Verse to Memorize: Revelation 7:15-17—"Therefore, they are before the throne of God and serve him day and night in his temple; and he who sits on the throne will spread his tent over them. Never again will they hunger; never again will they thirst. The sun will not beat upon them, nor any scorching heat. For the Lamb at the center of the throne will be their shepherd; he will lead them to springs of living water. And God will wipe away every tear from their eyes."

Prayer Suggestion: Pray for those who are hungry.

April 3
Holy Humor Month

Joy, laughter, happiness—all are byproducts of a Christian's life. Celebrate the joy Jesus Christ gives you this month, as well as a good sense of humor about life in general. Read Genesis 18:1–15 to find out about a particularly historic laugh.

Questions to Discuss: Why did Sarah laugh when she heard the words of the visitors? Do you believe anything is too hard for God? What do you think makes God happy?

Related Activity: Make Abraham and Sarah's tent. Cut pretzel logs into six four-inch pieces. Pair the logs and wrap rubber bands around the tops of each pair. Spread the unbound ends of each pair; stand them in clay bases. Stand the "legs" of the tent in a row, three inches apart. Let the clay harden a bit. Then drape a ready-to-use piecrust over the top of the pretzel rods. Tear part of the piecrust, between two pair of "tent stakes," to be the tent opening.

Curriculum Connection: Using *laugh* as the base word, add suffixes to make new words. Practice adding suffixes to base words using additional words.

Verse to Memorize: Genesis 18:14a—"Is anything too hard for the Lord?"

Prayer Suggestion: Ask God to help you trust in Him completely and believe, without a doubt, that nothing is too difficult for God.

April 4
Golden Rule Week

What a better place this world would be if everyone heeded Jesus' words and lived by the Golden Rule. You can make sure that you live by Jesus' words, and maybe others will follow your example.
Read 1 Samuel 24:1-22 to see if Saul lived by the Golden Rule.

Questions to Discuss: Was Saul treating David the way he wanted David to treat him? Have you lived by the Golden Rule today?

Related Activity: Write today's memory verse, with a permanent marker, on the ruler you use for math assignments.

Curriculum Connection: Study these measurements and memorize the equivalent formulas: inches, feet, yards, miles.

Verse to Memorize: Matthew 7:12a—"So in everything, do to others what you would have them do to you."

Prayer Suggestion: Ask God to help you treat others in the manner in which you would like to be treated.

April 5
National Library Month

Have you visited the library this month? Do you have your own library card? Do the librarians recognize you and call you by name? If you answered yes to any of the questions, you probably celebrate this holiday more often than just in April. Read John 21:25 to see how large the library would need to be to hold all of the information about Jesus Christ.

Questions to Discuss: What "other things" do you think Jesus did? What has Jesus done for you?

Related Activity: Make a book of the things Jesus has done for you, and illustrate the book. Make a family library of your books.

Curriculum Connection: Visit a library. Learn the Dewey decimal classification system. Practice finding books using a card catalog or computer information system.

Verse to Memorize: John 20:31—"But these are written that you may believe that Jesus is the Christ, the Son of God, and that by believing you may have life in his name."

Prayer Suggestion: Thank God for the words in the Bible that teach us about Jesus.

April 6
Passover

*The actual date of Passover is, like Easter, determined by the moon.
For this reason, the calendar date of Passover changes yearly. Most
people associate Passover with Jewish celebrations. However, many
Christians now celebrate Passover in addition to Easter, recognizing
Jesus' death on the cross as being foreshadowed at the first Passover
celebration. Read the following passages to learn more about the
first celebration and the fulfilling of prophecy through Jesus Christ.
Read Exodus 12:1-16, 21-29, 43-50; 1 Peter 1:17-21; John 19:31-37.*

Questions to Discuss: Why was the original Passover feast celebrated? Who became the Passover lamb? Compare God's instructions for
the lamb, in Exodus 12:5, to what happened later to Jesus.

Related Activity: Make a lamb to remind
you of Jesus' sacrifice on the cross. On a piece of
posterboard or cardboard, cut out a lamb-shaped
body and head. (An oval for the body with a circular
head attached will work fine.) Glue cotton balls onto
the body and head of your lamb. Attach two clothes-
pins to the bottom of the body for the lamb's legs.

Curriculum Connection: Learn more about the art of raising sheep.
Where are sheep raised in the United States? How and when are the sheep
sheared?

Verse to Memorize: 1 Corinthians 5:7—"Get rid of the old yeast
that you may be a new batch without yeast—as you really are. For Christ,
our Passover Lamb, has been sacrificed."

Prayer Suggestion: Thank God for His Passover lamb—Jesus Christ,
who saves us from our sins.

April 7
Palm Sunday

In Leviticus 23, God encourages His people to use palm fronds to "rejoice before the Lord." In Revelation 7:9, John sees in his vision a multitude of people holding palm branches as a sign of victory over tribulation. The palm has long been associated with festive celebrations, rejoicing in the Lord, and victory over death. How fitting that Jesus would be greeted by throngs of people with palm branches.
Read Psalm 92:12 and John 12:12–19.

Questions to Discuss: Why were there many people in Jerusalem during this time? Explain the symbolism of the crowd waving palm branches, using Leviticus, Revelation, John, and Psalm 92 as references.

Related Activity: Make a palm branch to praise Jesus. Wrap a dowel rod with florist tape. Cut a long sheet of green construction paper into a large, leafy outline. Cut in toward the stem of the leaf on either side, about every inch. Glue the uncut, stem part of the construction paper to the dowel rod. When the glue is dry, wave your palm branch and say today's verse.

Curriculum Connection: Use your Bible and a Bible dictionary to make a calendar of what happened to Jesus during the week of His crucifixion.

Verse to Memorize: Matthew 21:9b—"Blessed is he who comes in the name of the Lord! Hosanna in the highest."

Prayer Suggestion: Sing praises to Jesus by singing the chorus of "Blessed Be the Name." Wave your palm branches as you sing.

April 8
Mathematics Education Month

Is math your favorite subject? Is it your least *favorite subject? Whether you like math or not, you'll more than likely be using some form of math for the rest of your life. For that reason, celebrate this month with all the mathematicians throughout the country. Read Ephesians 3:14-19 to see what Paul has to say about using math to measure Jesus' love.*

Questions to Discuss: How long will God's love last? Is it possible to measure the love of Christ? Can you measure your parents' love?

Related Activity: Measure the largest room in your house by length, width, and height. If God's love was "poured" into the room, do you think the room would hold His love?

Curriculum Connection: Use flash cards to practice multiplication, division, addition, and subtraction facts.

Verse to Memorize: Psalm 136:26— "Give thanks to the God of heaven. His love endures forever."

Prayer Suggestion: Thank God that His love for us is so enormous that it can never be measured.

April 9
National Garden Month

*Do you know who had the very first garden? Of course you do. It was
Adam and Eve. Read about their splendid garden in Genesis 2:4-15.*

Questions to Discuss: Close your eyes and picture the Garden of
Eden. Describe its beauty.

Related Activity: Plant a garden, even if it's a small flower garden in
a window box.

Curriculum Connection: Name the three
main parts of a seed and the job of each part.

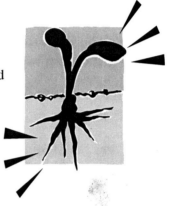

Verse to Memorize: Genesis 1:31a—"God
saw all that he had made, and it was very good."

Prayer Suggestion: Thank God for good
food that comes from the garden and for the
beauty of a flower garden.

April 10
National D.A.R.E. Day

D.A.R.E. (Drug Abuse Resistance Education) is a collaborative effort among police officers, school systems, parents, and community leaders. The D.A.R.E. program encourages young people, through education and fun activities, to keep their bodies drug-free. Read Ephesians 5:1–20 to see how God wants you to treat your body.

Questions to Discuss: How can you "imitate" God? Would God want you to abuse your body with drugs and alcohol?

Related Activity: Read the warnings on prescription and over-the-counter medicines that you have in your house.

Curriculum Connection: Write a report on the effects of drugs or alcohol on your body.

Verse to Memorize: Ephesians 5:15–18—"Be very careful, then, how you live—not as unwise but as wise, making the most of every opportunity, because the days are evil. Therefore do not be foolish, but understand what the Lord's will is. Do not get drunk on wine, which leads to debauchery. Instead, be filled with the Spirit."

Prayer Suggestion: Ask God to help you live wisely, and always make wise choices about drugs and alcohol.

April 11
Maundy Thursday

The word maundy *comes from the Latin word* mandatum, *meaning commandment. Read Matthew 26:17-46 and John 13:33-36 to find out what happened to Jesus on the Thursday before His death on Friday.*

 **Questions to Discuss:** Why did Jesus celebrate one last meal with His disciples? Why did Jesus spend time in prayer with God after the supper? Did Jesus want to do His Father's will? Was there ever a time you needed to obey God's will, even though it seemed difficult to do?

Related Activity: Make a prayer basket. Decorate a basket with spring-colored ribbons. Place the basket in a central location. Encourage family members to write prayer requests on slips of paper and drop them in the basket. Have each person remove a slip when he or she drops one in, and begin praying for that request immediately.

Curriculum Connection: Look for words like *fellowship* and *toward*—words with *-ship* and *-ward* suffixes.

Verse to Memorize: 2 Corinthians 5:21—"God made him who had no sin to be sin for us, so that in him we might become the righteousness of God."

Prayer Suggestion: Thank God for a sinless Savior.

April 12
Good Friday

On this day, many, many years ago, Jesus Christ gave up His life, in a miserable death on a cross, to pay for the sins of the world, once and for all. Did He die for you? Read Matthew 26:47–27:61 to see what you, your sins, and the sins of the world did to Jesus.

Questions to Discuss: Why did Judas betray Jesus? Why did God send Jesus to die on the cross? Imagine the crown of thorns that pierced Jesus' head. Picture each thorn as a sin you committed this week. Did Jesus die for your sins, too?

Related Activity: Use red, shoestring, peel-apart licorice like rope to make a cross. Cut a five-inch pretzel rod to be the horizontal piece. Use an uncut rod for the vertical piece. Form a cross with the two pieces, and wrap the licorice around the two pieces, criss-crossing the licorice strings to hold the pieces in place.

Curriculum Connection: Find symbols, other than the cross, that represent Jesus Christ or Christianity. What does the word *ichthus* mean?

Verse to Remember: 1 Peter 2:24—"He himself bore our sins in his body on the tree, so that we might die to sins, and live for righteousness; by his wounds you have been healed."

Prayer Suggestion: Thank God for sending Jesus Christ, His only son, to die for our sins.

April 13
Easter Even

Close your eyes. See and feel the darkness. How dark would your life be without Jesus? What would your life be like if Jesus had stayed in the tomb? Read Matthew 27:62-66.

Questions to Discuss: How do you think Jesus' disciples felt on this day? How did Jesus' family feel? What were they thinking?

Related Activity: Sing "Because He Lives." Talk about how your life is different because Jesus lives.

Curriculum Connection: Find ten synonyms for the word *dark*.

Verse to Memorize: Romans 6:4—"We were therefore buried with him through baptism into death in order that, just as Christ was raised from the dead through the glory of the Father, we too may live a new life."

Prayer Suggestion: In a very dark room, pray. Thank God for taking away the darkness of sin in your life. Thank God that Jesus rose from the dead.

April 14
Easter

The church began remembering the Resurrection every Sunday following its occurrence. Several hundred years later, early Christians set aside a special day just to celebrate the Resurrection. The timing of the celebration became dependent on the moon. Early on, Easter was celebrated on the Sunday following the first full moon after the vernal equinox. Pretty complicated! One thing's for sure: the reason for the celebration is not complicated. Read Luke 24:1-12.

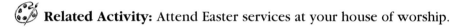 **Questions to Discuss:** How did Jesus' disciples, friends, and family feel on this day? How does this day make you feel? What did the women do first after leaving the empty tomb? Who can you tell about Jesus?

Related Activity: Attend Easter services at your house of worship.

Curriculum Connection: List synonyms for *rejoice*.

Verse to Memorize: 1 Peter 1:3-4— "Praise be to God and Father of our Lord Jesus Christ! In his great mercy he has given us new birth into a living hope through the resurrection of Jesus Christ from the dead, and into an inheritance that can never perish, spoil or fade—kept in heaven for you."

Prayer Suggestion: Thank God for a risen Savior.

April 15
Income Tax Day

Although the IRS looks forward to this day each year, many adults do not.
Read Luke 20:20-26 to see how Jesus felt about paying the government.

Questions to Discuss: What did Jesus say about paying Caesar? And what did He say about giving to God? What have you given to God recently?

Related Activity: Play a spinning money game. Each player uses a different coin. Spin the coins on the word *go* and see whose coin spins the longest. Exchange coins and try again.

Curriculum Connection: Who is on each coin and each bill? What is on the back of each coin and bill?

Verse to Memorize: Romans 13:6-7—"This is also why you pay taxes, for the authorities are God's servants, who give their full time to governing. Give everyone what you owe him: If you owe taxes, pay taxes; if revenue, then revenue; if respect, then respect; if honor, then honor."

Prayer Suggestion: Pray for the authorities who use the money generated from taxes that they might make wise decisions and use the money appropriately.

April 16
Eraser Day

*In 1770, a man discovered that pencil marks could be removed
from paper with a piece of latex. He coined the term eraser.
Read Acts 3:19-26 to see what Jesus "erases" from our lives.*

Questions to Discuss: What does it take to be forgiven of our
sins? When you have wronged another person, what do you say to that person, and what do you say to God?

Related Activity: Draw a heart. Write with a pencil some of the
events of the day—good and bad. (Record sins and shortcomings as well.)
Save your paper for prayer time.

Curriculum Connection: Practice subtraction or
"take away" problems on a chalk board by drawing
pictures with chalk. Use an eraser to find the
answer.

Verse to Memorize: 1 John 3:5a—"But you know that he appeared
so that he might take away our sins."

Prayer Suggestion: Ask God to forgive your sins. Name the ones
you wrote on your heart paper. Ask God to erase your sins from His mind.
Use an eraser to "take away" the sins on your paper. Thank God for His
forgiveness.

April 17
National Week of the Ocean

The water of the oceans covers more than 70 percent of the Earth.
Read about God's creation in Genesis 1:9-10, 13, 20-23.

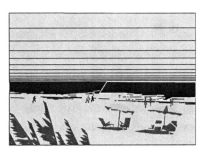

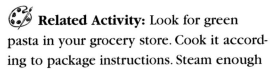 **Questions to Discuss:** On what day did God create the ocean? And when did He add creatures to the seas? What is your favorite ocean animal?

Related Activity: Look for green pasta in your grocery store. Cook it according to package instructions. Steam enough wieners for your family. When the wieners are cool enough to be handled, slice lengthwise, carefully with a knife, leaving the top third of the wiener uncut. Cut enough slices to make eight "legs." Top a bowl of green pasta with your "octopus." Use squirt mustard to add two eyes. Add whale- and dolphin-shaped crackers to the top of the pasta. Eat your miniature ocean and talk about the beauty of God's seas.

Curriculum Connection: Write a report on your favorite ocean animal. Draw a picture to accompany your report.

Verse to Memorize: Psalm 148:7—"Praise the Lord from the earth, you great sea creatures and all ocean depths."

Prayer Suggestion: Sit in a circle and play this prayer game. Have the first person say, "Thank you, God, for [name an ocean animal]." Have the next person repeat that line, adding another sea animal. Keep going until you can't remember what was said before you, then start the game all over with new sea creatures.

April 18
National Automobile Month

In biblical times, there was a custom of sending representatives out before royal visits to move all obstacles from the road so the royal person could proceed. The Old Testament prophecy of Isaiah 40:3-5 links this custom to John the Baptist's word, "Repent!" Repentance is necessary to prepare the way for the Royal Christ.

Questions to Discuss: What are you doing to prepare the way for Jesus' return? Have you made your road "straight" and "smooth"? What obstacles are in your road?

Related Activity: Make a celery car. Wash and clean a stalk of celery, removing the leafy end. Fill the cavity with egg salad, pimiento cheese, or some other favorite spread. Slice the large end of a carrot into four "wheels." Attach them to the celery car with a dab of cream cheese.

Curriculum Connection: Who is credited with the invention of the automobile? Make a timeline showing historical events in the history of the automobile.

Verse to Memorize: Matthew 3:2b—"Repent, for the Kingdom of heaven is near."

Prayer Suggestion: Ask God to help you prepare your life's path for Jesus' return, that you might remove obstacles and have a clear, smooth road.

April 19
National Coin Week

How many coins do you have in your piggy bank? Would you be sad if you lost any of your coins? Read about a woman who lost one coin and searched desperately until she found it. Read Luke 15:8-10.

Questions to Discuss: How did the woman feel when she lost her coin? Have you ever lost something really important? How did you feel?

Related Activity: Hide ten coins. Search for them. Rejoice when you find the tenth coin.

Curriculum Connection: Review the names of all the coins, and work on money word problems.

Verse to Memorize: Luke 15:10—"In the same way, I tell you, there is rejoicing in the presence of the angels of God over one sinner who repents."

Prayer Suggestion: Pray for those whose hearts are troubled.

April 20
National Poetry Month

The Bible is filled with beautiful poetry. What a poet is the mighty God in heaven. Read David's beautiful poetry, as inspired by the original Poet, in Psalm 23:1-6.

Questions to Discuss: How does David feel about God? Do you have a similar relationship with God? How can you improve your relationship with God?

Related Activity: Write a poem about your relationship with God. Begin with "The Lord is my [ ]." Fill in the blank with a word you want to use to describe God. Let your poem flow from there.

Curriculum Connection: Learn these poetic terms: *alliteration, assonance, blank verse, couplet, foot, free verse, limerick, meter, rhyme scheme, stanza.*

Verse to Memorize: Proverbs 3:5-6— "Trust in the Lord with all your heart and lean not on your own understanding; in all your ways acknowledge him, and he will make your paths straight."

Prayer Suggestion: Ask God to help you trust Him completely, as David did, to provide for your needs and to guide and protect you daily.

April 21
National Wildlife Week

No one except God knows exactly how many species of animals there are. To date, scientists have named more than one million five hundred thousand kinds of animals. Isn't that amazing? Read Genesis 1:24–31 to find out about the Creator who is responsible for each and every one of those wonderful tributes to His creativity.

Questions to Discuss: On what day were all the land animals created? What is your favorite animal?

Related Activity: Make a word search of lots of animal names..

Curriculum Connection: Name some examples of these classes of animals: mammals, fish, reptiles, amphibians, insects, birds.

Verse to Memorize: Psalm 104:24—"How many are your works, O Lord! In wisdom you made them all; the earth is full of your creatures."

Prayer Suggestion: Thank God for His wonderfully awesome animals.

April 22
"In God We Trust" Anniversary

The motto "In God We Trust" was added to U.S. coins, largely because of the increased religious sentiment that was brought about during the Civil War. On this date in 1864, Congress passed the legislation that enabled these words to be added to coins. Isn't it sad that it took a war to remind people to "Trust in God"? Read Psalm 56:3-4 to hear the psalmist's words about trust.

Questions to Discuss: What does this mean to you: "In God I trust"? Describe a time when you put your trust in God.

Related Activity: Find the words, "In God We Trust" on each coin and bill in your wallet or purse.

Curriculum Connection: Practice counting money, as if you were a salesclerk and were making change for a customer.

Verse to Memorize: Psalm 56:11a—"In God I trust; I will not be afraid."

Prayer Suggestion: Ask God to help you trust Him completely.

April 23
National Science and
Technology Week

What is your favorite invention, brought about by advances in technology? Is it your computer? A cell phone? Your calculator? Read Genesis 1:1 to see how "it all began."

Questions to Discuss: Why did God create the heavens and earth? How can you praise Him often for His wonderful world?

Related Activity: Using Genesis 1:1–31 as a guide, make a mural of God's creation, in order by days, and hang it in your room.

Curriculum Connection: Find out the history of the computer. How large was the first computer? Compare that to the size of hand-held computer gadgets of today.

Verse to Memorize: Jeremiah 10:6—"No one is like you, O Lord; you are great, and your name is mighty in power."

Prayer Suggestion: Thank God for His awesome creation. Pray for scientists that they might know the truth about God.

April 24
Feast of Unleavened Bread

In the Old Testament days, God established specific celebrations for His people. He gave them strict orders to follow. Little did His people know at the time that God was preparing their minds and hearts for the future Savior. Read about the Feast of Unleavened Bread, and find the correlation between this festival and Jesus Christ. Read Exodus 12:17-20, 37-39; Leviticus 23:6-8; 1 Corinthians 5:6-8.

Questions to Discuss: Why was the original Feast of Unleavened Bread celebrated? What does the "yeast" symbolize? How did Jesus become the "Unleavened Bread"?

Related Activity: Make bread with and without yeast. Compare and contrast the look and taste of the breads.

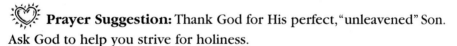

Curriculum Connection: Practice working with fractions.

Verse to Memorize: 2 Corinthians 7:1b—"Let us purify ourselves from everything that contaminates body and spirit, perfecting holiness out of reverence for God."

Prayer Suggestion: Thank God for His perfect, "unleavened" Son. Ask God to help you strive for holiness.

April 25
Seeing Eye Dog Anniversary

Dorothy Eustis witnessed dog training at a school in Germany whose purpose was to train German shepherds to assist blinded war veterans. Although the German school did not last, an article Ms. Eustis wrote for the Saturday Evening Post *in 1927 inspired Morris Frank, a young blind man. After training his own dog, he and Ms. Eustis worked together to form The Seeing Eye—the first dog guide school in America. The name of the program comes from Proverbs 20:12 (King James Version), "The hearing ear, and the seeing eye, the Lord hath made even both of them." Read John 9:1–41 to find out how a blind man's life was changed by "seeing" Jesus.*

Questions to Discuss: How did Jesus heal the blind man? Why were the Pharisees spiritually "blind"? Is there a part of your faith in which you do not see well?

Related Activity: Read about the guide dog program on the Internet. Who was the first American guide dog? Where is the closest guide dog school to you?

Curriculum Connection: Learn the parts of the eye and how the eye functions.

Verse to Memorize: 2 Corinthians 4:18—"So we fix our eyes not on what is seen, but on what is unseen. For what is seen is temporary, but what is unseen is eternal."

Prayer Suggestion: Pray for those who raise and train guide dogs.

116

April 26
Boston Marathon Day

The very first Boston Marathon was held on April 19, 1897.
Currently, the marathon is held every year on the third Monday in April.
Psalm 147:10–11 states that God is not concerned with the strength
of the runner's legs but rather the heart.

Questions to Discuss: How can you let God lead your life? What is the only way to "win the race of life?"

Related Activity: Have a Family Marathon. Run or walk a pre-established course. How long was your marathon?

Curriculum Connection: Learn the capital of all fifty states.

Verse to Memorize: Philippians 3:14—"I press on toward the goal to win the prize for which God has called me heavenward in Christ Jesus."

Prayer Suggestion: Pray for the marathon runners that they might see their need for Jesus.

April 27
Reading-Is-Fun Week

This week was established to highlight the importance, as well as the fun, of reading. Is reading your favorite subject? Read in Acts 8:26-40 about a man who was not necessarily enjoying what he was reading until God sent an "interpreter" his way.

Questions to Discuss: Why didn't the Ethiopian understand what he was reading? Do you read God's word often? Who can you tell about Jesus?

Related Activity: As a family, spend thirty minutes of silent reading for fun. Then take time to share orally what you have read.

Curriculum Connection: Talk about various phonics rules; include such rules as the sounds of blends and digraphs and the hard and soft "g" and "c."

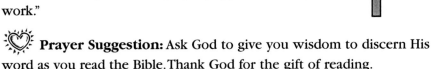

Verse to Memorize: 2 Timothy 3:16-17—"All Scripture is God-breathed and is useful for teaching, rebuking, correcting and training in righteousness, so that the man of God may be thoroughly equipped for every good work."

Prayer Suggestion: Ask God to give you wisdom to discern His word as you read the Bible. Thank God for the gift of reading.

April 28
Feast of Firstfruits

God commanded that His people recognize the Lord's bounty in the land. This was later fulfilled in the resurrection of Christ; Jesus is the beginning of God's harvest, with believers coming along after. Read about the original feast in the Old Testament, Leviticus 23:9-14, and the fulfillment in the New Testament, 1 Corinthians 15:20-28, 1 Thessalonians 4:13-18.

Questions to Discuss: Why is Jesus the "first" fruit? How will you feel when you see Jesus coming?

Related Activity: Play this thinking game. Have each person take a turn saying this sentence, filling in the blank with an earthly item: "I'm going to Heaven, and I won't need [ ]."

Curriculum Connection: Practice ordinals, from first to twenty-first. Learn to spell the words.

Verse to Memorize: 1 Thessalonians 4:16-18—"For the Lord himself will come down from heaven, with a loud command, with the voice of the archangel and with the trumpet call of God, and the dead in Christ will rise first. After that we who are still alive and are left will be caught up together with them in the clouds to meet the Lord in the air. And so we will be with the Lord forever. Therefore encourage each other with these words."

Prayer Suggestion: Thank God for coming back, one day, to take you to Heaven.

April 29
Zipper Day

This week, in 1913, a New Jersey man patented the zipper. What would your life be like without zippers? Do you have a tent with a zipper? Do you think tents in Jesus' day had zippers? Read Acts 18:1-11, 18:24-28 and take a guess about ancient zippers.

Questions to Discuss: What was Paul's profession? What does it mean to "dwell in God's tent"?

Related Activity: Count the zippers in your room. Don't forget jackets and jeans. Don't you feel blessed to have nice clothes to wear?

Curriculum Connection: Think of other means of fastening or closing, such as snaps, buttons, or hook-and-eye.

Verse to Memorize: Psalm 61:4a—"I long to dwell in your tent forever."

Prayer Suggestion: Thank God for letting you "dwell in His tent." "Camping out" with God is grand, isn't it?

April 30
National Honesty Day

Read Acts 16:16-40 to see what an honest man Paul was, even as he was being held prisoner and had the opportunity to escape.

Questions to Discuss: How did Paul save the jailer's life, physically as well as spiritually? How do you think the other prisoners felt before, during, and after the earthquake? Have you ever experienced an earthquake?

Related Activity: Remove the lid of a shoebox. Color and add construction paper cutouts to make the inside of the box resemble Paul's jail cell. (Lay the shoebox on its side.) Make cutout characters. Wrap twist ties around the hands and feet of your characters, like chains. Poke holes in the top and bottom of your scene. Insert spaghetti noodles into the holes, like prison bars. View your scene, then "rattle" the jail as if an earthquake were occurring. Move the top and bottom such that the "bars" are broken and Paul can be set free.

Curriculum Connection: Talk about words like *honesty* that begin with a silent "h."

Verse to Memorize: Proverbs 20:7—"The righteous man leads a blameless life; blessed are his children after him."

Prayer Suggestion: Pray that God will help you be an honest and righteous person.

May

May 1
Cheerio Day

In 1941, General Mills introduced a new oat grain cereal called Cheerios. Read in the book of Ruth about a grain field owner named Boaz. Read Ruth 3:1–18.

Questions to Discuss: How did God provide for Ruth? Was Ruth thankful for Boaz?

Related Activity: Make a batch of Cheerio party mix. Melt six tablespoons of margarine, and stir in three tablespoons of Worcestershire sauce and one teaspoon of salt. Add four cups of cereal squares, four cups of Cheerios, two cups of mini pretzels, and two cups of peanuts. Stir gently to coat. Bake for forty-five minutes, stirring frequently. Spread on paper towels to cool (yields twelve cups).

Curriculum Connection: "Cheerio" is an informal greeting, used mostly in England. What are some other greetings (formal, informal, and slang) used to say hello?

Verse to Memorize: 1 Thessalonians 5:16—"Be joyful always; pray continually; give thanks in all circumstances, for this is God's will for you in Christ Jesus."

Prayer Suggestion: Ask God to help you be mindful of people around you who take care of you and give thanks for those people.

May 2
King James Bible Publication Anniversary

Read Psalm 119:1-16. On May 2, 1611, a new translation of the Bible in English was published. King James I had appointed a committee to produce such a translation, and it was called the King James Version of the Bible. Do you make a habit of hiding God's word in your heart? God's word tells you to do so.

Questions to Discuss: How many Bibles are in your home? Do you have a King James Version? Do you have other versions? Does each family member have his or her own Bible? When is your favorite time of day to read God's word?

Related Activity: Read about James I in an encyclopedia or other reference book. After reading about King James, compare verses of scripture in different translations. Look for your favorite verse in several different translations.

Curriculum Connection: While working on math, encourage your children to count the books in the Old Testament, then count the books in the New Testament. How many books are in the entire Bible?

Verse to Memorize: 2 Timothy 3:16-17—"All Scripture is God-breathed and is useful for teaching, rebuking, correcting and training in righteousness, so that the man of God may be thoroughly equipped for every good work."

Prayer Suggestion: Have each family member hold his or her Bible. Give each person the opportunity to thank God for His word and ask God to speak to you through the scriptures.

May 3

National Barbecue Month

Family and friend barbecues call for good fellowship and good food.
Chicken, burgers, or hot dogs (usually prepared on the grill) accompany
most barbecues. King Herod probably held many feasts and celebrations
on a much grander scale than a neighborhood barbecue. One such feast led
to a very sad day for the friends and family of John the Baptist.
Read Matthew 14:1-5 and Mark 6:14-29.

Questions to Discuss: Why was John the Baptist persecuted?
Have you ever been persecuted or ridiculed for being a Christian? What can
help you be a strong and faithful Christian, even during times of suffering
for Christ?

Related Activity: Have a barbecue and invite a few friends.

Curriculum Connection: Have you ever
seen the word *barbecue* abbreviated as BBQ?
Find other abbreviations; learn their meanings
and correct spellings.

Verse to Memorize: 1 Peter
4:13—"But rejoice that you participate
in the sufferings of Christ, so that you
may be overjoyed when his glory is revealed."

Prayer Suggestion: Thank God for those
who are willing to tell others about Christ, especially those whose lives are
endangered by sharing the word of Jesus.

May 4

National Day of Prayer

Read Psalm 33:12-22. Celebrated on this day since 1981, National Day of Prayer was established by a presidential proclamation as a day of prayer, specifically for our nation and her leaders. If you do not already do so, take the time today to start a habit of praying for our country and those in authority.

Questions to Discuss: What can you do to be a good citizen? How does being a good citizen reflect your Christianity? How can you support the leaders in your community, state, and nation?

Related Activity: Research and find the names of national, state, county, and local leaders and officials. Make a list and keep it handy for daily prayer time.

Curriculum Connection: Discuss the differences between local, state, and federal government. What are some of the functions of each level?

Verse to Memorize: Psalm 33:12a—"Blessed is the nation whose God is the Lord."

Prayer Suggestion: Make a habit of praying for our country. Use the activity time list and pray specifically for one or two leaders each day. Thank God for our nation, and close your prayer by softly singing, "America the Beautiful" with eyes closed and heads bowed.

May 5
Older Americans Month

Paul wrote the books of Timothy as letters. They are known as the pastoral letters because they give instructions to Timothy on how to pastor and care for the church. Paul felt so strongly about the care of older people in the church that he addressed this area specifically in 1 Timothy 5:1-16. Read and heed Paul's advice.

Questions to Discuss: How does Paul feel about the elderly, especially those who have no one to take care of them? Is there an older person whom you should be taking care of?

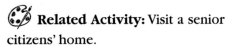

Related Activity: Visit a senior citizens' home.

Curriculum Connection: Use a Bible dictionary to find out about this saying: "as old as Methuselah." Make a family tree from Adam to Noah's sons.

Verse to Memorize: Job 12:12—"Is not wisdom found among the aged? Does not long life bring understanding?"

Prayer Suggestion: Ask God to show you an older person who needs your special attention. Pray for the elderly, especially those who are lonely and have no one to care for them.

May 6
National Tourism Week

The Queen of Sheba heard about Solomon's wisdom.
No doubt, she must have wanted to "see for herself" whether the
stories of him were true (she might have been the first tourist).
Read what happens to her in 1 Kings 10:1-13.

Questions to Discuss: Describe the Queen of Sheba. Why did she want to meet Solomon? How did she feel about "Solomon's God"?

Related Activity: Take an Internet trip. Decide on a place you want to visit; find information on the Internet about that location.

Curriculum Connection: Find these tourist attractions on a map: Mount St. Helens, Yellowstone National Park, Carlsbad Caverns, Everglades National Park. What tourist attractions are in your state?

Verse to Memorize: Psalm 72:18—"Praise be to the Lord God, the God of Israel, who alone does marvelous deeds."

Prayer Suggestion: Make a list of all the places you have visited. Thank God for the beauty of His world and for fun, family vacations.

May 7
Be-Kind-to-Animals Week

In the story of Numbers 22:1-23:12, Balaam had a rather unusual encounter with his donkey. Do you know what a female donkey is called? A jenny. And a male donkey is called a jack. Balaam does not tell us whether his donkey is male or female, but Balaam's donkey did have a few things to say to Balaam.

Questions to Discuss: Why was God angry with Balaam? Why did Balaam mistreat his donkey? Why do you think the donkey saw the angel but not Balaam? Do you have trouble paying attention to God?

Related Activity: Make a donkey sock puppet. Choose a brown knee sock, and add felt ears and mouth. Then add button eyes and smaller button nostrils. Let your puppet sing this song to the tune of "Found a Peanut": "Pay attention, pay attention, pay attention to God. God wants you to hear him, pay attention to God." Then change "pay attention" to "listen closely" and sing again. See if you can think of other verses.

Curriculum Connection: Visit an animal shelter. Find out how the shelter finds homes for animals. Pay special attention to one particular animal. When you return home, write an advertisement for that animal, as if you were going to place the ad in the newspaper. What writing style will you use?

Verse to Memorize: Proverbs 12:10—"A righteous man cares for the needs of his animal, but the kindest acts of the wicked are cruel."

Prayer Suggestion: Pray for the animals in the shelter that someone might adopt them and give them good homes.

May 8
National Raisin Week

Do you know where raisins come from? A raisin is actually a dried grape. Most raisins are natural raisins, that is, they are naturally dried by the sun. Raisins are mentioned often in the Old Testament. Read 1 Samuel 30:1-31, and see how David shared raisins with an Egyptian.

 **Questions to Discuss:** How did God use the Egyptian to carry out His will? Describe a time when God used another person to carry out His will through you.

Related Activity: Make oatmeal-raisin cookies.

Curriculum Connection: Use raisins as counters for your math assignment today.

Verse to Memorize: 1 John 2:17— "The world and its desires pass away, but the man who does the will of God lives forever."

Prayer Suggestion: Thank God for the people He uses to bless your life.

May 9
World Red Cross Day

The Red Cross provides emergency help to disaster victims and refugees in other countries. The Red Cross aids the armed forces, collects blood donations, and offers many safety, youth, and service programs. More than one hundred nations have their own Red Cross Societies; however, workers in all parts of the world unite in times of need. Had the Red Cross been in existence during the plagues on Egypt, volunteers would have certainly been sent to Egypt after the last plague. Read Exodus 11:1–10 to see why the Red Cross might have been needed to console Egyptian families.

Questions to Discuss: What was the last plague God sent to Egypt? Why did the hardening of Pharaoh's heart necessitate this plague? How did the people respond?

Related Activity: Watch a news broadcast. Are there countries dealing with a natural or man-made disaster? Was there mention of the Red Cross being involved? Do some chores around the house to earn extra money. Donate your earnings to a local Red Cross chapter.

Curriculum Connection: Look at a world map. Can you locate, name, and spell all of the continents?

Verse to Memorize: Psalm 77:13–15—"Your ways, O God, are holy. What god is so great as our God? You are the God who performs miracles; you display your power among the peoples. With your mighty arm you redeemed your people, the descendants of Jacob and Joseph."

Prayer Suggestion: Pray for Red Cross volunteers and areas in our world that are dealing with disasters.

May 10
Astronomy Week

Do you think Job was a stargazer? He appeared to know a lot about God's constellations. Read Job 9:8-9 to find out which constellations Job mentions.

 Questions to Discuss: Why do you think God created the stars in patterns, forming constellations?

Related Activity: Take a blanket outside tonight and look at the stars. See how many constellations you recognize.

Curriculum Connection: Learn to recognize many of the constellations.

Verse to Memorize: Psalm 147:4—"He determines the number of the stars and calls them each by name."

Prayer Suggestion: Pray for astronomers.

May 11
National Postcard Week

As far as holidays go, National Postcard Week is a relatively new holiday, only being in existence slightly over twenty years. Have you ever sent a postcard to someone? Read 2 Corinthians 5:1-10 to find out about a "dreamy destination."

Questions to Discuss: What do you think heaven looks like? How will it be to live with God forever? Who can you send a postcard to about spending eternity in heaven?

Related Activity: Let God "write" you a postcard from heaven. What would He say on the postcard? Have Him describe heaven and invite you to come live with Him one day.

Curriculum Connection: Learn to identify the fifty states in the United States.

Verse to Memorize: Philippians 3:20-21—"But our citizenship is in heaven. And we eagerly await a Savior from there, the Lord Jesus Christ, who, by the power that enables him to bring everything under his control, will transform our lowly bodies so that they will be like his glorious body."

Prayer Suggestion: Pray for people who are away from home.

May 12
National Windmill Day

*A windmill is a machine that operates by wind power.
In Matthew 14:22–33, Jesus walked across the water by "Jesus-power."
Peter had that same power—until a wind frightened him and he
began to sink. Read the passage to see what happened next.*

Questions to Discuss: What did Peter say to Jesus
when he (Peter) began to sink? What do you say to Jesus when
you have difficulties? Is your faith strong enough to allow you
to "walk on water"?

Related Activity: Re-create this scene as an edible
snack. Follow package directions to make blue gelatin
dessert. Pour the gelatin dessert into a nine-by-thirteen-
inch dish. Allow the gelatin "sea" to congeal. Meanwhile,
peel a banana. Carefully scoop out some of the banana to
make a boat. Stand bear-shaped crackers in the boat. Place the boat on the
congealed sea. Stand one bear-cracker in the gelatin for Jesus. Re-tell the
story, then snack.

Curriculum Connection: The basilisk lizard has a special way of
"walking on water." Read about the basilisk lizard in an encyclopedia.

Verse to Memorize: Hebrews 11:1—"Now faith is being sure of
what we hope for and certain of what we do not see."

Prayer Suggestion: Ask God to help you have a strong faith.

May 13
Mother's Day

Anna Jarvis, a Philadelphia Methodist Sunday School teacher and organist, originated this holiday as a tribute to her own mother after she passed away. Ms. Jarvis convinced church leaders of her day (1908) to hold special Mother's Day services on the second Sunday in May. The tradition caught on, and what was supposed to be a reverent, holy day for mothers has turned into a commercialized greeting-card, flower-shop holiday. Read Proverbs 31:10–31, and celebrate this day as Anna Jarvis first intended.

Questions to Discuss: What is special about your mother? What can you do today to let your mom know what a treasure she is?

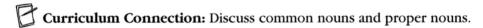

Related Activity: Paint and decorate a heart-shaped box (available from craft stores) or a shoebox. Ask your mother to keep the Mother's Day box in her room. Periodically, add notes, treasures, and treats to the box.

Curriculum Connection: Discuss common nouns and proper nouns.

Verse to Memorize: Proverbs 31:28—"Her children arise and call her blessed; her husband also, and he praises her."

Prayer Suggestion: Thank God for your mom.

May 14
Small Business Week

Many carpenters learn their trade by going to a technical or vocational school. Still others receive instruction in an apprenticeship program. And many, like Jesus, learn from on-the-job training. Read Matthew 13:53–58 to see what happened when the "carpenter's son" returned to His hometown.

Questions to Discuss: What was Joseph's occupation? Do you think Jesus was a carpenter, too? What do you think Jesus might have built when He was your age? Have you ever worked with wood? Do you know of someone who has a small business?

Related Activity: Purchase a wood-building craft kit from a building supply store or create a project of your own. Can you picture Jesus using a hammer, just like you?

Curriculum Connection: Learn the proper way to write a business letter. Write a sample letter. Be sure to include the heading, inside address, salutation, body, closing, and signature.

Verse to Memorize: Proverbs 22:29a—"Do you see a man skilled in his work? He will serve before kings."

Prayer Suggestion: Pray for small business owners, including carpenters.

May 15
National Bike Month

Read Isaiah 35:8–9. Can you remember your first "wheels?" Toddler-style bikes with huge, thick wheels probably came first. Tricycles likely came next, then small bikes with a pair of training wheels. Even when the training wheels were removed permanently, there was always a kickstand to keep a stationary bike from falling over. God is the ever-present support system. He's always there to keep you upright, from the time you are young and racing around with training wheels to that time in life when the training wheels are no longer needed. Have you thanked Him for His support today?

 Question to Discuss: Can you share a time when you especially felt God supporting you?

Related Activity: Go for a bike ride.

Curriculum Connection: As a bonus to Health and Safety study time, learn the proper hand signals for bicycle riding. Memorize these bike rules as well: (1) walk across busy intersections; (2) obey all traffic signs; (3) ride to the right of the flow of traffic; (4) ride in single file; (5) don't ride double on a single-passenger bike; (6) don't attempt stunts; and (7) don't hang on to moving vehicles to hitch rides.

Verse to Memorize: Proverbs 16:17—"The highway of the upright avoids evil; he who guards his way guards his life."

Prayer Suggestion: Pray for those who ride their bikes to school or work.

May 16
National Nurses' Week

Mephibosheth, grandson of Saul, was apparently lame from birth. The Bible mentions that he had a nurse to care for him. Mephibosheth must have been incapable of serving himself. Read 2 Samuel 4:4, 9:1-13 to see how his life changes when David remembers his friendship with Jonathan—Mephibosheth's father.

 Questions to Discuss: What kinds of things do you think the nurse did for Mephibosheth? How do you think Mephibosheth felt about his nurse? Who takes care of you when you are ill? Have you ever required the attention of a nurse?

Related Activity: Use cotton swabs as paint brushes and design a picture.

Curriculum Connection: Learn to read a thermometer. Check your temperature. What is the normal body temperature?

Verse to Memorize: James 5:16a—"Therefore confess your sins to each other and pray for each other so that you may be healed."

Prayer Suggestion: Pray for nurses.

May 17
Police Week

Take a look at the tips of your fingers. Did you know that no two fingerprints are exactly the same? Even if you have a twin brother or sister, both of you would have different prints. Police often use fingerprints as a method of solving crimes. Read in Genesis 3:1-24 to find out about the very first "crime" that was committed on earth.

Questions to Discuss: How did Satan trick Eve? Who did Eve blame for her sin? Who did Adam blame for his sin? Do you sometimes blame others for your "crimes" against God?

Related Activity: Make fingerprint animals. Press a fingertip on a stamp pad. Press the fingertip on white paper. Can you see the lines of your fingerprint? Use a thin marker to add legs, antennae, and other features to make fingerprint critters.

Curriculum Connection: Find out the qualifications and experience needed to become a police officer.

Verse to Memorize: James 4:7—"Submit yourselves then, to God. Resist the devil, and he will flee from you."

Prayer Suggestion: Pray for police officers.

May 18
National Strawberry Month

Did you know the strawberry plant belongs to the rose family?
Do you think Jesus snacked on strawberries in His day?
Read John 15:1–8 to hear the words of the Gardener's son.

Questions to Discuss: What does Jesus mean by "bear much fruit" in verse 5? Give examples of Jesus' "fruit" in your life.

Related Activity: Make sugar cookies topped with strawberry jam.

Curriculum Connection: Learn these parts of a plant: stem, seed, leaf, root, flower, fruit.

Verse to Memorize: John 15:8—"This is to my Father's glory, that you bear much fruit, showing yourselves to be my disciples."

Prayer Suggestion: Thank God for pruning you, even though it may seem difficult at the time. Ask God to prune you in such a way that you will bear much fruit and live a godly life.

May 19
International Museum Day

The Hope Diamond, the largest deep-blue diamond in the world, is on exhibit at the Smithsonian National Museum of Natural History in Washington, D.C. What other treasures do you think are housed there? Read about one of God's early treasures in Exodus 25:10-22.

Questions to Discuss: What was to be placed in the Ark of the Covenant? What made the ark so special?

Related Activity: Illustrate a picture of the ark by listening carefully to its description. Read to find out names that are synonymous with Ark of the Covenant (Numbers 10:33, Exodus 25:16, 1 Samuel 3:3).

Curriculum Connection: Learn to recognize common gems by their colors. Which gem is considered your birthstone?

Verse to Memorize: Psalm 132:8—"Arise, O Lord, and come to your resting place, you and the ark of your might."

Prayer Suggestion: Thank God for the rich and treasured history of His chosen people.

May 20
International Pickle Week

Some believe the origin of the phrase "in a pickle" is related to the old-fashioned pickle barrels that could be found in food markets. If one were not careful when leaning over to retrieve a pickle, he or she could wind up in the barrel with the pickles. That seems like quite a predicament to be in. Thus some believe the saying originates there. Jonah didn't find himself in a pickle barrel but rather found himself in an even more unusual situation. Read Jonah 3:1–4:11 to see what happened to Jonah after the fish spat him out.

Questions to Discuss: What made Jonah so "sour" about the people of Nineveh? What lesson did God teach Jonah using the vine? Tell about a time when you were sour with God? What lesson did you learn?

Related Activity: What else? Eat pickles. What kind is your favorite?

Curriculum Connection: Find out how pickles are made. What vegetable does a pickle come from?

Verse to Memorize: Ezekiel 18:32—"For I take no pleasure in the death of anyone, declares the Lord. Repent and live!"

Prayer Suggestion: Ask God to help you not be sour about His will but to rejoice in the ways of the Lord.

May 21
National Salvation Army Week

William Booth, a Methodist minister, founded the Salvation Army in London in 1865. The organization was first called The Christian Mission. By the time Booth died, the Salvation Army had spread to fifty-eight countries. William Booth had a compassion for the poor and needy, just as Jesus did. Read Matthew 4:23-25 to see a sampling of the many wonderful things Jesus did.

Questions to Discuss: What kinds of healing miracles did Jesus perform? How can you help people in need? How does God feel when you help others?

Related Activity: Gather clothes and food to donate to your local Salvation Army.

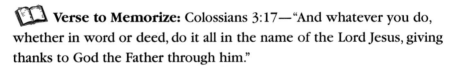

Curriculum Connection: Find out more about William Booth and the Salvation Army. What happened early in Booth's life to give him an appreciation for the poor and needy?

Verse to Memorize: Colossians 3:17—"And whatever you do, whether in word or deed, do it all in the name of the Lord Jesus, giving thanks to God the Father through him."

Prayer Suggestion: Pray for Salvation Army workers, as well as those who benefit from their services.

May 22
National Waitresses-Waiters Day

Have you ever wondered how a server can remember everything you ask for when you go to a restaurant? The next time you eat out, pay attention to your server's nametag. Be sure to call that person by name several times during your meal. It will mean a lot to him or her. Read John 12:1-8 to find out about one of Jesus' servers.

Questions to Discuss: What do you think Martha served to Jesus and his friends for dinner? What special act did Mary perform? Who do you think served Jesus more?

Related Activity: Have the children in the family serve as waiters and waitresses at tonight's meal. Don't forget to tip them.

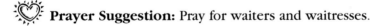

Curriculum Connection: Practice finding percents. Do word problems to find out how much tip a server needs.

Verse to Memorize: Philippians 2:9-11—"Therefore God exalted him to the highest place and gave him the name that is above every name, that at the name of Jesus every knee should bow, in heaven and on earth and under the earth, and every tongue confess that Jesus Christ is Lord, to the glory of God the Father."

Prayer Suggestion: Pray for waiters and waitresses.

May 23
Atlas Day

Do you use a map when you visit a new place? Do you think Joseph used a map when he traveled? Read Matthew 2:13-23 and think about how he might have known which way to go.

Questions to Discuss: How did Joseph know that he should go to Egypt? Why was Joseph afraid? How did God protect Jesus? Where did Jesus' family go next?

Related Activity: Make a board game. Decide on a real or pretend destination. Draw that destination on one side of a piece of posterboard. Draw your starting point and label it. Draw spots along the way, then roll the dice to get to your destination.

Curriculum Connection: Joseph and his family went to Egypt at God's command. Learn the countries of Africa.

Verse to Memorize: Psalm 56:3-4—"When I am afraid, I will trust in you. In God, whose word I praise, in God I trust; I will not be afraid. What can mortal man do to me?"

Prayer Suggestion: Ask God to guide you and comfort you when you are afraid.

May 24
Ascension Day

Ascension Day is observed forty days after Easter and signifies Christ's departure from earth and His return to heaven. Read about Jesus' ascension to heaven in Mark 16:19-20 and Acts 1:7-11.

Questions to Discuss: What do you think it will be like to see Jesus sitting at the right hand of God? Who can you tell about that awesome sight?

Related Activity: Trace your right hand. Write five things you can do to tell others about Jesus.

Curriculum Connection: Start with *write* and *right*. Think of other homophones. Make sure you know the meaning of each word in a homophone pair.

Verse to Memorize: Hebrews 10:12—"But when this priest had offered for all time one sacrifice for sins, he sat down at the right hand of God."

Prayer Suggestion: Ask God to show you someone who needs to hear about Jesus sitting at the right hand of God.

May 25
National Photo Month

Do you think Thomas would have believed it was Jesus if he had seen a photograph? Read about doubting Thomas in John 20:19-31.

Questions to Discuss: Why do you think the disciples doubted? Do you sometimes need proof of Jesus' love and glory?

Related Activity: Spend some time today looking through family photo albums. If you have not done so recently, schedule an appointment with a friend or professional to have a family portrait made.

Curriculum Connection: Make a timeline of your family's history.

Verse to Memorize: John 20:29—"Then Jesus told him, 'Because you have seen me, you have believed; blessed are those who have not seen and yet have believed.'"

Prayer Suggestion: Ask God to help you overcome the times that you are like a doubting Thomas.

May 26
National Backyard Games Week

How big is your backyard? Is your frontyard larger? Do you have a fence around your yard? What is special about your yard? Celebrate your family's play-place this week, and thank God for the opportunity to spend quality time with your family outside. Read 2 Timothy 4:1–8 to find out what Paul says he will receive when he finishes his race.

Questions to Discuss: What "race" was Paul referring to? How are you doing on your "race"?

Related Activity: Play a relay race game outside. Set up cones with obstacles; stop and do jumping jacks, and so on. Cheer on your teammates.

Curriculum Connection: What interjections did you use when you played your game outside? What is an interjection? Can you think of more interjections?

Verse to Memorize: Hebrews 10:38—"But my righteous one will live by faith. And if he shrinks back, I will not be pleased with him."

Prayer Suggestion: Ask God to help you have a strong faith like Paul, so that you may "finish the race."

May 27
National Egg Month

In the first few weeks of life, chicks require a very warm environment, perhaps as warm as 90 degrees. The mother hen gathers her chicks under her wings for warmth, as well as security, protection, and comfort. Jesus must have seen hens doing this, for He compares Himself to a mother hen in Luke 13:31-35. Read how Jesus longs to comfort Jerusalem.

 Questions to Discuss: How does a baby chick feel when the mother hen wraps herself around it? What did Jesus want to do for the people of Jerusalem? Tell about a time that you felt Jesus' love wrapped around you.

Related Activity: Boil and prepare deviled eggs. Use food coloring to color the egg mixture different colors for a springy, rainbow-colored effect.

Curriculum Connection: What is the meaning of the word *poultry?* Name other birds that are categorized as poultry.

Verse to Memorize: Psalm 5:11— "But let all who take refuge in you be glad; let them ever sing for joy. Spread your protection over them, that those who love your name may rejoice in you."

Prayer Suggestion: Thank God for His protection.

May 28
Memorial Day

The original Memorial Day celebration honored those who lost their lives in the Civil War. As time went on and other wars were fought, this day became a time to honor victims of each additional war. Read Acts 6:1–15 and 7:48–8:1 to find out how Stephen became a "victim" of the "war" against early Christians.

Questions to Discuss: Who was Stephen? Why was he put to death? How did Stephen feel about his suffering, and what did he feel toward his accusers?

Related Activity: Paint stones white. Place them on your bedside table to remind you that you may suffer for Christ.

Curriculum Connection: Read about one of the wars in which America was involved, such as the Gulf War.

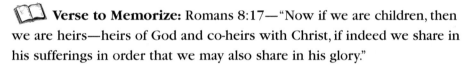

Verse to Memorize: Romans 8:17—"Now if we are children, then we are heirs—heirs of God and co-heirs with Christ, if indeed we share in his sufferings in order that we may also share in his glory."

Prayer Suggestion: Ask God to help you see the glory in your suffering for Christ.

May 29
National Salad Month

Read John 4:31–34. No one knows exactly when people first ate lettuce leaves, but there is evidence that ancient Greeks and Romans held lettuce in high esteem. A Greek proverb states, "Eat cress [salad leaves] and gain wit." The emperor Caesar Augustus put up a statue in honor of lettuce because he believed it cured him from an illness. Jesus told His disciples that His sustenance came from God, that His "food is to do the will of him who sent me and to finish his work" (John 4:34). God desires that you hold "doing the will of him who sent [Jesus]" in as high esteem as ancient Greeks and Romans did lettuce.

Questions to Discuss: Why did Jesus call "doing the will of" God His "food"? Are there things in your life that you hold in higher esteem than doing the will of God?

Related Activity: Make a salad for lunch. As you wash, chop, and prepare the vegetables, toppings, and dressing, play this memory game. Have the first person say, "A salad I'm making for lunch. I'll put in [tomatoes] to crunch." The next person repeats the first person's words and adds another ingredient to the salad. The rhyme continues until someone cannot remember all the previously named ingredients.

Curriculum Connection: Look for other salad recipes in favorite cookbooks. Make a "Salad Recipe Book" of recipes that your family wants to try. Take turns making at least one new salad recipe a week during Salad Month.

Verse to Memorize: Matthew 5:6—"Blessed are those who hunger and thirst for righteousness, for they will be filled."

Prayer Suggestion: Thank God for farmers and good food to eat.

May 30
National Book Month

May is set aside as a month to enjoy the pastime of reading. What is your all-time favorite book? How many times have you read that book? Do you own a copy of the book? Is your name written in the front of the book? Read Luke 10:17-20 to find out where Jesus says your name should be written.

 Questions to Discuss: What did Jesus say warrants great rejoicing? Is your name written in heaven's book?

Related Activity: Count the books in your house. Choose a new book to start reading, or write a book of your own.

Curriculum Connection: Find out information about your favorite author. Is he or she a Christian? Give an oral report about the author you choose.

Verse to Memorize: Revelation 3:5—"He who overcomes will, like them, be dressed in white. I will never blot out his name from the book of life, but will acknowledge his name before my Father and his angels."

Prayer Suggestion: Thank God for your salvation.

May 31
National Moving Month

God told Abram to leave his country, his friends, his family—everything that Abram knew and loved. God said to Abram, "Go." Guess what Abram did? He went. Read about Abram's obedience in Genesis 12:1-9.

Questions to Discuss: Have you ever moved to a new place? Recall your moving experience. Was Abram obedient to the word of God? How can you be obedient to God?

Related Activity: Pretend you are moving to a new place. Plot your course on a map.

Curriculum Connection: Learn how to read a compass. Which direction is north? south? east? west?

Verse to Memorize: Psalm 119:57—"You are my portion, O Lord; I have promised to obey your words."

Prayer Suggestion: Pray for families who are moving or have recently moved that they might find a church home and new Christian friends.

June

June 1
Donut Day

Would you throw your jelly-filled donut in the water and then wait to see if it washes back to you on shore? The writer of Ecclesiastes (possibly Solomon) suggests doing just that. If the donut comes back to you, then you've not lost anything. (Well, you have a soggy donut.) But if the donut does not come back, perhaps you will take a risk, be adventurous, and go after it. Who knows what you will see along the way or who you will meet? Maybe the donut will feed a very hungry bird. You may never know that your donut saved the life of a starving bird; your risk blessed another being without you even knowing. Take a chance—cast your bread upon the water and see what happens. (Read Ecclesiastes 11:1 first.)

Questions to Discuss: What are some things about life that are uncertain? Whose love can you depend on, no matter the uncertainty of your circumstances? Who or what have you taken a risk on recently?

Related Activity: Have a donut snack. Better yet, be adventurous; take a risk; try a donut or pastry you have never tried before.

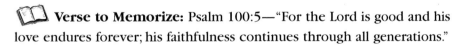

Curriculum Connection: Find these seas on a map: Caspian Sea, Mediterranean Sea, Black Sea, Arabian Sea, Aegean Sea, Baltic Sea, North Sea, Norwegian Sea, Red Sea.

Verse to Memorize: Psalm 100:5—"For the Lord is good and his love endures forever; his faithfulness continues through all generations."

Prayer Suggestion: Praise God for His goodness.

June 2
Feast of Weeks

The Feast of Weeks was established as a harvest festival in the Old Testament. A harvest feast known also as Pentecost, the Feast of Weeks took place fifty days after the offering of the firstfruits. Read Leviticus 23:15-22 to see God's instructions for this festival.

Questions to Discuss: Why did God want the Israelites to celebrate this feast? What future celebration was this feast a precursor of? Why do you think God mandated, in the Old Testament, that this feast be held exactly fifty days after the Feast of Firstfruits? Why was bread used that contained yeast?

Related Activity: Bake a loaf of bread or biscuits with yeast. Talk about how your sins affect other people.

Curriculum Connection: Identify some molds and fungi. Who was Sir Alexander Fleming? Do a report on his findings.

Verse to Memorize: Romans 5:12, 18—"Therefore, just as sin entered the world through one man, and death through sin, and in this way death came to all men, because all sinned—consequently, just as the result of one trespass was condemnation for all men, so also the result of one act of righteousness was justification that brings life for all men."

Prayer Suggestion: Thank God for sending His Son so that your sins can be forgiven.

June 3
Pentecost

What a wonderful day for the Christian church! Not only was this the day God chose to send the Holy Spirit to work in mankind's life but one could also say this was the birthday of the original church. And God, in His infinite wisdom, had the timing planned out long before this day arrived. Remember the Feast of Weeks? How many days after the Feast of Firstfruits was the Weeks Feast to be held? How many days after Easter is Pentecost celebrated? Isn't God amazing? Read John 16:5-16 and Acts 1:12-2:41 to be further amazed.

Questions to Discuss: Why were the disciples and others assembled together in one place? What did they hear first? What did they see next? What gift did the people receive during Pentecost? How many people "joined the church" after Peter's message?

Related Activity: Tear red and orange tissue paper into strips. Stand in a chair and drop the "tongues of fire" to see what it might have looked like when the Holy Spirit came upon the people.

Curriculum Connection: Learn about the taste buds on your tongue. What are the four kinds of taste that we generally speak of when referring to taste buds?

Verse to Memorize: Titus 3:4-7—"But when the kindness and love of God our Savior appeared, he saved us, not because of righteous things we had done, but because of his mercy. He saved us through the washing of rebirth and renewal by the Holy Spirit, whom he poured out on us generously through Jesus Christ our Savior, so that having been justified by his grace, we might become heirs, having the hope of eternal life."

Prayer Suggestion: Thank God for the gift of the Holy Spirit.

June 4
National Iced Tea Month

Not much is known about Stephanas, as mentioned in 1 Corinthians 16:15-18. All the information given in the New Testament about this person is contained in just a couple of verses in Corinthians. But what a joy he must have been to Paul. For Paul specifically points out that Stephanas' entire household was serving the Lord, after recently being baptized in Christ, and Paul mentions that Stephanas and a couple of other new Christians "refreshed" his spirit greatly. Have you ever had the opportunity to refresh someone's spirit? Like a cool iced tea on a hot summer's day is the refreshing love of Jesus. Share both today.

Questions to Discuss: How do you think Stephanas and his family served the saints? Why did Paul say the men "refreshed" his spirit? How can you, through service to God, refresh someone's spirit?

Related Activity: Make iced tea. Have you ever made sun tea?

Curriculum Connection: Learn these liquid measurements and their equivalent formulas: cup, pint, quart, half-gallon, gallon.

Verse to Memorize: Romans 15:17—"Therefore I glory in Christ Jesus in my service to God."

Prayer Suggestion: Make a list of those in your church or neighborhood who serve you in the name of God. Give thanks specifically for those people. Then ask God to help you serve others.

June 5
National Fishing Week

Fish live almost anywhere there is water. About three-fifths of the known fish live in the ocean; thus they are saltwater or marine animals. The rest of the fish live in non-saltwater environments and are called freshwater fish. Have you ever been fishing? Read about the greatest Fisherman of all times in Matthew 4:18–22.

Questions to Discuss: What was Peter and Andrew's occupation? What did Jesus mean by "fishers of men"? Is there someone you need to "fish for"?

Related Activity: Use an empty wrapping paper tube as a fishing pole. Tie yarn onto one end; tie a magnet on the other end of the yarn. Use gingerbread-boy cookie cutters to trace and cut out people-patterns. Add details to the cutouts and write your family members' names on each one. Write other friends' names and family members' names on the others. Place a paper clip on top of each "person." Then pretend to "fish for men," as Jesus mentioned in today's story.

Curriculum Connection: What are the distinguishing characteristics of fish? Learn to recognize several kinds of saltwater and freshwater fish.

Verse to Memorize: Matthew 4:19—"'Come, follow me,' Jesus said, 'and I will make you fishers of men.'"

Prayer Suggestion: Pray for people who make their living as fishermen, as well as people who fish for fun.

June 6
National Fragrance Week

Take a "smelling" tour of your house. Walk in the kitchen, close your eyes, and sniff. What do you smell? Go to the family room. Take a whiff. What do you smell? Walk in the laundry room. What does it smell like? How does your room smell—or do you really want to know? Paul wanted Christians to "smell" like Christ. Read 2 Corinthians 2:14-16a to see what he meant.

Questions to Discuss: Describe the "aroma of Christ." What can you do to exhibit this "fragrance" of Christ to those around you?

Related Activity: Make a potpourri bag. Trace around a dinner plate onto fabric or lace. Cut with pinking shears. Place potpourri in the center of the circle, and tie up the sides with ribbon. Place it in your room to remind you to have the aroma of Christ.

Curriculum Connection: Read about the sense of smell and how it works. What is an olfactory nerve?

Verse to Memorize: 2 Corinthians 2:15a—"For we are to God the aroma of Christ."

Prayer Suggestion: Ask God to help you give the aroma of Christ to those around you.

June 7
Boone Day
(Honors Daniel Boone)

Daniel Boone is one of the most famous pioneers in the history of the United States. He blazed many trails from Virginia to Kentucky. Read about another "trail-blazer" in Joshua 1:1–18.

Questions to Discuss: Who took Moses' place as leader of God's people? What did God promise Joshua? Did Joshua obey God?

Related Activity: Play a follow-the-leader game outside. Try to find a new trail near your home to explore.

Curriculum Connection: Read about Daniel Boone's life. Do an oral report on his adventures.

Verse to Memorize: Psalm 119:35—"Direct me in the path of your commands, for there I find delight."

Prayer Suggestion: Ask God to direct your path daily and to help you obey His word, just as Joshua did.

June 8
Vacuum Cleaner Day

The vacuum cleaner was patented today in 1869. Do you welcome that invention? Read in Mark 7:1-23 about a group of people who were obsessed with cleanliness.

Questions to Discuss: What did Mark say makes a man unclean? Is there something in your life that needs "cleaning up"?

Related Activity: Sing this song to the tune of "The Farmer in the Dell": "I'm cleaning up the house; I'm cleaning up the house. It's vacuum cleaner day—Hooray!—I'm cleaning up the house. I'm cleaning up my life; I'm cleaning up my life. I'm getting rid of all my sin; I'm cleaning up my life." (Then vacuum.)

Curriculum Connection: Practice dividing words into syllables. How many syllables does *vacuum* have?

Verse to Memorize: Proverbs 4:23—"Above all else, guard your heart, for it is the wellspring of life."

Prayer Suggestion: Ask God to help you "vacuum" your heart and "clean up" the evils that make you unclean.

160

June 9
Children's Sunday

This holiday first started in the mid-1800s as a day to christen children into the church. Many Christian churches today celebrate the second Sunday in June as a day to concentrate on children. Read Matthew 19:13–15 to see how Jesus felt about children.

Questions to Discuss: Why did the disciples discourage the children from coming to Jesus? What was Jesus' response? How does Jesus feel about children?

Related Activity: Sing "Jesus Loves the Little Children," replacing "red and yellow, black and white" with children's names in the family, and sing "we are precious in His sight."

Curriculum Connection: Discuss the growth stages of a baby, from infancy to toddlerhood.

Verse to Memorize: Matthew 19:14—"Jesus said, 'Let the little children come to me, and do not hinder them, for the kingdom of heaven belongs to such as these.'"

Prayer Suggestion: Thank God for a "kid-friendly" Savior.

June 10
Ball Point Pen Anniversary

In 1943, a Hungarian man patented the first ball point pen. Jesus told His disciples that He did not come to do away with the law or the prophets—not even the slightest pen-mark would He do away with— yet He came to fulfill the law and prophecy of the Old Testament. Read Jesus' words in Matthew 5:17-20.

Questions to Discuss: What does Jesus mean by "the law"? How did Jesus fulfill the law?

Related Activity: Use colored pens to draw a picture.

Curriculum Connection: What two colors combine to make purple? orange? green? What happens when you add white to a color? When you add black?

Verse to Memorize: Colossians 2:16-17— "Therefore do not let anyone judge you by what you eat or drink, or with regard to a religious festival, a New Moon celebration or a Sabbath day. These are a shadow of the things that were to come; the reality, however is found in Christ."

Prayer Suggestion: Give thanks to God for Jesus' fulfilling of the prophecies of the Old Testament.

June 11
National Little League
Baseball Week

*This week was established by presidential proclamation and has
been celebrated since 1959. Do you think Paul ever played baseball?
Likely, he didn't. But he does have some valuable words to say in
1 Corinthians 9:24-27 about running.*

Questions to Discuss: What is the prize for winning the race that
Paul speaks of? What do you need to do to win "the crown"?

Related Activity: Make crowns from construction paper. Wear your
crown while you play a game of baseball.

Curriculum Connection: Learn the rules of
baseball. Be able to name all the players' positions.

Verse to Memorize: James 1:12—"Blessed
is the man who perseveres under trial, because
when he has stood the test, he will receive the
crown of life that God has promised to those
who love him."

Prayer Suggestion: Say this prayer of thanksgiving: "Thank you,
Lord, for the crown I won, When I accepted Jesus, your only Son."

June 12
Dairy Month

*Have you had a glass of milk today? Have you eaten any cheese?
Did you spread butter on anything at breakfast? Did you have ice cream
for dessert? Was cream cheese on your bagel? If you've partaken of any
of these delicacies, you have already celebrated this holiday. Milk has
almost all of the nourishing substances that people need for growth
and good health. No wonder Mom reminds you often to drink your milk.
Read Hebrews 5:11–14. Paul talks about "infant" Christians and the
"milk" they need for growing as a Christian.*

Questions to Discuss: Why did the Christians need "milk, not solid food"? What can you do in your walk with Christ to grow and mature?

Related Activity: Make a milkshake.

Curriculum Connection: Name as many dairy products as you can think of. Research to see what vitamins and minerals are contained in each product.

Verse to Memorize: 1 Peter 2:2–3—"Like newborn babies, crave pure spiritual milk, so that by it you may grow up in your salvation, now that you have tasted that the Lord is good."

Prayer Suggestion: Ask God to help you grow and mature in your spiritual walk.

June 13
American Rivers Month

The Missouri River is the longest river in the United States and flows over twenty-five hundred miles from beginning to end. This beautiful river is the home for a variety of wildlife: bears, deer, moose, elk, muskrats, skunks, weasels, foxes, and many others. Bass, rainbow trout, carp, and catfish are just some of the fish that teem in the upper and lower portions of the river. Although many people and animals enjoy the beauty of the Missouri River, nothing can top the splendor of the river described in Revelation 22:1–21.

Questions to Discuss: Have you ever been to a river? Did you swim, fish, or picnic? Describe how beautiful you think the River of Life in Heaven is? Why is it called the water of life?

Related Activity: Make bean bag fishes. Cut fish-shapes from felt. Decorate with fabric paints. When the paints are dry, seal both sides of your fish together with craft glue or hot glue, leaving a small opening. Use a funnel to fill the fish with dried beans. Seal the opening.

Curriculum Connection: Find the American rivers on a map. Which river is the second longest? Are there rivers in your state?

Verse to Memorize: Revelation 22:17—"The Spirit and the bride say 'Come!' And let him who hears say 'Come!' Whoever is thirsty, let him come; and whoever wishes, let him take the free gift of the water of life."

Prayer Suggestion: Thank God for salvation, so that you may live in Heaven with Him forever.

June 14
Flag Day

The flags belonging to the nations of the world are as varied as the people who inhabit each nation. On June 14, 1777, the Continental Congress accepted the first U.S. flag as having thirteen stripes and thirteen stars on a blue field. As the United States changed, so did the flag. Flag Day, as a holiday, was first celebrated in 1877. Read Mark 16:14-18. Jesus hoped His disciples would get to see the flags of many nations. Jesus wanted His word spread across the world.

Questions to Discuss: Have you ever been to a foreign country? What "good news" is Jesus talking about? Where does Jesus want you to spread the good news?

Related Activity: Make a flag with paints and a sheet. (This activity is best done outside on a flat surface.) On a white sheet, paint a blue square in the top left corner. Pour red paint in a shallow container. Remove shoes and socks; have family members step in the paint and walk across the sheet, forming the red stripes of the flag. Discuss the fact that many people have walked on this great land. Use hands dipped in white paint to make stars in the blue field. Remind your family that it takes many people working together to have a successful family, community, nation, and world.

Curriculum Connection: Look in an encyclopedia to see the various flags of the United States. Why did the flag keep changing?

Verse to Memorize: Mark 16:15-16—"He said to them, 'Go into all the world and preach the good news to all creation. Whoever believes and is baptized will be saved, but whoever does not believe will be condemned.'"

Prayer Suggestion: Ask God to show you how you can help spread the "good news" of salvation.

June 15
Cracker Jacks Day

A new popcorn, peanuts, and molasses concoction was introduced at the Chicago World's Fair in 1893. By 1896, the company had named the invention Cracker Jacks, and they've been on the market ever since. Do you like to snack on Cracker Jacks? Read Mark 2:23-28 and find out why the disciples got in "hot water" for snacking.

 **Questions to Discuss:** Why did the Pharisees disapprove of the disciples' action? What do you do on the Sabbath for spiritual restoration?

Related Activity: Snack on Cracker Jacks.

Curriculum Connection: Make a list of Jesus' twelve disciples. Learn to spell their names, and find out interesting facts about Jesus' companions.

Verse to Memorize: Exodus 20:8—"Remember the Sabbath day by keeping it holy."

Prayer Suggestion: Thank God for the Sabbath, a day of spiritual, mental, and physical rest.

June 16
Father's Day

This special day came about after the origination of the Mother's Day celebration. Many people wanted to honor both parents, not just one. Although the holiday began to be celebrated around 1910, it took over sixty years for it to be declared a national holiday. President Nixon signed Father's Day into a holiday in 1972. Read John 3:16-21 in honor of your Heavenly Father.

Questions to Discuss: What is special about your father? What can you do for your dad on his special day? What special thing did our Heavenly Father do for us?

Related Activity: Using permanent markers, write notes on a handkerchief for Dad.

Curriculum Connection: Make a family tree. Be sure to include extended family members on both sides of the family.

Verse to Memorize: John 3:16—"For God so loved the world that he gave his one and only Son, that whoever believes in him shall not perish but have eternal life."

Prayer Suggestion: Thank your Heavenly Father for the gift of His son. Thank God also for your earthly father.

June 17
World Juggling Day

Juggling is defined as "keeping two or more objects in the air simultaneously." Martha was busy preparing a meal for Jesus and other guests. She was alone in the kitchen and probably felt like she was juggling dishes, flour, oil, and what-have-you. Martha was flustered that Mary was not helping her. Read about this "juggling" incident in Luke 10:38–42.

Questions to Discuss: What do you think Martha was doing? What was Mary doing? Why did Martha get upset? What did Jesus say to her? Are you sometimes too busy "juggling" other things to pay attention to Jesus?

Related Activity: Attempt to juggle two balls, then try three.

Curriculum Connection: Add three numbers, then four, then try five.

Verse to Memorize: Colossians 3:23–24— "Whatever you do, work at it with all your heart, as working for the Lord, not for men, since you know that you will receive an inheritance from the Lord as a reward. It is the Lord Christ you are serving."

Prayer Suggestion: Ask God to help you do everything, from juggling to schoolwork, with all your heart, as working for the Lord.

169

June 18
Aquarium Month

Do you like finding coins and money on the ground when you are walking? Don't you feel incredibly blessed when that happens to you? How would you feel if you opened a fish's mouth and found a coin? Pretty blessed, huh? Well, that probably only happens to Jesus. Read about this miracle of Jesus in Matthew 17:24-27.

Questions to Discuss: Did Jesus give money to the temple? Do you give regularly to your church? What does your church do with your money?

Related Activity: Spend some time watching your fish swim around in their aquarium. If you do not have an aquarium, make an edible one. Prepare blue and green gelatin dessert in separate containers and chill until firm. Scoop spoonfuls of congealed gelatin and drop them into a medium-size, washed and cleaned aquarium. Add Gummy fish and Gummy worms as you go. Squirt whipped topping across the top of the "water" when you're finished. Snack on your creation.

Curriculum Connection: Discuss water in these three forms: solid, liquid, and gas.

Verse to Memorize: Proverbs 3:9a—"Honor the Lord with your wealth."

Prayer Suggestion: Ask God to help you give generously to your church.

June 19
Juneteenth

This is a day specifically for the state of Texas, although many Southern states celebrate the day as well. In 1865, Union General Granger proclaimed the slaves of Texas free. Read Genesis 37:12-36 to find out how Joseph was sold into slavery.

Questions to Discuss: Why were Joseph's brothers jealous of Joseph? How did God use Reuben to save Joseph's life? What happened to Joseph?

Related Activity: Cut construction paper into nine-by-two-inch strips. Write a sin you committed or a shortcoming you have on each strip. Tape or staple the strips together, linking each strip into the other like a paper chain. Put several links together, then wear the chains on your wrist. Talk about how you can be released from the chains of sin. (Save the chain for prayer time.)

Curriculum Connection: There were twelve boys in Joseph's family. Learn to multiply by 12.

Verse to Memorize: John 8:34—"Jesus replied, 'I tell you the truth, everyone who sins is a slave to sin.'"

Prayer Suggestion: Wearing the chains you made earlier, ask God to free you from the slavery of sin. Pray specifically for the sins on your construction paper chains. Thank God for the forgiveness of sins, then break free from your chains by pulling your hands apart quickly.

June 20
Bald Eagle Day

Did you know the bald eagle is not really bald? The feathers on the top of his head are white, thus giving the appearance of baldness. The bald eagle is found only in North America and is the national bird. People in biblical days must also have thought highly of the eagle. Read what Isaiah says about eagles in Isaiah 40:27–31.

Questions to Discuss: What does it mean to "hope in the Lord"? How does God give you "wings like eagles"? Have you ever seen an eagle where you live? Was it a bald eagle?

Related Activity: Have an eagle relay race. Race in the back yard, flapping your extended arms like an eagle as you run.

Curriculum Connection: Read about the animals on the endangered and threatened list.

Verse to Memorize: Isaiah 40:31—"But those who hope in the Lord will renew their strength. They will soar on wings like eagles; they will run and not grow weary, they will walk and not be faint."

Prayer Suggestion: Give thanks for the eagle—one of God's many majestic animal creations.

June 21
Summer

Hallelujah! Summer is finally here—at least, according to the calendar. Is it still cool where you live? Or has it felt like summer arrived weeks ago? Celebrate the gift of summer by praising God with Psalm 74:17.

Questions to Discuss: What do you like best about summer? What do you like least about summer? Why are you glad that God gave you the warm months of summer?

Related Activity: Take a walk and admire the beauty of summer.

Curriculum Connection: Look at a national temperature map for today. What city has the highest temperature? The lowest? Are there states that still have snow on the ground?

Verse to Memorize: Psalm 143:5—"I remember the days of long ago; I meditate on all your works and consider what your hands have done."

Prayer Suggestion: Thank God for the gift of summer.

June 22
National Rose Month

Do you ever stop to marvel at God's creativity? Do you wonder how He came up with so many beautiful flowers for your enjoyment? God took such care and delight in creating the plant life; however, God took even more care in creating His children. Read in Matthew 6:28-34 the words of Jesus as He tells us how much God cares for us.

Questions to Discuss: What is your favorite flower? Why do you think God created so many beautiful flowers? How do you know that God cares for you? How has He shown that to you today?

Related Activity: Take a field trip to a local florist or plant nursery. Admire the beauty of the flowers.

Curriculum Connection: Name as many flowers as you can think of. Put the names in alphabetical order.

Verse to Memorize: Matthew 6:33—"But seek first his kingdom and his righteousness, and all these things will be given to you as well."

Prayer Suggestion: Thank God for His beautiful flowers.

June 23
National Forgiveness Day

Jacob was a sneaky schemer. He sought ways to gain advantage over others, even if his acts were devious and sinful. Jacob tricked his brother into selling his birthright to him, then he tricked his blind father into giving Jacob his brother's blessing. Jacob had every reason to believe that Esau might still be angry with him. Read Genesis 32:1-21 and 33:1-20 to see what happened with the two brothers.

Questions to Discuss: Did Esau forgive Jacob? How do you know that from what you read? Is there someone you need to forgive? Is there someone you need to seek forgiveness from?

Related Activity: Play a sheep game. Use two different colors of cotton balls. Let one color be Esau's sheep and one color be Jacob's. Place the sheep together in the middle of the table, with one person standing on each side of the table. Each person will need a straw. On "Go," both players try to get their own sheep to the other side of the table, to their "pen" by blowing with a straw. The first person to get his or her sheep in the pen is the winner.

Curriculum Connection: Discuss suffixes. Find other words that have the *-ness* suffix and the *-ful* suffix.

Verse to Memorize: Ephesians 1:7—"In him we have redemption through his blood, the forgiveness of sins, in accordance with the riches of God's grace."

Prayer Suggestion: Thank God for His Son, Jesus, that through Him you can be forgiven for your sins.

June 24
Insect Appreciation Day

*Out of the more than one million, five hundred thousand animal
species that scientists have identified, about one million are insects.
Insects live almost everywhere on earth. Although most people despise
many insects, there are a great number of beneficial insects. During
the warm summer months when bugs seem to be rampant, take the
time to appreciate this part of God's creation. John the Baptist did.
Read in Matthew 3:1-12 why he appreciated insects.*

Questions to Discuss: What did John the Baptist eat? What did he wear? What did John the Baptist preach?

Related Activity: Go on a nature walk. See how many insects you can find. Keep a list or draw pictures of the insects you see.

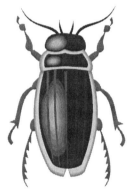

Curriculum Connection: Use an encyclopedia or the Internet to find out more about insects. What distinguishes an insect from other animals? How many legs does an insect have? What is a person called who studies insects? Find the insects that are beneficial to man.

Verse to Memorize: Psalm 104:24—"How many are your works, O Lord! In wisdom you made them all; the earth is full of your creatures."

Prayer Suggestion: See if you can name an insect for each letter of the alphabet. Thank God for insects, A to Z.

June 25
Fork Day

Knives and spoons were used as eating utensils long before forks were invented. Even after their invention, forks took a while to catch on. Would you like to try eating without a fork? Read Genesis 2:15-17 about a couple who ate without a fork.

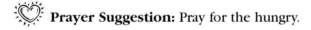

Questions to Discuss: Do you think Adam and Eve used forks and spoons? What foods did God give to Adam and Eve? What is your favorite food to eat with a fork? What is your favorite food to eat *without* a fork?

Related Activity: Cut up pieces of fruit with a plastic knife, then eat the pieces with a fork.

Curriculum Connection: Learn the proper way to set a table.

Verse to Memorize: Philippians 4:12b—"I have learned the secret of being content in any and every situation, whether well fed or hungry, whether living in plenty or in want."

Prayer Suggestion: Pray for the hungry.

June 26
Beautician's Day

Do you go to someone regularly to have your hair trimmed or cut? Today is the day to thank and appreciate that person. Read in Esther about a group of women who went through an intensive beauty treatment. Read Esther 2:1-18.

Questions to Discuss: Explain the saying, "Beauty is only skin deep."

Related Activity: Draw portraits of each family member. Write their names on slips of paper and draw names to determine whose picture you will draw. On a large sheet of freezer paper or drawing paper, draw and color a portrait of your selection. Write on the paper a list of qualities that make that person beautiful on the outside and a list of qualities that make that person beautiful on the inside.

Curriculum Connection: Use math formulas to practice converting months to years, hours to days, days to years, and so on.

Verse to Memorize: 1 Peter 3:3-4—"Your beauty should not come from outward adornment, such as braided hair and the wearing of gold jewelry and fine clothes. Instead, it should be that of your inner self, the unfading beauty of a gentle and quiet spirit, which is of great worth in God's sight."

Prayer Suggestion: Thank God for the qualities that make you beautiful, inside and out. Ask God to help you see others' inner beauty.

June 27
National Recycling Month

Despite a presidential proclamation in 1990 by President George Bush recognizing June as recycling month, it is estimated that only 10 percent of the nation's solid waste is recycled. Why not start this month and pay even closer attention to how much garbage you toss and what perhaps could be used again? Read Exodus 32:1–14 to see how some of God's people recycled gold in a manner that was not appropriate.

Questions to Discuss: How did the Israelite people use recycling in an inappropriate way? What items do you recycle in your home? What else can you recycle that you are not currently reusing?

Related Activity: Find something in your house to reuse. Turn a milk jug into a birdhouse or an empty oatmeal box into a pencil holder. Use your imagination and create something fantastic.

Curriculum Connection: What is the phonics rule for adding suffixes to words ending in a silent "e"? Add suffixes to the word *recycle,* as well as other similar words.

Verse to Memorize: John 6:12—"When they had all had enough to eat, he said to his disciples, 'Gather the pieces that are left over. Let nothing be wasted.'"

Prayer Suggestion: Ask God to help you be mindful of His gifts, be thankful, and not wasteful.

June 28
Zoo Month

Close your eyes. Pretend you are on an ark with two or more of every kind of animal that God created. You've been on the boat for one hundred fifty days! Use your imagination. What do you hear? What do you see? How do you feel? What do you smell? Don't you think Noah thought, "This place is a zoo!" Read Genesis 8:1–21 to find out what happened to the very first (well, second, if you count Adam) zookeeper.

Questions to Discuss: What is your favorite animal? Why do you think God created so many spectacular animals? What do you think is the noisiest animal? The friendliest? The most elegant? The slimiest?

Related Activity: Make an edible zoo. Mix one part peanut butter with one part nonfat dry milk to make an edible dough. Spread the dough on a cookie sheet for the ground. Add shredded wheat cereal and green-tinted coconut for hay and grass. Build animal cages with graham crackers and pretzel log pieces, using frosting for glue. Stand animal crackers around in your zoo. Build fences with pretzel sticks and frosting-glue. For added fun, take a field trip to a nearby zoo.

Curriculum Connection: Find the nearest zoo to your house and locate it on a map. Locate other zoos in the United States. Where is the National Zoo?

Verse to Memorize: Psalm 36:6b—"O Lord, you preserve both man and beast."

Prayer Suggestion: Play a charades game. Act out an animal. When someone guesses your animal, say this prayer: "Thank you, God, for [zebras], oh my! Thank you, God, O Lord on High!"

June 29
Fireworks Safety Month

In preparation for the upcoming Independence Day celebration,
an entire month on the safety of fireworks was established.
Read Genesis 18:16-19:29 to find out about the "fireworks" that
rained down on Sodom and Gomorrah.

Questions to Discuss: Why did God want to destroy Sodom and Gomorrah? Why do you think Lot's wife looked back as she was fleeing? Is there a sin in your life that you need to "flee from" and not look back?

Related Activity: Pretend to shoot off fireworks with this activity. Place a handful of colorfully wrapped hard candies in the middle of a sheet. Have the family stand around the edge of the sheet, holding on to the sheet with both hands. Toss the candies in the air on the count of three and watch the fireworks.

Curriculum Connection: Discuss adverbs and their grammatical role in sentences. Start with these examples: turn *quickly*, run *swiftly*, change *immediately*.

Verse to Memorize: Psalm 34:14a—"Turn from evil and do good."

Prayer Suggestion: Act out this prayer: "Dear God, Please help me turn from evil and sin. Help me do good— Amen—Amen!" (Physically turn around on the word *turn*, and fold your hands in prayer and look up on the words *Help me.*)

June 30
Tightrope Walk Day

On June 30, 1859, funambulist Jean Francois Gravelet, of European circus fame, became the first person to walk a tightrope across Niagara Falls. Do you know what funambulism *means? It's the art of tightrope walking, of course. Well, it wasn't exactly a tightrope, but Joshua's spies did dangle from a suspended rope in Jericho. Read about their exploits in Joshua 2:1–24.*

Questions to Discuss: Why did Rahab hide the spies? Why was that a particularly brave and faithful thing for her to do? Tell about a time when God helped you be especially brave.

Related Activity: Stretch out a rope on the ground and be a funambulist. (Use a jump rope or long piece of yarn, if necessary.)

Curriculum Connection: Talk about verbs like *walk, hide, spy.* Look for the verbs in today's passage.

Verse to Memorize: James 2:26. Read 25, also: "As the body without the spirit is dead, so faith without deeds is dead."

Prayer Suggestion: Ask God to help you be brave and faithful, like Rahab.

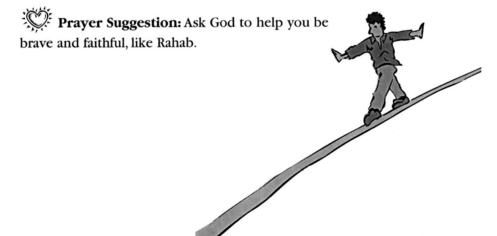

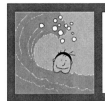

July

July 1
International Joke Day

In Chapter 18 of Genesis, Abraham and Sarah received three special visitors. The men announced to the couple that they would have a child within a year. Because they were both elderly, Sarah thought this had to be a joke. She laughed. Read Genesis 21:1-7 to see what happened to Sarah almost a year later.

Questions to Discuss: What was funny about Isaac's birth? Does God ever joke about His plans or promises?

Related Activity: Tell jokes. What is your favorite joke?

Curriculum Connection: Discuss pronouns. Find the pronouns in today's passage.

Verse to Memorize: Luke 1:37—"For nothing is impossible with God."

Prayer Suggestion: Thank God for the gift of laughter.

July 2
Halfway Point of Year

Today marks exactly the halfway point of the year. Have you accomplished the goals you wanted for this year? How is your schoolwork progressing? How is your job progressing? Are your spiritual goals up-to-date? Have you taken that vacation you wanted? If you answered no to these questions, you better get busy. Half the year has gone by. Read Joshua 3:1–4:24 to find out about some men who wound up in the halfway point of the Jordan River.

Questions to Discuss: Read verse 5. Can you imagine the excitement the camp must have experienced, knowing that God was going to "do amazing things among" them? Describe how the men must have felt? What amazing thing did God do? Do you ever wonder why God had the men choose the stones from the *middle* of the river?

Related Activity: Give each person twelve sugar cubes. Have them build a monument, like the one in today's passage. Have one person ask another, "What do these stones mean?" and have the builder respond with something amazing God has done for him or her.

Curriculum Connection: Discuss these math terms and do sample problems: middle, median, mode, average.

Verse to Memorize: Joshua 4:24—"He did this so that all the peoples of the earth might know that the hand of the Lord is powerful and so that you might always fear the Lord your God."

Prayer Suggestion: Thank God for all the things He's done for you, especially the things you shared during today's lesson.

July 3
I Forgot Day

This is a special day set aside to remember all the things you forgot to do during the first half of the year. Of course, if you forgot them, who's to say you'll remember them today? Just remember that you forgot something and try not to forget to remember for the second half of the year. Read Hebrews 10:1–18 to see what God does not remember.

Questions to Discuss: Does God remember your sins? What do you have to do in order for God to forget your sins? How can you show your appreciation to God for His forgiveness?

Related Activity: Write down your shortcomings and the sins you committed today. Bow your head and ask God for forgiveness for each specific sin. After you finish praying, wad the paper you wrote on and throw it into the garbage.

Curriculum Connection: What are the three main parts of the brain? Describe the function of each part.

Verse to Memorize: Hebrews 8:12—"For I will forgive their wickedness and will remember their sins no more."

Prayer Suggestion: Thank God for His forgiveness.

July 4
Independence Day

Independence Day is the holiday that celebrates the birth of America. On July 2, 1776, the Continental Congress declared the American colonies free and independent. The Declaration of Independence was signed just two days later. Read Exodus 13:1-16 to find out about the "independence" of God's people.

Questions to Discuss: Whom did America fight in the War for Independence?

Related Activity: Make a fireworks display with paint. Dip a new bug swatter in bright colors of paint. Splat the swatter on a large sheet of drawing paper. This activity is best done outside in a large clear area. Make sure you use washable paints and wear old clothes and shoes—better yet, no shoes.

Curriculum Connection: Make a timeline of the important dates and events leading to America's independence. Begin with the Boston Massacre in 1770 and end with the Treaty of Paris in 1783.

Verse to Memorize: John 8:31b-32—"Jesus said, 'If you hold to my teaching, you are really my disciples. Then you will know the truth, and the truth will set you free.'"

Prayer Suggestion: Thank God for your freedom in His Son, Jesus Christ. Thank God also that you live in a free country.

July 5
Travel Agency Day

Upon the stoning death of Stephen, a great persecution of the church began. Believers scattered to other places for safety. Those who opposed the church probably thought they had won the battle. But in the words of Joseph, "You intended to harm me, but God intended it for good to accomplish what is now being done, the saving of many lives." The stoners had every intention of harming the Christians, but God intended for the believers to scatter throughout the world so that "the saving of many lives" could take place through the knowledge of Jesus Christ. Read in Acts 13:1-14:28 about some of Barnabas and Saul's travel experiences.

Questions to Discuss: What is a travel agent's job? How did Paul and Barnabas spread the news about Jesus? How can you spread the news about Jesus?

Related Activity: Make a boat for Barnabas and Saul to sail to Cyprus. Use a bar of soap. Carefully carve a hull. Glue cloth onto craft sticks and insert the sticks into the soap. Have boat races in the tub.

Curriculum Connection: What countries border the United States? What popular tourist attractions do the countries boast of?

Verse to Memorize: Acts 13:49—"The word of the Lord spread through the whole region."

Prayer Suggestion: Pray for travel agents.

July 6
National Postal Worker Day

When the letter carrier needs a signature in order to release a package to you, he or she knocks on your door. If you do not come right away, the letter carrier knocks persistently, hoping to find you home. Read Matthew 7:7-8 to find out what Jesus says about persistence.

 Questions to Discuss: How does Jesus tell His disciples to pray? Are you persistent when you pray? Why do you think Jesus uses three different verbs: *ask, seek, knock?*

Related Activity: Write a thank-you note to your mail carrier. Thank him or her for delivering your mail.

Curriculum Connection: Discuss verbs.

Verse to Memorize: Philippians 4:6—"Do not be anxious about anything, but in everything, by prayer and petition, with thanksgiving, present your requests to God."

Prayer Suggestion: Pray for postal workers.

July 7
Sunglasses Day

In 1929, Mr. Sam Foster sold his first pair of sunglasses on an Atlantic City boardwalk. Just one year later, these eye protectors became extremely popular. Read about a time when Peter, James, and John might have thought they needed sunglasses. Read Matthew 17:1-13.

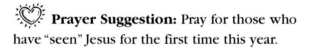 **Questions to Discuss:** What do you think Jesus, Moses, and Elijah talked about? (See also Luke 9:31.) Close your eyes and try to imagine Jesus in all His splendor. Describe the scene.

Related Activity: Use puffy paints, beads, and permanent markers to decorate the rims of a pair of sunglasses.

Curriculum Connection: Count by threes.

Verse to Memorize: Luke 9:35—"A voice came from the cloud, saying, 'This is my Son, whom I have chosen; listen to him.'"

Prayer Suggestion: Pray for those who have "seen" Jesus for the first time this year.

July 8
Stamp Day

The first adhesive postage stamps were issued in this month in 1847 by the U.S. Postal Service. Over the years, many people have enjoyed collecting stamps. Some stamps, especially older ones, have accumulated quite a lot of value. Read in Ephesians 1:1–14 about a "seal" or "stamp," if you will, that God wants you to "collect."

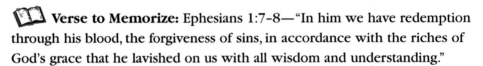

Questions to Discuss: Do you have God's stamp or seal? How does that make you feel?

Related Activity: Design a new stamp. What will you put on your stamp?

Curriculum Connection: How much does a stamp cost? How much would two stamps cost? Three? Five? Ten?

Verse to Memorize: Ephesians 1:7–8—"In him we have redemption through his blood, the forgiveness of sins, in accordance with the riches of God's grace that he lavished on us with all wisdom and understanding."

Prayer Suggestion: Pray for stamp collectors.

July 9
National Peach Month

*Do you like to eat peaches? Do you know what state is called the
Peach State? Do you think Paul ate peaches? Read what Paul says
about olive branches in Romans 11:11-24.*

Questions to Discuss: Who are the "branches" referred to in this
passage? And who are the "wild olive shoots"? According to this passage,
why should the Gentiles be grateful to the Jews, especially the patriarchs?

Related Activity: Make a peach pie.

Curriculum Connection: Draw a flower and label these parts: sepal,
petal, stamen, pistil. What is the job of each part?

Verse to Memorize: Romans 11:20-21—"Granted. But they were
broken off because of unbelief, and you stand by faith. Do
not be arrogant, but be afraid. For if God did not
spare the natural branches, he will not spare you
either."

Prayer Suggestion: Thank God for the history of the Jewish people that's contained in the
Old Testament.

July 10
Air Conditioning Day

This celebration is held annually for most of July and part of August—the hottest time of the year in the Northern Hemisphere. Do you have air conditioning in your house? Do you have a fan? Have you ever visited a desert? Read about Jesus' time spent in the hot desert in Luke 4:1-13.

Questions to Discuss: How did Jesus resist the devil's temptations? How can you resist the temptation to sin?

Related Activity: Sit in front of an air conditioner vent (or fan). Talk about how having Jesus in your life makes you feel "cool" and comfortable.

Curriculum Connection: Identify these imaginary lines: equator, Arctic Circle, Tropic of Cancer, Tropic of Capricorn, Antarctic Circle. Why are the temperatures warmer near the equator?

Verse to Memorize: 1 Peter 5:9a— "Resist [the devil], standing firm in the faith."

Prayer Suggestion: Ask God to help you resist the temptation to sin.

July 11
National Bison Month

In 1889, there were barely over five hundred bison known to be alive in the United States. Protective measures were put into place in order to prevent the herds from being wiped out. Because of these measures and specific wild game laws, bison now number well over eighteen thousand. Read Psalm 50:10 to see to whom the bison belong.

Questions to Discuss: Why does God call all the animals His? Do you remember to thank God for "loaning" you His animals?

Related Activity: Look for bison in a box of animal crackers. See how many bison are included in the package. Spread some frosting on the back of one bison and match it to the front of another bison. Do this with all the bison. Then stand the "herd" on your table to admire. (Save some for prayer time.)

Curriculum Connection: Name the characteristics common to all mammals.

Verse to Memorize: Psalm 148:7a, 10a—"Praise the Lord from the earth . . . wild animals and all cattle."

Prayer Suggestion: Eat animal crackers. Thank God for each animal represented in your box.

July 12
National Picnic Month

Think back to your last picnic. How many people attended the picnic? Have you ever been to a picnic with over four thousand people in attendance? What if you were the one in charge of feeding that many people? Read about the miraculous way Jesus feeds the multitude in Matthew 15:29–39.

Questions to Discuss: Compare and contrast the feeding of five thousand (Matthew 14:13–21) and this passage.

Related Activity: Pack a picnic for your family—and take off.

Curriculum Connection: Talk about place value. Can you recognize numbers with digits in the million's place?

Verse to Memorize: Psalm 77:11–12—"I will remember the deeds of the Lord; yes, I will remember your miracles of long ago. I will meditate on all your works and consider all your mighty deeds."

Prayer Suggestion: Pray for those who have never heard the words of Jesus.

July 13
International Town Criers' Day

Long before newspapers were in existence, a town crier was appointed to make public announcements. It was the town crier's job to walk the streets, disseminate newsworthy items, and make public announcements about upcoming meetings or important events. Town criers were particularly popular in England and the American colonies during the 1600s. With the invention of the printing press, these "walking newspapers" were soon without jobs. Read Isaiah 6:1-13. Isaiah, the prophet, was a little like an early town crier.

Questions to Discuss: What message did God want Isaiah to give His people? How is that like the message God wants you to proclaim?

Related Activity: Make a horn to get the crowd's attention before you make an announcement. Use an empty paper towel holder for a base. Slide an ice cream cone into one end of the base, bottom first. Use cream cheese to "seal" the cone in place. Let the cream cheese harden a bit, then you have a horn to blow before you start your "town crying."

Curriculum Connection: Discuss the changes in the forms of communication since biblical days.

Verse to Memorize: Isaiah 6:8—"Then I heard the voice of the Lord saying, 'Whom shall I send? And who will go for us?' And I said, 'Here am I. Send me.'"

Prayer Suggestion: Pray for those who tell others the message of God.

July 14
Tape Measure Anniversary

On July 14, 1868, the tape measure was patented. Have you used this helpful invention today? Read Isaiah 40:12 to see how God "measures" the earth.

Questions to Discuss: Close your eyes and imagine God holding an ocean in His cupped hands. Now imagine God measuring the heavens, using His hand as a tape measure. Picture God weighing the mountains in a scale. Describe how magnificent and enormous God must be.

Related Activity: Measure your hand, your waist, your arm, your Bible, and your room, using a tape measure. Who has the biggest room? The smallest hand?

Curriculum Connection: Study the metric system.

Verse to Memorize: Psalm 111:2–3—
"Great are the works of the Lord; they are pondered by all who delight in them. Glorious and majestic are his deeds, and his righteousness endures forever."

Prayer Suggestion: Thank God for His splendor and majesty that can never be measured.

July 15
Cow Appreciation Day

Have you ever been told to chew slowly or chew your food before you swallow? That's one thing a mother cow would never ever tell her calf. Cows belong to a group of animals called ruminants. God designed the cow's stomach with four compartments. This kind of stomach allows them to chew their food only enough to swallow it quickly, then later they bring the swallowed food back into their mouth to be chewed and swallowed again. Sound gross? Well, God's creation is His alone, and He had specific plans for each and every animal He created. The next time someone tells you to chew your food before you swallow it, you can appreciate the cow and giggle quietly. Read Psalm 147:7–9.

Questions to Discuss: How does God supply food for the cows? What food products does God supply you with His gift of cattle?

Related Activity: Drink milk and sing this song to the tune of "Old McDonald": "God created a wonderful world. W-O-R-L-D. And on this world He gave me a cow. W-O-R-L-D. With a moo-moo here and a moo-moo there, here a moo, there a moo, everywhere a moo-moo. God created a wonderful world. W-O-R-L-D." Add other animals to your song and appreciate all of God's creation.

Curriculum Connection: Practice classifying. Group animals into these categories: farm animals, domestic animals, wild animals, zoo animals, sea animals. Will some animals fit into more than one category?

Verse to Memorize: 2 Peter 1:3—"His divine power has given us everything we need for life and godliness through our knowledge of him who called us by his own glory and goodness."

Prayer Suggestion: Thank God for providing for all your needs. Don't forget to appreciate cows, too.

July 16
Lavender Season

Lavender belongs to the mint family and has pale-purple flowers and long pale-green leaves. When dried, lavender flowers can keep their fragrance for a very long time. The writer of Ecclesiastes 7:1a says, "A good name is better than fine perfume." Is your name "better" than a bush of lavender?

Questions to Discuss: Why does the author think a good name is important? What exactly does he mean by "good name"? How can you keep a good name? What happens when you "call on the name of the Lord"?

Related Activity: Make a fragrant lavender stem for your room. Place a small amount of clay in a baby food jar, enough to hold a small dowel rod in place. Wrap the dowel rod with green florist tape. Cut strips of green construction paper for leaves. Roll the leaves around a pencil to make them curl. Wrap the tape around the base of the leaf to attach it to the stem. Cut many small strips of lavender-colored paper, and curl them. Attach them in a bunch at the end of the dowel rod, using the florist tape. Add lavender-scented soap to the baby food jar for fragrance.

Curriculum Connection: Research the Internet to find out which countries in Europe are known for growing lavender. Find out what state in the United States produces a great deal of lavender.

Verse to Memorize: Acts 2:21—"And everyone who calls on the name of the Lord will be saved."

Prayer Suggestion: Ask God to help you live your life such that you will always have a good name.

July 17
Wrong-Way Day

On July 17, 1938, an unemployed airplane mechanic named Douglas Corrigan left New York and headed for Los Angeles. Over twenty-eight hours later, he landed in Dublin, Ireland, claiming he had followed the wrong end of his compass needle. He was later nicknamed Wrong-Way Corrigan and seemed to have a light-hearted attitude about his now-famous mistake. Read Genesis 13:1–14:24 to find out about a man who was headed in the wrong direction but knew exactly what he was doing.

Questions to Discuss: How was Lot headed down the "wrong way" on the path of life? Why was Abram willing to risk his life for Lot? What do you do when you start heading down the wrong path?

Related Activity: Make a board game on posterboard. Choose a starting and ending location. Have several landing spots that have words such as this: "Spoke unkindly; go back two spaces." Play the game and discuss how sinning makes you "go backwards" in life.

Curriculum Connection: Study the grammatical rules for using hyphens. Make a list of commonly used words containing hyphens.

Verse to Memorize: Ezekiel 33:11—"Say to them, 'As surely as I live, declares the Sovereign Lord, I take no pleasure in the death of the wicked, but rather that they turn from their ways and live. Turn! Turn from your evil ways!'"

Prayer Suggestion: Ask God to help you follow the right path—the path of righteousness and not sin.

July 18
Shark Awareness Day

God created over three hundred kinds of sharks. The whale shark, the largest, grows up to forty feet long. The smallest shark measures only about six inches long and weighs about one ounce. Why do you think God created such a vast array of fish that would eventually become one of the most feared animals in the ocean? Read Psalm 148:7.

Questions to Discuss: How can a shark give "praise to the Lord"? What part of the miraculous way in which you were made can give praise to the Lord? How do you verbally give praise to God?

Related Activity: Play with a beach ball. Try not to let the ball touch the ground. When it falls to the ground, yell "Shark!" and run out of bounds.

Curriculum Connection: Name, locate, and spell the oceans.

Verse to Memorize: Psalm 147:1— "Praise the Lord. How good it is to sing praises to our God; how pleasant and fitting to praise him!"

Prayer Suggestion: Sit in a circle. Have the first person hold the beach ball and say, "Thank you, God, for [ ]." Fill in the blank with something special about the ocean or one of God's sea creatures. Pass the ball to the next person and continue. When you've thought of all the ocean-related thanksgivings, continue with other offers of thanks.

July 19
Space Week

Space Week is held each year to commemorate space milestones.
The greatest space milestone, without a doubt, is God's very creation
of space. Read Psalm 108:4–5 to see how the psalmist uses the
idea of space to express God's love for man.

Questions to Discuss: How does God show His love to you? How can you show your love to God? Who can you tell about God's love?

Related Activity: Follow the poetic pattern of the psalmist and answer this question: How big is God's love? Here are a few examples: longer than a bear hibernates in the winter; higher than an airplane can fly. Now it's your turn. Encourage each person to come up with several poetic answers to the question.

Curriculum Connection: Define these terms: *asteroid, comet, meteorite, shooting star, meteor.*

Verse to Memorize: Romans 8:38–39—"For I am convinced that neither death nor life, neither angels nor demons, neither the present nor the future, nor any powers, neither height nor depth, nor anything else in all creation, will be able to separate us from the love of God that is in Christ Jesus our Lord."

Prayer Suggestion: Thank God for His wonderful love.

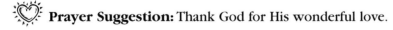

July 20
Moon Day

July 20, 1969, two astronauts made the first landing on the moon. Neil Armstrong and Edwin Aldrin walked around on the moon's surface for more than two hours. Read Genesis 1:14–19 to see who made their moonwalk possible.

Questions to Discuss:
What is your favorite thing to do at night? What was God's purpose for creating the moon?

Related Activity: Stay up to watch the moonrise. Do a story-telling activity as you watch the moon. Start your story like this: "When I go to the moon. . . ."

Curriculum Connection: How many moons does each planet have?

Verse to Memorize: Psalm 74:16—"The day is yours, and yours also the night; you established the sun and moon."

Prayer Suggestion: Thank God for the moon.

July 21
Captive Nations Week

In 1959, President Eisenhower signed the Captive Nations Resolution to make the American people aware of countries that do not know freedom and independence in their homeland. Each year, Captive Nations Week is held during the third week of July. Read Exodus 1:1–22 and 5:1–6:1 to find out how God's people were being held captive by the Egyptians.

Questions to Discuss: Why did the Egyptian king despise the Israelites? How did the Egyptians treat the Israelites? How would it feel to live in a country where you were mistreated or not allowed to worship freely?

Related Activity: Play a relay game. Form two teams. Give each team an equal number of small bricks or large rocks. Establish a "finish line." On "Go," the first person from each team carries one brick to the finish line, runs back to the team, and tags the next person. That person then runs with a brick. The first team to have all of their bricks across the finish line wins.

Curriculum Connection: Locate the countries of the Middle East on a map.

Verse to Memorize: Jeremiah 7:6–7—"If you do not oppress the alien, the fatherless or the widow and do not shed innocent blood in this place, and if you do not follow other gods to your own harm, then I will let you live in this place, in the land I gave your forefathers forever and ever."

Prayer Suggestion: Pray for nations whose people do not know freedom, either physically or through Jesus.

July 22
National Baked Bean Month

Summers are filled with picnics, barbecues, and family reunions; often hot dogs, hamburgers, and baked beans, along with watermelon and fresh vegetables, are served. Read Luke 8:40-56 to hear how astonished a young girl's parents are when Jesus mentions food for their daughter.

Questions to Discuss: Why did the people laugh at what Jesus said in verse 52? Why were the girl's parents astonished? Why do you think Jesus ordered her family not to tell others about the miracle? Is it difficult for you to keep Jesus' miracles to yourself?

Related Activity: Cook baked beans.

Curriculum Connection: Discuss singular and plural nouns. Find singular and plural nouns in today's passage.

Verse to Memorize: Jeremiah 17:14—"Heal me, O Lord, and I will be healed; save me and I will be saved, for you are the one I praise."

Prayer Suggestion: Pray for those who are traveling this summer to a family reunion. Give thanks to God for your family.

July 23
National Recreation and Parks Week

Do you like to go to the park? Do you have a park near your house? What is your favorite thing to do at the park? This week is set aside to encourage families to play together and enjoy the facilities offered by recreational parks. Read John 5:1–15. Does your park have a swimming pool? The pool at Bethesda was not particularly for recreational use but for invalids who expected to be cured by the "healing waters." Read the passage to see who became the "healing waters" for a man who had been crippled for almost forty years.

Questions to Discuss: Why did Jesus first ask the man if he wanted to be healed? How do you let God know of your petitions and requests?

Related Activity: Visit a park near your home, preferably one with a swimming pool. Remember to praise God for fun times with your family.

Curriculum Connection: Discuss the tenses of verbs. What is the present tense of *to heal?* Past tense? Future tense?

Verse to Memorize: 1 John 5:14—"This is the confidence we have in approaching God: that if we ask anything according to his will, he hears us."

Prayer Suggestion: Pray for those who work outside in the summer time.

July 24
National Ice Cream Month

This has to be a favorite holiday of many Americans. Nothing can be more refreshing in the middle of the summer than a delicious bowl of ice cream. Paul looked forward to getting "refreshed" by other Christians. Read Romans 15:30–33 to see what he says.

Questions to Discuss: What refreshes you on a hot summer day? What refreshes you, spiritually, when you are weary? How can you refresh a fellow Christian? Does your family refresh you?

Related Activity: Make homemade ice cream or take a field trip to your nearby ice cream store.

Curriculum Connection: Today's passage is filled with prepositional phrases. Find each phrase. Circle the preposition and underline the object of the preposition in each phrase. How many prepositions can you name?

Verse to Memorize: Hebrews 3:13a— "But encourage one another daily."

Prayer Suggestion: Pray for those whose spiritual life needs to be refreshed.

July 25
Blueberry Month

The parable of the workers in the vineyard is contained only in the gospel of Matthew. Vineyards are mentioned often in the Bible. Even before Israel took possession of Palestine, vineyards were prolific in the land. It is no wonder that vines, vineyards, and grapes are used figuratively quite often in God's word. Read this parable in Matthew 20:1-16. Pay careful attention to the figurative language used.

 Questions to Discuss: What message was Jesus teaching in this parable? Who are the early workers? Who are the latecomers?

Related Activity: Make blueberry muffins.

Curriculum Connection: Blueberries grow wild in many parts of the world and are grown commercially in the United States and Canada. Look on the Internet to find out what careers are available for those interested in any branch of agriculture.

 Verse to Memorize: Matthew 4:17—"From that time on Jesus began to preach, 'Repent, for the Kingdom of heaven is near.'"

Prayer Suggestion: Pray for migrant workers.

July 26
National Hot Dog Month

Did you know that Americans consume more than twenty billion hot dogs per year? On the Fourth of July alone, Americans will enjoy over one hundred fifty million hot dogs. Did you also know that more hot dogs are eaten at the Los Angeles Dodgers Stadium than in any other major league ballpark in the country? And if you live in Los Angeles, New York, or Chicago, people in your city eat the most hot dogs; they are first, second, and third, respectively, in hot dog consumption. So if you haven't contributed to the hot dog statistics during National Hot Dog Month, you only have a couple of days left. Read 2 Kings 4:8-17 and decide if you think Elisha ate hot dogs.

 Questions to Discuss: What do you think the rich woman served Elisha? How did God use the Shunamite woman to further His will through Elisha? How did Elisha reward the woman for her kindness?

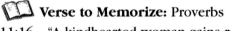 **Related Activity:** Eat hot dogs.

Curriculum Connection: Look for these kinds of sentences in today's passage: declarative, imperative, interrogative, exclamatory.

Verse to Memorize: Proverbs 11:16—"A kindhearted woman gains respect, but ruthless men gain only wealth."

Prayer Suggestion: Ask God to help you be kind and compassionate to all but especially to those in need.

July 27
Parents' Day

Early in the Bible, God established devotion to parents as a religious duty. Children were to be respectful and obedient to their parents. In turn, parents were expected to lovingly discipline their children and raise them until either the sons could provide a living for themselves or the daughters were married. A great deal of value was placed on the blessing of a parent. Mary and Joseph must have felt so honored to be Jesus' earthly parents. Read Matthew 1:18-25, the passage in which Joseph finds out the role he will play in Jesus' life.

Questions to Discuss: Parents, share what you like best (and least) about your role as a parent. Children, share the godly characteristics that you see in your parents. Everyone: How have your parents helped you come to know Christ?

Related Activity: Do a good deed for your parents today: wash their cars, clean the bathrooms, or weed the lawn.

Curriculum Connection: Discuss singular possessives. Start with "Mary's son" and "Joseph's boy," then write other singular possessives.

Verse to Memorize: Ephesians 6:1-3—"Children, obey your parents in the Lord, for this is right. Honor your father and mother—which is the first commandment with a promise—that it may go well with you and that you may enjoy long life on the earth."

Prayer Suggestion: Make a list of the things about your parents that you are thankful for. Give thanks to God for each item.

July 28
Beatrix Potter Day

Beatrix Potter was born on this day in 1866. She was an English author who became famous for her stories about a rabbit named Peter. Peter Rabbit was a mischievous rabbit, who was forever in trouble. Usually, his troubles came about because he was trying to snitch vegetables from Mr. McGregor's vegetable garden. Although these tales are lighthearted and are about talking animals, read 1 Kings 21:1-28 to find out about a very serious incident that involved taking something that belonged to another person.

Questions to Discuss: Have you ever been envious of something someone else had? Have you ever thought of taking something that didn't belong to you? Why would that be wrong?

Related Activity: Read a Beatrix Potter story. Snack on raw carrots while you read.

Curriculum Connection: Choose a favorite children's book. Do a story map of your book to include the setting (characters, place, time), the problem, the events leading to resolution, and the resolution. Do an oral book report.

Verse to Memorize: Exodus 20:15—"You shall not steal."

Prayer Suggestion: Ask God to help you always obey His commandments.

July 29
NASA Anniversary

*In 1958, the National Aeronautics and Space Administration (NASA)
was established as a U.S. government agency. Its task was to
conduct and carry out research on flight in space and within the
earth's atmosphere. Read Psalm 148:1–6. The psalmist sounds as if
he might have enjoyed a job with NASA.*

Questions to Discuss: Would you like to take a ride in a spaceship? Do you think you would feel closer to God? What makes you feel close to God?

Related Activity: Make a spaceship from ice cream cones. Stack two cake cones, upside-down, on your work area. Spread white frosting over the entire spaceship. Cut wafer sandwich cookies into triangles, and add four to the bottom of the spaceship, spaced evenly. Use colored frosting to add windows and doors; write "NASA" on the side, and add a few candies for decoration.

Curriculum Connection: Study the phases of the moon. When is the next full moon?

Verse to Memorize: Psalm 148:1a—"Praise the Lord."

Prayer Suggestion: Pray for astronauts.

July 30
National Tennis Month

Do you know what the word love *means in relation to tennis?* Love *is the scoring term for* zero *in a tennis game. When playing tennis, if you have zero, you've got love. Aren't you glad that it is just the opposite where God is concerned? If you have God's love, you are the winner—you have it all. Read Romans 5:6-11 to confirm.*

 Questions to Discuss: How much does God love you? How can you be sure God loves you?

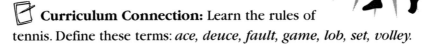

Related Activity: Play a game of tennis. If you do not have the equipment or if no courts are available, go to the park and play with tennis balls.

Curriculum Connection: Learn the rules of tennis. Define these terms: *ace, deuce, fault, game, lob, set, volley.*

Verse to Memorize: Romans 5:8—"But God demonstrates his own love for us in this: While we were still sinners, Christ died for us."

Prayer Suggestion: Thank God for His love.

July 31
National Foreign Language Month

One would think that God's people would have learned their lesson after the flood that devastated the world. However, years later, humans were at it again. With their self-centered, egotistical attitudes, men decided to "leave God out" of their lives and take destiny into their own hands. They blatantly disobeyed God by not scattering abroad; they also wanted to make a name for themselves by erecting a monument to rival all monuments. Read about the Tower of Babel in Genesis 11:1-9.

Questions to Discuss: How did God prevent the people from finishing their tower? Why did He cause them to speak different languages? How were the different ethnic groups formed? Do you know anyone who speaks a different language than your family? Have you told that person about Jesus?

Related Activity: Use the Internet to find out how to say hello in five other languages.

Curriculum Connection: Locate and learn to spell the countries of Asia.

ASIA

A **Verse to Memorize:** Romans 12:1-2—"Therefore, I urge you brothers, in view of God's mercy, to offer your bodies as living sacrifices, holy and pleasing to God—this is your spiritual act of worship. Do not conform any longer to the pattern of this world, but be transformed by the renewing of your mind. Then you will be able to test and approve what God's will is—his good, pleasing and perfect will."

Prayer Suggestion: Pray for people in your neighborhood, city, or church who have a different ethnic background than you.

August

August 1
National Inventor's Month

Uzziah had every right to be proud of his accomplishments. By the age of sixteen, he was a king. King Uzziah fortified his army and supplied them with great weapons and materials, some of which were relatively new inventions for that time. He was quite successful. However, as Proverbs 16:18 ("pride goes before destruction, a haughty spirit before a fall") warns, King Uzziah allowed his success to go to his head. Read 2 Chronicles 26:1–23 to see how Uzziah's pride became his downfall.

Questions to Discuss: Describe King Uzziah's reign when he was faithful to the Lord. Compare and contrast that time with Uzziah's reign when he became proud and unfaithful to the Lord.

Related Activity: Be an inventor. Devise a plan for a new invention—real or pretend. Then carry out your plan. How does your invention work? Is it time to apply for a patent?

Curriculum Connection: Choose any item. Use the Internet, encyclopedia, or other resource materials to find out when that item was invented, who invented it, and when it was patented.

Verse to Memorize: Proverbs 16:3—"Commit to the Lord whatever you do, and your plans will succeed."

Prayer Suggestion: What are your plans for today? Pray silently, committing your plans to God. Ask Him for His wisdom, guidance, and instruction in your plans.

August 2
First Lincoln Penny Anniversary

Although the penny was first authorized to be minted in 1787, the first penny to depict President Abraham Lincoln was not produced until 1909. Noteworthy about the new penny was the fact that no other coin had featured a historic figure at that time. The Lincoln penny was the first coin with the words "In God We Trust." When the Lincoln Memorial was added to the back of the penny, it became the first coin to highlight the same person on both sides. Look carefully at a Lincoln penny. Can you see the statue of Lincoln inside the memorial? Read Luke 21:1-4 to hear a story about a woman with a small amount of money.

Questions to Discuss: Why did Jesus praise the widow's small offering? What have you given to God recently?

Related Activity: Cut the top out of an empty, clean milk jug. Try to toss a penny into the container. (Use a basket if you have no empty jug.) How many can you get in?

Curriculum Connection: Do addition and subtraction problems that involve money.

Verse to Memorize: Malachi 3:10—"'Bring the whole tithe into the storehouse, that there may be food in my house. Test me in this,' says the Lord Almighty, 'and see if I will not throw open the floodgates of heaven and pour out so much blessing that you will not have room enough for it.'"

Prayer Suggestion: Pray for widows and widowers.

August 3
5th Avenue Opens in New York City

5th Avenue opened in New York in 1824. It soon became one of the most famous streets in the world. Read about another famous road, the road to Emmaus, in Luke 24:13-35.

Questions to Discuss: Why do you think the two men did not recognize Jesus at first? What is significant about the men "inviting Jesus in" to their home? Have you invited Jesus into your home and life?

Related Activity: Go for a walk on a street in your neighborhood. Compare and contrast your road with what you know about the road to Emmaus and what you know about 5th Avenue in New York City.

Curriculum Connection: Draw a map of your neighborhood, labeling streets, houses, stores, and so on.

Verse to Memorize: Acts 16:31b— "Believe in the Lord Jesus, and you will be saved."

Prayer Suggestion: Pray for people who live in big cities, that they might not get so caught up in the rush of the city and the throngs of people that they miss seeing Jesus along the road.

August 4
American Family Day

There are very few events recorded in the Bible about Jesus' life as a boy. One particular event involves the family's trip to Jerusalem for Passover. The Bible mentions that Jesus' family made the trip every year. Read about their trip in Luke 2:21–40.

Questions to Discuss: What is your favorite activity to do with your family? Where is your favorite place to go with your family? In what ways does your family worship God?

Related Activity: Have a family council meeting and discuss options for what you can do today to celebrate Family Day. Take a vote, then go for a family adventure.

Curriculum Connection: Give directions from your house to your house of worship. Use a map search, if necessary, to give accurate mileage and street names.

Verse to Memorize: 1 John 3:1a—"How great is the love the Father has lavished on us, that we should be called children of God!"

Prayer Suggestion: Hold hands in a circle. Pray silently for each person in your family, thanking God for that person and for your loving family.

August 5
National Fresh Breath Day

Paul was preaching to the people in Athens. Many Athenians worshipped idols, and this greatly disturbed Paul. Read in Acts 17:24-28 to see who Paul tells the Athenians gave them the very breath they breathe.

Questions to Discuss: Take a deep breath. Who gave you the breath of life?

Related Activity: Eat a peppermint in silence as you meditate on all the things God has given you. When the peppermints are gone, share some of your thoughts.

Curriculum Connection: Look at a picture of the lungs. What are these body parts: the diaphragm, pharynx, larynx, trachea?

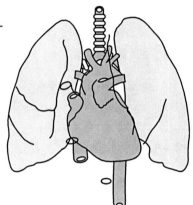

Verse to Memorize: Acts 17:25c—"Because he himself gives all men life and breath and everything else."

Prayer Suggestion: Thank God for the breath of life.

August 6
Halfway Point of Summer

In Psalm 32:1-5, David says that when he does not confess his sins to the Lord, he feels as "sapped as in the heat of the summer." What do you think he means by that? What happens to you on a really hot, summer afternoon, perhaps after much play or work outside? Do you feel drained of energy, lifeless? Read David's words in today's passage.

Questions to Discuss: How do you feel when you sin against God? How do you feel when you confess your sin to God?

Related Activity: Play in a sprinkler.

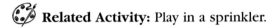

Curriculum Connection: Define these terms: *savanna, tropical rain forest, desert, steppe.*

Verse to Memorize: 1 John 1:9—"If we confess our sins, he is faithful and just and will forgive us our sins and purify us from all unrighteousness."

Prayer Suggestion: Is there a sin that you need to confess to God? Pray silently, confessing and asking for forgiveness.

August 7
National Scuba Diving Day

For many years, people have enjoyed diving underwater. Early divers, using no equipment, dove for food, pearls, shells, and other treasures. It was not until the early 1800s that breathing equipment was used while diving and even later when masks and goggles began to be used.
Read Psalm 107:23-31. The psalmist exclaims that early sea goers witnessed the marvels and beauty of God's creation in the sea.

Questions to Discuss: What is the psalmist describing? Who can calm the storms on the sea?

Related Activity: Play this memory game to remind you of God's marvels in the ocean. Let each person say the rhyme and fill in the blank with an ocean animal. "I'm going scuba diving in God's great sea. I'm going scuba diving; won't you come with me? I see a [ ]."

Curriculum Connection: Identify plankton, nekton, benthos.

Verse to Memorize: Psalm 148:7—"Praise the Lord from the earth, you great sea creatures and all ocean depths."

Prayer Suggestion: Thank God for His great sea creatures.

August 8
Clown Month

Glance at the concordance in the back of your Bible; look at the entries for the word joy. *Why do you think the word* joy *is used so often in the Bible? When most people see a clown, they smile, laugh, or feel happy. There is a difference, however, between joy and happiness. Happiness can often be a temporary state of being. True joy, brought about in Jesus Christ, is a permanent feeling and attitude of the heart. Joy in Jesus means that, even during a difficult or very sad situation, you can still rest in His love and salvation and your eternity in Heaven. Read John 15:9–17 and see what Jesus says about joy.*

Questions to Discuss: How does a clown make you feel? Does the happiness that a clown gives you last forever? What does joy mean to you? What makes you happy? Who can give you an everlasting feeling of joy?

Related Activity: Make a silly clown using an ice cream cone. Scoop your favorite kind of ice cream into a sugar cone. Turn the cone upside down on a small plate. Add candies to turn your cone into a clown face with a pointy hat.

Curriculum Connection: Use a thesaurus to find synonyms and antonyms of the word *joy.*

Verse to Memorize: John 15:10–11—"If you obey my commands, you will remain in my love, just as I have obeyed my Father's commands and remain in his love. I have told you this so that my joy may be in you and that your joy may be complete."

Prayer Suggestion: Thank God for the joy that Jesus brings.

August 9
National Lighthouse Day

The first American lighthouse was built in Boston Harbor in 1716. Hundreds more followed thereafter. The Lighthouse Preservation Society persuaded Congress to proclaim a National Lighthouse Day to bring about awareness of this part of America's treasured maritime history, to remember those lives saved by lighthouses, and to honor the beauty of lighthouse architecture. Read Mark 4:21–23 to find out how you can have your own personal lighthouse.

Questions to Discuss: Who is the "lamp"? Would your life be dark without Jesus?

Related Activity: Use flowerpots to make a lighthouse. For each lighthouse, you'll need a one-and one-half-inch terra pot, a two-inch terra pot, and a three-inch terra pot. Turn the pots upside down and stack them, largest pot on bottom. This will be your lighthouse. Decide what colors you want to paint it. (You'll want to paint yellow windows on the top, smallest pot.) Unstack the pots for painting. Use acrylic paints. When the paint is completely dry, glue the pots together, using craft glue.

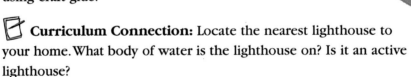

Curriculum Connection: Locate the nearest lighthouse to your home. What body of water is the lighthouse on? Is it an active lighthouse?

Verse to Memorize: Colossians 1:13–14—"For he has rescued us from the dominion of darkness and brought us into the kingdom of the Son he loves, in whom we have redemption, the forgiveness of sins."

Prayer Suggestion: Turn off all the lights in the room except for a small lamp. Place it in the middle of the floor. Thank God for allowing Jesus to be the light of the world. Ask Him to shine through you.

August 10
Mall Day

On this day in 1992, the largest mall in America opened its doors in Bloomington, Minnesota. This enormous mall houses not only any kind of store you could imagine but the largest indoor family theme park, Minnesota's largest aquarium, theaters, restaurants, and several other attractions. One could spend a fortune in a short amount of time at a place like this. Read Matthew 6:24 to heed a warning about money.

Questions to Discuss: How can money be a master? Do you let money master your life? How can you be a wise steward of God's money?

Related Activity: Take a field trip to the mall for fun, just to look around. Make a list of the stores in your mall.

Curriculum Connection: Use the list you made to practice classifying. Group the stores under such headings as clothing, kitchen and bath, novelty, toys.

Verse to Memorize: Hebrews 13:5—"Keep your lives free from the love of money and be content with what you have, because God has said, 'Never will I leave you; never will I forsake you.'"

Prayer Suggestion: Ask God to help you worship Him—not money.

August 11
Food Stamp Act Anniversary

The 1960s brought about a national interest in hunger and poverty problems in the United States. A Food Stamp Act of 1964 enabled low-income families to use coupons in retail stores to purchase certain nutritionally sound food items. Read Luke 16:19-31 to find out about a poor man who sought help for his hunger problems.

Questions to Discuss: Why do you think the rich man would not share food with the beggar? What regrets did the rich man have when he died? How can you help those in need?

Related Activity: Donate food to a shelter or your church's food pantry.

Curriculum Connection: Make an outline of the lives of the rich man and the beggar. Use what you know and information from the story to fill in such things as the food they both ate, how they slept, the clothes they wore, the friends they had, their attitude toward others.

Verse to Memorize: Proverbs 21:13—"If a man shuts his ears to the cry of the poor, he too will cry out and not be answered."

Prayer Suggestion: Ask God to help you open your eyes to the needy in your community.

August 12
Phonograph Anniversary

The first phonograph, for all practical purposes, was invented in 1877 by Thomas Edison. Soon after, other inventors improved Edison's phonograph, yet Edison is still known as the inventor of the phonograph. A phonograph is a device that plays pre-recorded sounds and is also called a record player. Read John 21:15-24, then answer the questions that follow.

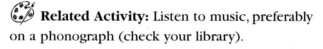 **Questions to Discuss:** Explain the meaning of the saying "like a broken record." (Parents, you may have to help your children with this one; many youngsters today have never even seen a record player.) Why does this passage sound as if Jesus' words are a broken record? Why do you think Jesus asked Peter that question three times?

Related Activity: Listen to music, preferably on a phonograph (check your library).

Curriculum Connection: Discuss consonant digraphs—two consonants that are sounded together to make one sound, such as *ph*, *sh*, *ch*, *th*, *wh*, *ck*.

Verse to Memorize: Matthew 22:37-38—"Jesus replied: 'Love the Lord your God with all your heart and with all your soul and with all your mind. This is the first and greatest commandment.'"

Prayer Suggestion: Read this rhyme together, then make up one of your own: "Dear God, Help me love you with my whole heart; For that's the very best place to start. Help me love you with all my soul; For you, dear God, can make me whole. Help me love you with all my mind; For that was part of your design. Help me love you—heart, soul, and mind; For I love you, God—all the time!"

August 13
Lawyer Day

*The American Bar Association was founded on this day in 1878.
This voluntary association is made up of lawyers, judges, law students,
and law teachers of the United States. Its goal is to promote justice
and uphold the standards of legal education and ethics. Read Jesus'
parable in Luke 18:1-8 about a judge and a destitute woman
in which Jesus teaches us more about how to pray.*

Questions to Discuss: Did the judge in the story know God? How many times do you think the widow made requests from the judge? What was the result of her persistence? How did Jesus use the parable of the judge and widow to encourage His disciples to pray without ceasing?

Related Activity: Start or continue writing in a prayer journal. Write requests, and make notes when prayers are answered.

Curriculum Connection: Find out the educational requirements needed to become a lawyer or judge. If possible, interview a person with one of these professions.

Verse to Memorize: Ephesians 6:18a—"And pray in the Spirit on all occasions with all kinds of prayers and requests."

Prayer Suggestion: Using your prayer journal, pray silently. Pray for lawyers that they might make wise decisions.

August 14
National Relaxation Day

Two oxen were often yoked together to pull a plow for agricultural purposes. A wooden yoke formed a frame for the oxen's heads to fit into. Jesus says, in Matthew 11:25–30, that if a person takes His yoke (meaning to trust Him as Savior), Jesus will bring him or her rest for the soul—salvation for all eternity.

Questions to Discuss: Close your eyes and picture yourself in a yoke. Imagine yourself pulling a large cart. Inside that cart are all your cares and worries—jobs, chores, schoolwork, relationships, loan payments, allowances, church commitments, and so on. Try pulling that wagon alone. How do you feel? Now picture Jesus in the yoke with you. Strong, powerful, loving, patient, kind, caring Jesus—yoked together with you. Picture Jesus carrying the weight of the load; you just seem to be there next to Him. How do you feel now? Jesus says His burden is light. Can you feel His rest?

Related Activity: In a hammock, on a blanket outside, or on the floor in a cool room, lie quietly, as a family, and meditate on Jesus.

Curriculum Connection: Practice writing the tenses of irregular verbs such as *lie-lay*, *sit-set*, *rise-raise*.

Verse to Memorize: Matthew 11:28—"Come to me, all you who are weary and burdened, and I will give you rest."

Prayer Suggestion: While relaxing, give your cares and worries to God, and ask Him to give you rest.

August 15
Roller Coaster Anniversary

The first roller coaster built in the United States was built in 1884 at Coney Island in Brooklyn, New York. Coaster rides built in other countries before this date often consisted of two parts. Riders could ride down a hill in a car but only to the bottom of the hill. Then the patrons walked up the next hill, while attendants lugged the coaster up, and riders would come back down again. Uphill, downhill; uphill, downhill. That must have been how God's people felt of their attempt to leave Egypt. Read Exodus 9:13–35 to see what a roller-coaster ride that time was for the Israelites.

 Questions to Discuss: Describe the storm that brought the Plague of Hail. Why was Pharaoh's heart hard? How did God plan to use Pharaoh's hardened heart to His glory?

Related Activity: Use blocks, posterboard, toy cars, and other accessories to make your own roller coaster ride. (If you have several empty paper towel holders, join them altogether and send a marble coasting downhill.)

Curriculum Connection: Work on comparative and superlative forms of adjectives: *fast, faster, fastest; hard, harder, hardest.*

Verse to Memorize: Exodus 9:16—"But I have raised you up for this very purpose, that I might show you my power and that my name might be proclaimed in all the earth."

Prayer Suggestion: Praise the Lord for His mighty works.

August 16
International Left-Hander's Day

Are you left-handed? Are you right-handed? Are you ambidextrous?
Read Matthew 6:1–4 to see what Jesus says about your hands
"keeping secrets from one another."

Questions to Discuss: What does Jesus mean about not letting your left hand know what you are doing? Why does Jesus want you to keep quiet about your good deeds? Does God want you to boast about your works?

Related Activity: If you are left-handed, work, eat, and play right-handed today. If you are right-handed, work, eat, and play left-handed.

Curriculum Connection: Find the pronouns in today's passage.

Verse to Memorize: Ephesians 2:8–9—"For it is by grace you have been saved, through faith—and this not from yourselves, it is the gift of God—not by works, so that no one can boast."

Prayer Suggestion: Give thanks to God for His saving grace.

August 17
David "Davy" Crockett's Birthday

Davy Crockett was a very famous frontiersman in U.S. history. He held leadership positions in the Tennessee legislature and the U.S. House of Representatives. Crockett died in the war for Texas independence. Read in Joshua 23:1–24:33 about another famous leader.

Questions to Discuss: Why do you think Joshua was a good leader? What are the qualities of a good leader? How can you exhibit good leadership qualities at home?

Related Activity: Take turns leading your family on a walk or hike through the neighborhood or park.

Curriculum Connection: Learn more about Davy Crockett. Look for some of the tall tales that have been written about him. Write a report about his life.

Verse to Memorize: Joshua 24:14a—"Now fear the Lord and serve him with all faithfulness."

Prayer Suggestion: Thank God for the "explorers" in our past, biblical ones as well as post-biblical ones.

August 18
Klondike Gold Rush Begins

This week in 1896, George Carmack, his wife, Kate, and their relatives found gold in a creek near his home. Miners from a nearby town moved to the area shortly after news of the gold findings. However, it was not until almost a year later, when a steamship arrived in Seattle with gold from the area, that the gold rush began. One of the world's greatest gold rushes then took place in the Yukon Territory of northwestern Canada. Read in Acts 3:1-16 about a "prospector" who found something greater than gold when he met Jesus' disciples, Peter and John.

Questions to Discuss: What did the lame man ask of Peter and John? What gift (a gift more valuable than gold) did the man receive?

Related Activity: Paint rocks gold. Hide them in the yard and have a gold rush hunt. When you finish the hunt, sing the old Sunday School favorite, "Silver and Gold Have I None."

Curriculum Connection: Read more about the Klondike Gold Rush. Read about the California Gold Rush. Who were the "'49ers"?

Verse to Memorize: 2 Corinthians 9:15—"Thanks be to God for his indescribable gift!"

Prayer Suggestion: Place inside a box a sheet of paper with the word *Jesus* written on it. Wrap the box with as many layers of paper as there are people in the family. As each person unwraps a layer, have him or her say, "Thank you, God, for your indescribable gift!" The last person opens the box to find "Jesus" inside.

August 19
Hurricane Season

Hurricane season begins June first and lasts until November thirtieth. Peak activity seems to be from mid-August until mid-October, with many of the hurricanes in the past making landfall in the early fall. Read about Jonah's escapades with "a great wind" in Jonah 1:1–2:10.

Questions to Discuss: Why did Jonah run away from God? Is it possible to hide from God? Why did God discipline Jonah? Have you ever wished you could hide from God?

Related Activity: Put a floating toy in a bucket with water. Using a large wooden spoon, spin the water around quickly to see how Jonah might have felt on board that ship.

Curriculum Connection: Look in a dictionary to see what these words mean: *hurricane, tsunami, tropical depression, tropical storm.*

Verse to Memorize: Hebrews 12:5b–7a—"My son, do not make light of the Lord's discipline, and do not lose heart when he rebukes you, because the Lord disciplines those he loves, and he punishes everyone he accepts as a son. Endure hardship as a discipline."

Prayer Suggestion: Ask God to lovingly discipline you when necessary so that you might become a more godly person.

August 20
Alaska Discovered

In 1741, a Danish navigator sailing for Russia gained sight of and discovered Alaska while on an expedition to explore the North Pacific region. Russia soon laid claim to the island and began a destructive fur-trading business with sea otter furs. When the fur trade declined in the 1850s and several other business attempts failed, Russia sold Alaska to the United States for a little less than two cents per acre. Although initially many people thought this purchase was folly, the deal turned out to be an advantageous one. Read about a couple in the Bible who sold their property (Acts 5:1–11) and what turned out to be their "folly."

Questions to Discuss: Why did Ananias and Sapphira lie to Peter? Who else did they wrong? Why should you never lie to God?

Related Activity: Cool off your summer. Pretend you're in Alaska and have a snowball fight with crumpled paper.

Curriculum Connection: Read about the native Alaskans.

Verse to Memorize: Jeremiah 17:9—"The heart is deceitful above all things and beyond cure. Who can understand it?"

Prayer Suggestion: Ask God to help you always be honest and truthful.

August 21
Truck Driver's Week

The only forms of transportation mentioned in the Bible are walking,
riding in chariots, or riding on animals such as horses, donkeys,
or camels. So when the Philistines wanted to return the stolen Ark
of the Lord, they had no kind truck driver to do the job for them.
Read 1 Samuel 4:1b-18, 5:1-6:21 to see how they solved their dilemma.

Questions to Discuss: Why was the Ark of the Lord special? Why did the Philistines want to return the Ark to the Israelites? How did the cows know just where to go to deliver the Ark?

Related Activity: Go for a drive to be a "traffic watcher." Keep a record of the kinds of vehicles you see, such as vans, station wagons, cars, eighteen-wheelers, small trucks. Graph your results.

Curriculum Connection: Make a list of the forms of transportation available today. How many are available in your city?

Verse to Memorize: Psalm 118:1—
"Give thanks to the Lord, for he is good; his love endures forever."

Prayer Suggestion: Pray for truck drivers and other people who make their living by driving.

August 22
Liquid Soap Anniversary

William Shepphard first patented liquid soap on this day in 1865. Do you have any liquid soap in your house? Read Psalm 51:1-17 to see why David felt he needed to be cleansed.

Questions to Discuss: Why does the psalmist want to be "whiter than snow"? Do you feel dirty and unclean when you sin? What can you do to feel clean again?

Related Activity: Fill empty detergent bottles with water, and "paint" the sidewalk. Can you write your name in cursive with the water?

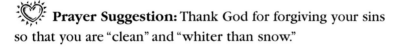

Curriculum Connection: Look in your pantry. Categorize the items there as to how they would be found in your grocery store.

Verse to Memorize: Psalm 51:7b—"Wash me, and I will be whiter than snow."

Prayer Suggestion: Thank God for forgiving your sins so that you are "clean" and "whiter than snow."

August 23
National Smile Week

Have you ever heard the saying that it takes more muscles to frown than it does to smile? This is your chance, then, to let some muscles atrophy. Try not to use the "frowning" muscles all week. Smile instead. Read John 11:1-44 to discover when several of Jesus' friends used their "sad muscles" at the beginning of the story. See how their joy returns in the end.

 Questions to Discuss: How did Mary and Martha feel at the beginning of this story? Why did Jesus cry? How did the sisters feel at the end of this passage? How does it make you feel that you have an eternal life in Heaven with Jesus?

Related Activity: Paint a pillowcase with smiley faces. Write on the case, "Smile! Jesus loves you!"

Curriculum Connection: Read about the muscles in your body. What are the three kinds of muscles?

Verse to Memorize: John 11:25-26a—"Jesus said to her, 'I am the resurrection and the life. He who believes in me will live, even though he dies; and whoever lives and believes in me will never die.'"

Prayer Suggestion: Give thanks to God for the gift of eternal life.

August 24
National Mustard Day

*Mustard, as a condiment, is produced from the mustard plant.
There are a variety of species of mustard plant. Jesus, as described in
Mark 4:30-34, uses the mustard plant as the source of a parable.*

Questions to Discuss: What happens to the tiny mustard seed?
How is that like spreading the news about Jesus? How can you
help the mustard seed "grow" to phenomenal proportions?

Related Activity: Eat a hot dog with mustard.

Curriculum Connection: Describe these parts of
a tree and their function: crown, trunk, root.

Verse to Memorize: 2 Corinthians 5:20—
"We are therefore Christ's ambassadors, as though
God were making his appeal through us. We implore you
on Christ's behalf: Be reconciled to God."

Prayer Suggestion: Ask God to show you someone who needs to
hear about His Kingdom.

August 25
Friendship Day

Jonathan and David's friendship probably formed soon after David came to the palace to play the harp for King Saul, Jonathan's father. They probably spent a great deal of time together and shared lots of happy moments. Read more about their friendship in 1 Samuel 19:1–20:42.

Questions to Discuss: How did Jonathan and David feel about each other? What makes your best friend special? How can you show your friend how you feel about him or her?

Related Activity: Draw a picture of you and your friend. Write a note or poem on the picture. Give or mail your note to your friend, and wish that person a "Happy Friendship Day."

Curriculum Connection: Talk about conjunctions, that is, connecting words. The most common conjunctions are *and, but, or.* Other words sometimes used as conjunctions are *as, so, because, however.* Look for conjunctions in today's passage.

Verse to Memorize: Proverbs 17:17a—"A friend loves at all times."

Prayer Suggestion: Pray for your friends by name. Thank God for friendships.

August 26
Mother Teresa's Birthday

On August 29, 1910, Agnes Gonxha Bojaxhiu was born in Macedonia. By the time she was twelve, she knew she wanted to help the poor. At eighteen, she joined a community of Irish nuns with mission work in Calcutta. She worked in a high school in Calcutta for years, then moved to the slums of Calcutta to start a school for children. It was here that she began to be called Mother Teresa instead of Sister Teresa. Mother Teresa's accomplishments are a tribute to her love of God; she worked with or started orphanages, homes for the dying, a leper colony, and dozens upon dozens of other projects. In 1979, she won the Nobel Peace Prize. God called her home in 1997. Read what Matthew says about the meek and humble in Matthew 5:1-12.

Questions to Discuss: What does *meek* mean? What does it mean to depend on God? How did Mother Teresa depend on God? How do you show your dependence on God?

Related Activity: Visit a retirement home. Ask the caretakers whether there are residents who never receive visitors. Give those persons special attention.

Curriculum Connection: Read about the religious groups in India.

Verse to Memorize: Matthew 5:5—"Blessed are the meek, for they will inherit the earth."

Prayer Suggestion: Thank God for people like Mother Teresa— meek, kind, and loving disciples for God. Pray for missionaries in foreign countries who do humanitarian work in the name of Jesus.

August 27
National Veterinary Week

Doctors who treat animals are called veterinarians. Had veterinarians been in practice in biblical days, the Egyptians would certainly have thought they needed one. Read to see what happens in Exodus 9:1-7.

 Questions to Discuss: What happened to the animals in today's passage? Why did God bring this plague on Egypt? What does God want us to learn from the plagues on the Egyptians and the exodus of His people?

Related Activity: Take your pet to your veterinarian for a check-up. Thank your veterinarian. If you have no pet, visit a pet shop for fun.

Curriculum Connection: Explain the difference between vertebrates and invertebrates.

Verse to Memorize: Romans 15:4— "For everything that was written in the past was written to teach us, so that through endurance and the encouragement of the Scriptures, we might have hope."

Prayer Suggestion: Pray for veterinarians.

August 28
Dream Day

On August 28, 1963, Martin Luther King Jr. led a peaceful march to Washington, D.C., to protest racism and discrimination. On the steps of the Lincoln Memorial, he gave a stirring speech titled "I Have a Dream." Read John 4:1-30, 39-42 to find out Jesus' views about discrimination.

Questions to Discuss: Why was the woman surprised that Jesus was talking to her? How did Jesus feel about people who were different in one way or another?

Related Activity: Read Martin Luther King Jr.'s speech. Write on the topic, "I Have a Dream About Heaven." Include in your dream what it will be like with people from all over the world joining hands in Heaven.

Curriculum Connection: Use Luke to make a list of Jesus' miracles. Were all of the people involved of Jewish descent?

Verse to Memorize: 1 John 4:11, 21b—"Dear Friends, since God so loved us, we also ought to love one another. Whoever loves God must also love his brother."

Prayer Suggestion: Ask God to help you find ways to end discrimination.

August 29
Goose Day

Wild geese live mostly in Asia, Europe, and North America.
There are well over forty species of wild geese. Read about another
bird, the dove, in Matthew 3:13–17.

Questions to Discuss: Why was John uncomfortable, at first, with the idea of baptizing Jesus? What did God say when Jesus was baptized? What does the dove symbolize? Why did God send the dove when Jesus was baptized?

Related Activity: Make an edible dove. Split a bagel. Spread cream cheese on both halves, filling in the whole in one half. Cut one half in half again, making two wings. Place the "body" on a plate and put the wings in place on either side. Place a powdered-sugar "donut hole" on top for a head.

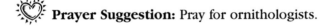

Curriculum Connection: Work with irregular plurals such as *goose-geese, foot-feet*.

Verse to Memorize: Matthew 3:17— "And a voice from heaven said 'This is my son, whom I love; with him I am well pleased.'"

Prayer Suggestion: Pray for ornithologists.

August 30
National Water Quality Month

God performed miracle after miracle for the Israelite people through Moses, and yet they continued to find reasons to grumble. Read Exodus 17:1-7.

Questions to Discuss: Why were the Israelites grumbling this time? Read verse 4. Why do you think Moses called the Israelites "these people"? How did the people feel after God gave them water? Do you sometimes forget God's blessings, grumbling and complaining about something else instead?

Related Activity: Drink bottled water. Talk about God's blessings.

Curriculum Connection: Read to see how water is purified.

Verse to Memorize: James 1:17a—"Every good and perfect gift is from above, coming down from the Father."

Prayer Suggestion: Make a list of as many of your blessings as you can name. Give thanks for each one.

August 31
National Back-to-School Month

*Have you started a new school year yet? Did you take a summer
vacation? Have you had your first quiz for the new year?
Read about Job's "tests" in Job 1:1–2:13, 38:1–42:17.*

Questions to Discuss: What were some of the hardships and trials
that Job endured? What hardships have you endured? Did Job remain faithful to God?

Related Activity: Gather your schoolbooks. Give thanks to God for
each subject, and ask His blessings in each area of study for the year.

Curriculum Connection: Make an
outline of what you will study this year.

Verse to Memorize: Romans
5:3-4—"Not only so, but we also rejoice
in our sufferings because we know that
suffering produces perseverance; perseverance, character; and character, hope."

Prayer Suggestion: Pray for those
who are suffering.

September

September 1
Save-the-Tiger Month

The tiger is the largest member of the cat family and is an endangered species. Those that remain in the wild live in Asia. Most people fear tigers because they have been known to kill and eat people. However, tigers are easy to breed and raise in captivity; thus many tigers live in zoos and are trained for circus acts. Tigers can be trained to jump through hoops and even allow riders. Perhaps the wild tiger can be trained, but James says that "no man can tame the tongue." Read his words in James 3:1–12.

Questions to Discuss: Why does James say that no man can tame the tongue? What evil words or lies have you spoken this week? How can you learn to keep your tongue from doing wrong?

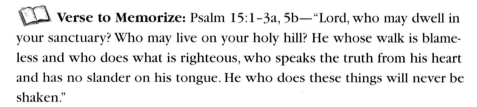

Related Activity: Paint a tiger. Write on your paper, "Watch your tongue!"

Curriculum Connection: Read about other animals in the cat family.

Verse to Memorize: Psalm 15:1–3a, 5b—"Lord, who may dwell in your sanctuary? Who may live on your holy hill? He whose walk is blameless and who does what is righteous, who speaks the truth from his heart and has no slander on his tongue. He who does these things will never be shaken."

Prayer Suggestion: Ask God to help you use your tongue to say kind words and stay away from unkind, dishonest, and disrespectful words.

September 2
All-American Breakfast Month

Do you remember when Jesus served His disciples breakfast?
Do you remember what they ate? Read John 21:1-14.

Questions to Discuss: What happened when the disciples did as Jesus requested? Why do you think Jesus provided so many fish for the disciples? Tell about a time when you obeyed God and were rewarded handsomely.

Related Activity: Go out for breakfast or cook a breakfast buffet at home as a family.

Curriculum Connection: Talk about contractions. Find the contractions in today's passage, and give the two words represented by each contraction.

Verse to Memorize: James 1:22— "Do not merely listen to the word, and so deceive yourselves. Do what it says."

Prayer Suggestion: Ask God to help you obey His word.

September 3
National History Month

*A very important event in the history of Christianity took place
on a hill in Moriah. Read about Abraham's obedience in
Genesis 22:1-19 and James 2:20-24.*

Questions to Discuss: How did Abraham obey God? How do you think Abraham felt about sacrificing Isaac? What did God do for Abraham? How did God reward Abraham's obedience? How can you obey God? Explain the symbolism of Abraham's sacrifice of his firstborn and God's sacrifice of His Son, Jesus.

Related Activity: Parents, ask your children to do a task: clean a room, fold clothes, put away toys. Instruct them to be obedient. Reward their obedience with a simple but tangible treat.

Curriculum Connection: Choose a time in history that you want to learn more about. Use encyclopedias, the Internet, and the library for research. Give an oral report, using visuals.

Verse to Memorize: Hebrews 5:8-9—"Although he was a son, he learned obedience from what he suffered and, once made perfect, he became the source of eternal salvation for all who obey him."

Prayer Suggestion: Ask God to help you be obedient.

September 4
National Chicken Month

Several kinds of birds are mentioned in the Old and New Testaments of the Bible. Many of the birds mentioned are referenced because of eating instructions. Birds such as vultures, eagles, kites, ravens, owls, gulls, ospreys, storks, and herons, to name a few, are specifically mentioned in Leviticus 11:13 as birds that are unclean and should not be eaten. Other birds mentioned in various places in the Bible include the chicken, sparrow, and dove. Read what Jesus says about a sparrow in Luke 12:1-12.

Questions to Discuss: How important are you to God? How important is God to you? Is God valuable enough to you for you to acknowledge Him publicly?

Related Activity: Use the instructions on a package of food coloring to prepare egg dye. Color eggs; draw designs on the eggs with waxed crayons before coloring if you wish.

Curriculum Connection: Find out about birds that are now extinct, like the dodo bird.

Verse to Memorize: Luke 12:8-9—"I tell you, whoever acknowledges me before men, the Son of Man will also acknowledge him before the angels of God. But he who disowns me before men will be disowned before the angels of God."

Prayer Suggestion: Ask God to help you boldly acknowledge Him to your friends, family, and others.

248

September 5
Be-Late-for-Something Day

This may be a fun, silly celebration to participate in, but there is one thing for sure that Jesus does not want us to be late for: His second coming. Read Matthew 24:36–51 to hear Jesus' warnings.

Questions to Discuss: How can you "keep watch" and be ready for Jesus' return? What do you need to do today to get ready?

Related Activity: Be late for something today, within reason, of course. Serve breakfast at 10:00 A.M. or dinner at 9:00 P.M.

Curriculum Connection: Look at the different time zones in the United States. What time zone are you in?

Verse to Memorize: Matthew 24:36, 42— "No one knows about that day or hour, not even the angels in heaven, nor the Son, but only the Father. Therefore keep watch, because you do not know on what day your Lord will come."

Prayer Suggestion: Ask God to help you be ready, at all times, for the return of Jesus.

September 6
National Courtesy Month

The very name of Ruth, the Moabite woman, suggests friendship.
And what a dear and courteous friend she was to Naomi.
Read about their relationship in Ruth 1:1–22.

Questions to Discuss: How did Ruth show kindness to Naomi? How can you be courteous to others?

Related Activity: Make a tree with autumn-colored leaves in preparation for the new season to decorate your wall. Add fruits to the tree, writing a fruit of the spirit on each piece of fruit. On the leaves, write specific ways you can be courteous to friends and family members.

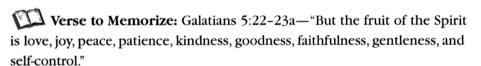

Curriculum Connection: How many books in the Bible are named after women? Who is your favorite woman in the Bible?

Verse to Memorize: Galatians 5:22–23a—"But the fruit of the Spirit is love, joy, peace, patience, kindness, goodness, faithfulness, gentleness, and self-control."

Prayer Suggestion: Before you put the fruit pieces on the tree, turn them all face-down on the floor. "Pick" fruit and ask God for that fruit, saying, "Dear God, Please give me love." Allow each person a chance to pick each fruit.

September 7
Grandma Moses Day

September 7, 1860, Anna Mary Robertson was born in New York. She later married a painter and became Mrs. Moses. When Anna Mary Moses was seventy-eight years old, she began a painting career that would eventually see her simple country scenes exhibited throughout the world. When she was one hundred years old, New York State proclaimed her birthday as Grandma Moses Day. She died a year later. Read about another person who accomplished great things at an advanced age. Read Deuteronomy 34:1–12.

Questions to Discuss: Why didn't Moses go into the land God promised Abraham's descendants? How old was Moses when he died? How did God use Moses to bless His people? What kinds of things can you do for God, whether you are young or not-so-young?

Related Activity: Try to find a picture of one of Grandma Moses' paintings. Paint a country scene using her style.

Curriculum Connection: Who is your favorite painter? What painting is he or she famous for? Write a brief report on that painter's life.

Verse to Memorize: Ecclesiastes 9:10a—
"Whatever your hand finds to do, do it with all your might."

Prayer Suggestion: Ask God to use you to bless others all the days of your life.

September 8
National Rice Month

Rice, one of the world's most important food crops, is the main part of the meal for over half the people in the world. Rice is a cereal grain and belongs to the grass family. In Isaac's family, Esau, the hunter, often smelled like a "field that the Lord has blessed," according to his father. In fact, Isaac's blessing consisted of a prayer for his son that he would have "an abundance of grain" in his future. Find out how this blessing was given to the wrong son in Genesis 27:1–28:5.

Questions to Discuss: How did Rebekah and Jacob deceive Isaac? How did their actions hurt their family? As a result, how did Esau sin? Do your sins and disobedience affect other people? Tell about a time when your wrong actions have affected another person in your family.

Related Activity: Try a new rice recipe.

Curriculum Connection: Talk about the use of quotation marks. Find the quotation marks in today's passage and determine which person is speaking in each incident.

Verse to Memorize: Ephesians 5:6—"Let no one deceive you with empty words, for because of such things God's wrath comes on those who are disobedient."

Prayer Suggestion: Ask God to keep you from being disobedient to God and to your family.

September 9
Labor Day

On June 28, 1894, President Grover Cleveland signed an act making the first Monday in September a legal, federal holiday. However, many Americans had been celebrating the holiday for years prior. This holiday honors working people across the country and is the unofficial end of summer. Read Genesis 29:14b-30 to see what the labor of one particular Old Testament worker netted him.

Questions to Discuss: What kind of work did Jacob do for Laban? Why did Jacob work another seven years? What kind of work do you enjoy doing?

Related Activity: Discuss the professions or occupations that are represented in your extended family.

Curriculum Connection: Practice multiplying by sevens.

Verse to Memorize: Ecclesiastes 5:18-19— "Then I realized that it is good and proper for a man to eat and drink and to find satisfaction in his toilsome labor under the sun during the few days of life God has given him—for this is his lot. Moreover, when God gives any man wealth and possessions, and enables him to enjoy them, to accept his lot and be happy in his work—this is a gift of God."

Prayer Suggestion: Thank God for the occupations represented in your family. Ask Him to prepare your heart and mind for a future career.

September 10
Sew-Be-It Day

Sew-Be-It Day is held on this day in September, during National Sewing Month, to bring public awareness to those who work with their hands to produce clothing and other articles. Read about a handmade robe in 1 Samuel 18:1–30.

Questions to Discuss: Who do you think made Jonathan's robe? Why did he give it to David? Have you ever given something really special to a dear friend? Why was Saul jealous of David? How did Saul's jealousy lead to sinful acts?

Related Activity: Draw an outline of a bear, gingerbread boy, dog, or some other simple shape. Trace the outline onto a piece of construction paper. Cut out two shapes. Punch holes around the outside of the shape. Using long shoestrings or yarn, sew your outlines together.

Curriculum Connection: Talk about the use of the colon as a punctuation mark. Find the colon in this passage.

Verse to Memorize: Romans 8:3c–4—"And so he condemned sin in sinful man, in order that the righteous requirements of the law might be fully met in us, who do not live according to the sinful nature but according to the Spirit."

Prayer Suggestion: Ask God to keep you from sinful acts and wrongdoing.

September 11
9/11 Day

Before the tragic events of September 11, 2001, this day recognized the establishment of the 911 emergency phone number. After the great emergency on this day in 2001, Americans will forever remember the loss of over twenty-five hundred lives. More than four hundred of the dead were uniformed rescuers. Read in 1 Corinthians 15:1-58 to see why death for a Christian is only the beginning of an eternity with Christ.

Questions to Discuss: Why is death a victorious time for a Christian? What happens to a Christian when he or she dies?

Related Activity: Visit a fire station, police station, or other emergency personnel locale. Take cookies or treats, and thank the men and women for their services.

Curriculum Connection: Find the education requirements needed to be a firefighter, police officer, paramedic, sheriff's deputy.

Verse to Memorize: 1 Corinthians 15:3b-4, 55—"That Christ died for our sins according to the Scriptures, that he was buried, that he was raised on the third day according to the Scriptures. Where, O death, is your victory? Where, O death, is your sting?"

Prayer Suggestion: Pray for emergency workers, paramedics, ambulance drivers, firefighters, police officers, sheriff's deputies.

September 12
National Biscuit Month

Do you like to eat biscuits? What is your favorite addition to a biscuit? Butter? Jelly? Sausage? Read 2 Kings 4:42–44 about some men who might have added something to their bread to make it tastier.

Questions to Discuss: Who provided enough bread for all of the men? Who provides for your needs?

Related Activity: Make homemade biscuits, and save some for tomorrow.

Curriculum Connection: Practice rounding numbers to the nearest ones, tens, hundreds.

Verse to Memorize: 1 Timothy 6:17—"Command those who are rich in this present world not to be arrogant nor to put their hope in wealth, which is so uncertain, but to put their hope in God, who richly provides us with everything for our enjoyment."

Prayer Suggestion: Thank God for providing for your needs.

September 13
National Honey Month

Bees store nectar in tiny, six-sided cells in their hives. When water evaporates from the nectar, it changes into honey. God designed the bee to do just that. God promised the Israelites land "flowing with milk and honey." Read Numbers 13:1–14:38 to see if the land really was that wonderful.

Questions to Discuss: Why was this land described as flowing with milk and honey? Why did the spies give a bad report about the land? Which of the spies trusted God? Do you trust God?

Related Activity: Using biscuits you cooked yesterday, eat biscuits and honey, along with a tall glass of milk.

Curriculum Connection: Read to find out the details of how bees make honey. What is nectar? How do the bees get nectar?

Verse to Memorize: John 14:1—"Do not let your hearts be troubled. Trust in God; trust also in me."

Prayer Suggestion: Ask God to help you trust in Him completely.

September 14
Soccer Season

Have you ever played soccer? Have you ever scored a goal? How did you feel when you scored a goal? Read about goal scoring in Philippians 3:12-4:1.

 Questions to Discuss: What goal should you strive toward, according to Philippians 3:14? How does it feel to know that, as a Christian, you have already won the prize of eternal life?

Related Activity: Play soccer as a family.

Curriculum Connection: Learn the rules of soccer. What do these terms mean: *save, dribble, drop ball, trap, volley?*

Verse to Memorize: 1 Timothy 6:12—"Fight the good fight of the faith. Take hold of the eternal life to which you were called when you made your good confession in the presence of many witnesses."

Prayer Suggestion: Thank God for the prize of eternal life.

September 15
Grandparents' Day

*By presidential proclamation, the first Sunday in September following
Labor Day is set aside for honoring and remembering grandparents.
Read Proverbs 17:6.*

 Questions to Discuss: What makes your grandparents special?
Do your grandparents know the Lord? Can you share
Jesus' love with them today?

Related Activity: Call or write your grandparents.

Curriculum Connection: How old are your
grandparents? What year were they born? How
much younger are you than each of your grandparents? Use subtraction problems to answer these
questions.

Verse to Memorize: Titus 2:11–13—"For the grace of God that
brings salvation has appeared to all men. It teaches us to say 'No' to ungodli-
ness and worldly passions, and to live self-controlled, upright and godly
lives in this present age, while we wait for the blessed hope the glorious
appearing of our great God and Savior, Jesus Christ."

Prayer Suggestion: Pray for your grandparents.

September 16
Mayflower Day

A ship called the Mayflower left Plymouth, England, on this day in 1620 to sail for a new world in which they could set up their own church. The voyage across the sea met with storms and other difficulties. Read about a storm on a boat in Jesus' day in Matthew 8:23-27.

Questions to Discuss: What was Jesus doing when the storm came up? How did the disciples feel? What do you do when you are afraid? Tell about a recent time when you were frightened.

Related Activity: Make sub-boats, using submarine rolls. Scoop out some of the bread on top. Fill with chicken salad. Use pretzel sticks and pressed fruit rolls to make sails.

Curriculum Connection: Read about the adventures of the Pilgrims. Why were some of the Pilgrims called Separatists? Where did they land in America?

Verse to Memorize: 1 Peter 5:7—"Cast all your anxiety on him because he cares for you."

Prayer Suggestion: Thank God for comforting you during your times of fear.

September 17
National Tie Week

Does your father wear a tie to work? Does your father wear a tie to church? Read what Paul says in Romans about "holy clothing."
Read Romans 13:14a.

Questions to Discuss: How do you "clothe" yourself with Jesus?

Related Activity: Use Dad's old ties. In pairs, have a three-legged race.

Curriculum Connection: Compare and contrast the clothing styles of today and the clothing styles of your parents' younger days.

Verse to Memorize: Ephesians 2:10—"For we are God's workmanship, created in Christ Jesus to do good works, which God prepared in advance for us to do."

Prayer Suggestion: Ask God to help you show Christ, inside and out.

September 18
National Housekeepers' Week

A week to recognize housekeeping staff and to appreciate the work they do.
If you do housekeeping work in your home, then this is your week, also.
Read about a difficult time in some "housekeepers'" lives in Exodus 8:1–15.

Questions to Discuss: What would it be like to have frogs piled up all over your home? Why did God cause this plague? Why did God allow Pharaoh's heart to be hardened?

Related Activity: Do housekeeping chores together, but save the laundry for another day. Play Christian music as you work.

Curriculum Connection: Describe the distinguishing characteristics of an amphibian.

Verse to Memorize: Psalm 145:13b—"The Lord is faithful to all his promises and loving toward all he has made."

Prayer Suggestion: Pray for housekeepers—professional and nonprofessional.

September 19
National Student Day

In Matthew 10:1–42, Jesus warned His disciples that, as students of the great Teacher, they would probably suffer some of the same difficulties He had suffered. But He urged them to continue to be good "students" of His word and continue to do His work. Are you a good student of Jesus?

Questions to Discuss: Why did Jesus send out the disciples? What advice did Jesus give to the twelve men? What did Jesus mean by "A student is not above his teacher"? How can you be a good student of Jesus and a good student of your schoolwork?

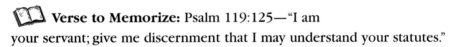

Related Activity: Bake cupcakes and sing, "Happy Student Day to me; Happy Student Day to me; Happy Student Day, God loves me; Happy Student Day to me."

Curriculum Connection: Talk about subject-verb agreement. Look at the sentences in today's passage in relation to this agreement.

Verse to Memorize: Psalm 119:125—"I am your servant; give me discernment that I may understand your statutes."

Prayer Suggestion: Ask God to help you be a good student of His word.

September 20
National Laundry Workers' Week

How often do you do laundry? Would you like to make a living doing laundry? Many folks do, and today is the day to honor them. Read about a launderer's "nightmare" in Exodus 7:14-24.

Questions to Discuss: How do you think the Egyptians felt during this plague? How did it affect their daily lives? How did God comfort the Israelites during their trials? How does God comfort you?

Related Activity: Do laundry together as a family. How many towels do you have? Washcloths? Tablecloths? Socks? Do you feel blessed to have so many clothes to wash?

Curriculum Connection: Discuss the uses of the semicolon, colon, and comma. Can you find these punctuation marks in today's passage?

Verse to Memorize: 2 Corinthians 1:3-4a—"Praise be to the God and Father of our Lord Jesus Christ, the Father of compassion and the God of all comfort, who comforts us in all our troubles."

Prayer Suggestion: Pray for laundry workers, including the person in charge of laundry in your home.

September 21
National Farm Awareness Week

Have you thanked a farmer today? You cannot survive without food, and nearly all of the food you eat comes from crops and livestock raised on farms. People in biblical days were well aware of making a living as a farmer. That is why Nathan knew David could relate to a story told to him about a farmer's lamb. Read 2 Samuel 11:1-12:25 to hear Nathan's words.

Questions to Discuss: How did Nathan scold David for his sinful behavior? What was David's punishment for his sin? How do you feel when reprimanded for doing wrong?

Related Activity: Take a field trip to a farm. If you do not live near farms, go to your local grocery store's produce department and observe the many products produced on farms.

Curriculum Connection: Research to find out what farm animal is raised predominantly in your state.

Verse to Memorize: James 4:8—"Come near to God and he will come near to you. Wash your hands, you sinners, and purify your hearts."

Prayer Suggestion: Ask God to keep you close to Him so that you will not sin against Him.

September 22
Children's Good Manners Month

Very little is known of Jesus' life as a child. The incident in Luke 2:41-52 shows that Jesus most likely lived His boyhood days just like His adult days, that is, in obedience to God and in a kind and respectful manner to others. Read evidence of Jesus' good manners as a child in today's passage.

Questions to Discuss: Why did Jesus stay at the temple? Using what you know about Jesus, tell what kinds of things Jesus did to obey His parents. How are good manners a sign of obedience?

Related Activity: Make a list of good manners at church, good manners at mealtimes, good manners at playtime, and good manners in public.

Curriculum Connection: Discuss the difference between concrete and abstract nouns. Find examples of both in the passage.

Verse to Memorize: Proverbs 20:11—"Even a child is known by his actions, by whether his conduct is pure and right."

Prayer Suggestion: Ask God to help you have good manners and be respectful toward your family members.

September 23
Autumn

According to the calendar, this is the first day of autumn. Does it still feel like summer where you live? Does it already feel like winter where you live? Read James' words about waiting patiently for autumn in James 5:7-11.

Questions to Discuss: How should we wait for the Lord's return? What is your favorite part about autumn?

Related Activity: Go on a walk and enjoy the beauty of fall. Collect leaves that have fallen off the trees. Press them with an iron between pieces of waxed paper.

Curriculum Connection: Find out why the leaves change colors and fall off the trees. What is an evergreen tree?

Verse to Memorize: Psalm 27:14— "Wait for the Lord; be strong and take heart and wait for the Lord."

Prayer Suggestion: Thank God for the beautiful colors of autumn.

September 24
Good Neighbor Day

According to the dictionary, a neighbor *is defined as one who "lives near or next to another." However, in the story of the Good Samaritan in Luke 10:29-37, Jesus defines* neighbor *as meaning "all the world." Read how Jesus feels about neighbors in His opinion of the word, in Matthew 22:34-40.*

Questions to Discuss: How does Jesus say to treat neighbors? What have you done for a neighbor this week? Do you have a neighbor on your street who does not know Jesus?

Related Activity: Bake cookies or bread for someone who lives near you.

Curriculum Connection: Learn to spell words with the "eigh" phonics pattern.

Verse to Memorize: Matthew 22:39b—"Love your neighbor as yourself."

Prayer Suggestion: Draw a map of your neighborhood. Label houses with names of people you know. Pray specifically for each family.

September 25
Rabbit Day

Most rabbits live in shallow holes, hiding themselves from their prey with weeds and grasses. In the northern United States, rabbits often live in dens or burrows during the winter. Sometimes they move into abandoned holes of other animals. Rabbits, like other animals, have places they call home. Jesus told His disciples that He had no earthly home and that those that followed Him would have to give up their homes as well. Read Matthew 8:18-22.

Questions to Discuss: What "costs" of following Jesus are mentioned in this passage? What costs have you experienced by being a follower of Jesus? Are the benefits worth the costs?

Related Activity: Make a rabbit puppet, using a white lunch sack. Cut pink ears and nose; cut whiskers and eyes. Glue the facial features in place. Glue a make-up powder puff to the back of the puppet.

Curriculum Connection: Talk about the vocabulary words used to mean various homes for animals. Who lives in a den? A bed?

Verse to Memorize: Luke 6:23a—"Rejoice in that day and leap for joy, because great is your reward in heaven."

Prayer Suggestion: Thank God for your reward: eternal life in heaven with Him.

269

September 26
Deaf Awareness Week

Deaf Awareness Week, held the last full week in September annually, was established to bring attention to deaf people, their achievements, and the issues they face in daily life. Hearing-impaired Americans can thank an energetic Congregational minister named Thomas Hopkins Gallaudet for the first school for the deaf, which opened in 1817 in Hartford, Connecticut. Jesus had a healing heart and spirit for the deaf as well. Read about some of His miracles for the hearing-impaired and other illnesses and diseases in Matthew 11:1–19.

Questions to Discuss: What kinds of miracles did Jesus perform? Do you occasionally have doubts about Jesus, just as John did while in prison? How can you know for sure that Jesus is Lord of your life?

Related Activity: Go on-line or check out a book from the library on American sign language. Learn to sign "Jesus Loves Me."

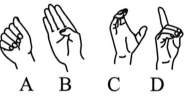

A B C D

Curriculum Connection: Learn more about Thomas Gallaudet. How and why did he first become interested in the hearing-impaired? Learn the alphabet in sign language.

Verse to Memorize: 1 John 5:1a—"Everyone who believes that Jesus is the Christ is born of God."

Prayer Suggestion: Pray that God will help you be more aware and sensitive toward the hearing-impaired.

September 27
Answering Machine Anniversary

The first answering machine was over three feet tall. Willy Muuler
invented the first automatic answering machine in 1935.
Read about a young boy's answer to God in 1 Samuel 3:1-4:1a.

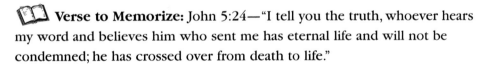

Questions to Discuss: Who called Samuel?
Why did he think it was Eli calling? Do you listen for
God to speak to you? Share with your family a time
you heard God's words.

Related Activity: Leave a message on your
answering machine about Jesus.

Curriculum Connection: Learn how
the ear works. What are the three main parts
of the ear?

Verse to Memorize: John 5:24—"I tell you the truth, whoever hears
my word and believes him who sent me has eternal life and will not be
condemned; he has crossed over from death to life."

Prayer Suggestion: Ask God to help you hear when He speaks to you.

September 28

Dog Week

There are more than three hundred kinds of purebred dogs. The American Kennel Club (AKC) classifies them into seven major groups for shows and exhibitions. Although today they are considered man's best friend, dogs in the Bible were not as highly regarded. Read about a dog eating leftover crumbs in Mark 7:24-30.

Questions to Discuss: Why did Jesus give the message to the Jews first? How did Jesus reward the woman's faith? What makes your faith strong?

Related Activity: Visit a humane shelter and volunteer to take dogs for a walk.

Curriculum Connection: What are the seven major groups recognized by the AKC? Give examples of dogs in each group. Learn to recognize various dog breeds.

Verse to Memorize: Romans 10:17— "Consequently, faith comes from hearing the message, and the message is heard through the word of Christ."

Prayer Suggestion: Pray for dog handlers and animal shelter employees.

September 29

Festival of Trumpets

*The Festival of Trumpets, as designated by God, was a presentation of
Israel for the Lord. The day was to be commemorated with rest and
trumpets. Read Leviticus 23:23-25, Joel 2:1-3:21 to see how
God meant for this festival to be prophetic of the future.*

Questions to Discuss: Why was the
festival originally celebrated? How is this festival prophetic of Jerusalem's future? When will
the trumpet sound?

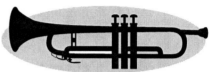

Related Activity: Borrow a tape or CD
from the library that contains trumpet music. Listen to
the trumpet sounds.

Curriculum Connection: Read about Dizzy Gillespie.

Verse to Memorize: 1 Corinthians 15:51b-52—"We will not all
sleep, but we will all be changed in a flash, in the twinkling of an eye, at the
last trumpet. For the trumpet will sound, the dead will be raised imperish-
able, and we will be changed."

Prayer Suggestion: Thank God for His promise that Jesus will
come again.

September 30
Day of Atonement

In Leviticus 16:1-34, God established the instructions for the Day of Atonement—a day set aside to sacrifice atonement for priests and people and the tabernacle and altar. The Day of Atonement was established as a day of cleansing and purifying. In establishing this holy festival, just like other Old Testament festivals, God foresees the future and prophetically links the Old Testament celebrations to the celebration of Jesus Christ. Read the words in Romans 3:21-30 about Jesus' sacrifice of atonement.

Questions to Discuss: What does *atonement* mean? How do you know your sins are forgiven?

Related Activity: Make a list of sins and wrongdoings that you committed this week.

Curriculum Connection: Define these words: *atonement, propitiation, redemption, justification.*

Verse to Memorize: 1 John 2:1c-2—"Jesus Christ, the Righteous One. He is the atoning sacrifice for our sins, and not only for ours but also for the sins of the whole world."

Prayer Suggestion: Using your list, ask for forgiveness for each wrong act. Thank God for His Son, Jesus, who made the one-time atoning sacrifice for the sins of the world.

October

October 1
Computer Learning Month

Many inventors contributed to the history of computers. One would have a difficult time picking out a single person's name as the sole inventor of the computer. Computer Learning Month is held each October to raise awareness of the importance of this invention. In this day and age, if you do not know how to operate a computer, you might be considered unschooled and ordinary. Read about two men who were accused of being unschooled and ordinary for different reasons. Read Acts 4:1-22.

Questions to Discuss: Why were Peter and John anything but ordinary? What did they tell the rulers, elders, and teachers of the law?

Related Activity: Play a computer game as a family. Visit your library if you don't have a computer at home.

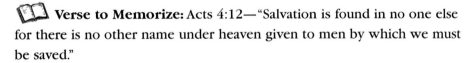

Curriculum Connection: Learn to do something new on your computer.

Verse to Memorize: Acts 4:12—"Salvation is found in no one else for there is no other name under heaven given to men by which we must be saved."

Prayer Suggestion: Give thanks to God for the people and things that contribute to your education, such as your parents, siblings, church leaders, computers, books, and so on.

October 2
National Go-on-a-Field-Trip Month

King Ahab blamed the drought his country was experiencing on the prophet Elijah, who correctly told Ahab that his country was in trouble because of their abandonment of the Lord's commands. Despite a miraculous display of God's powers, King Ahab, his wife, Jezebel, and others were unchanged in their worshipping of Baal. Elijah decided it was time for a "field-trip," and he made a hasty exit.
Read about his conversations with God in 1 Kings 19:1–18.

Questions to Discuss: Why did Elijah run away? Why did Elijah feel as though he was the only one left who believed in God? How many God-fearing believers did God speak of in verse 18? Have you ever felt as though you were all alone as a Christian?

Related Activity: Go with your family on a field trip.

Curriculum Connection: Plot on a map all the field trips or vacations that you have taken with your family.

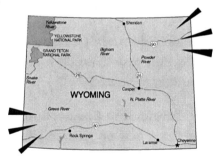

Verse to Memorize: James 1:2—
"Consider it pure joy, my brothers, whenever you face trials of many kinds, because you know that the testing of your faith develops perseverance."

Prayer Suggestion: Thank God for your trials and difficulties, for they strengthen your faith. Ask God to comfort you when you feel alone as a Christian.

October 3
International Dinosaur Month

Information that exists about dinosaurs is based on excavations of dinosaur bones. Scientists classify dinosaurs into two main groups, according to the structure of their hips. One group has a hip structure like that of other reptiles; the other group's hip structure resembles birds' hips. Read who made their hips this way in Psalm 24:1-2.

Questions to Discuss: What would it have been like to live at the same time as the dinosaurs?

Related Activity: Play with toy dinosaurs in the mud. Make chocolate pudding. Once it has chilled, pour some into low-sided, shallow containers. Spread a cloth on the floor, and let your dinosaurs play in the mud.

Curriculum Connection: What do these terms mean: *herbivore, carnivore, omnivore?*

Verse to Memorize: Psalm 24:1— "The earth is the Lord's and everything in it."

Prayer Suggestion: Thank God for His creations— those we can see today and those we cannot.

October 4
National Housing Week

National Housing Week, as proclaimed by President Ronald Reagan in 1982, seeks to bring awareness that "all Americans deserve the opportunity to live in decent, affordable housing." Read John 14:1-4 to find out about your future home.

Questions to Discuss: What do you like best about your home? What is your favorite room? What do you think "God's house" looks like? How do you think it feels to be homeless?

Related Activity: Serve a meal at a homeless shelter or donate food and clothing.

Curriculum Connection: Draw blueprints of your home on graph paper.

Verse to Memorize: John 14:2-3—"In my Father's house are many rooms; if it were not so, I would have told you. I am going there to prepare a place for you. I will come back and take you to be with me that you also may be where I am."

Prayer Suggestion: Pray for those who have no place to call home.

October 5
Bank Teller Appreciation Week

Do you have a piggy bank at home? Do you have a savings account at a bank? This is the week to say thank you to the person who takes care of your money at the bank. Read Matthew 25:14-30 and see what Jesus says about banking.

Questions to Discuss: What does God want you to do with the gifts and talents He's given you? Are you using your talent for Him?

Related Activity: Count your money. Take out your tithe and offerings, then take some money to the bank for deposit in your account. If you do not have an account, start one this week.

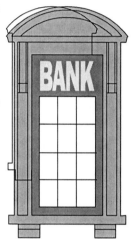

Curriculum Connection: Practice changing percents to decimals and decimals to percents.

Verse to Memorize: 1 Peter 4:10, 11c—"Each one should use whatever gift he has received to serve others, faithfully administering God's grace in its various forms. So that in all things God may be praised through Jesus Christ."

Prayer Suggestion: Ask God to help you use your gifts, talents, and money wisely.

October 6
World Communion Sunday

Many churches have observed World Communion Sunday for over sixty-five years now. This celebration, held annually on the first Sunday in October, was originally called the World Wide Communion Sunday. Read Acts 2:42-47, 1 Corinthians 11:17-34.

Questions to Discuss: What does *communion* mean to you? Try to imagine Jesus serving the cup and breaking the bread. How would you feel to be in His presence?

Related Activity: Participate in communion at your house of worship.

Curriculum Connection: Locate and learn to spell the names of the countries of South America.

Verse to Memorize: 1 Corinthians 10:16—"Is not the cup of thanksgiving for which we give thanks a participation in the blood of Christ? And is not the bread that we break a participation in the body of Christ?"

Prayer Suggestion: Give thanks to God for allowing you to participate in communion with the blood and body of Christ.

October 7
National Roller Skating Month

This month-long celebration recognizes the joy that roller skating has brought to many people for many years. Do you own a pair of roller skates? Do you own roller blades? How about a scooter? Read 2 Kings 4:15-37 to find out why a woman was in need of fast transportation.

Questions to Discuss: What happened to the Shunammite woman's son? What did Elisha do for the boy?

Related Activity: Take your family to a roller skating rink or roller blade park, or ride scooters in your neighborhood.

Curriculum Connection: Find out about another wheeled vehicle. Read about the first transcontinental railroad, completed at Promontory Point, Utah.

Verse to Memorize: John 3:36—"Whoever believes in the Son has eternal life, but whoever rejects the Son will not see life, for God's wrath remains on him."

Prayer Suggestion: Thank God that physical death, for a Christian, is not the end.

October 8
Fire Prevention Week

Fire Prevention Week is held annually during the week of the anniversary of the Great Chicago Fire. The origin of this fire, causing extensive damage, has never been determined. In 1920, President Woodrow Wilson issued the very first National Fire Prevention Day proclamation, and since 1992, this celebration has been celebrated for an entire week. The purpose of the campaign is to enlighten the public on fire safety rules and to keep the public informed of the importance of fire prevention. Read about a "fiery" experience in the Old Testament, 1 Kings 18:1-46.

Questions to Discuss: How were the people going to know who the One True God was? How did Elijah know God would answer his request? Does God answer your prayers?

Related Activity: Either outdoors or inside in a fireplace, under careful parental supervision, roast marshmallows.

Curriculum Connection: Talk about fire safety rules and fire prevention techniques. Discuss the instruction: "stop, drop, and roll." Read about the two great fires in American history—the Great Chicago Fire and the Peshtigo Fire. Who gets blamed for the Great Chicago Fire in most cases? Has that ever been proven?

Verse to Memorize: John 15:7—"If you remain in me and my words remain in you, ask whatever you wish, and it will be given to you."

Prayer Suggestion: As a family, make a list of answered prayers. Thank God for each answer.

October 9
Feast of Tabernacles

Read about this festival in Leviticus 23:33-43, John 7:1-13, 37-39.
Originally, God established this time to celebrate the harvest and
commemorate the journey from Egypt to Canaan. Read to find the
prophetic meaning of the celebration.

Questions to Discuss: Compare the redemption from Egypt to Canaan with the redemption from present-day to the reign of Christ. Why is this festival also called the Festival of Booths?

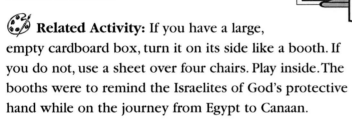

Related Activity: If you have a large, empty cardboard box, turn it on its side like a booth. If you do not, use a sheet over four chairs. Play inside. The booths were to remind the Israelites of God's protective hand while on the journey from Egypt to Canaan.

Curriculum Connection: This festival had several different names. In the New Testament, Jesus has several names also. Look in a Bible dictionary, commentary, or concordance to find the different names for Jesus.

Verse to Memorize: 1 John 2:25—"And this is what he promised us—even eternal life."

Prayer Suggestion: Wrap a box with bright-colored paper. Sit on the floor in a circle. Take turns holding the gift in your hand and saying, "Thank you, God, for the gift of eternal life."

October 10
National Spinning and Weaving Week

Read Genesis 37:1-4. So begins the story of Joseph, the young man who would be responsible for saving his family from the famine while a ruler in Egypt. Read how a woven garment played a part in the history of God's people.

Questions to Discuss: Why did Israel love Joseph more than his brothers? How did that make his brothers feel about Joseph? What happens to Joseph?

Related Activity: Braid several colors of yarn together to make a belt.

Curriculum Connection: Joseph had eleven brothers. Learn the elevens multiplication facts.

Verse to Memorize: Romans 8:28—"And we know that in all things God works for the good of those who love him, who have been called according to his purpose."

Prayer Suggestion: Thank God for always taking care of you.

October 11
National Newspaper Week

When God needed to make an announcement in the Old Testament, He didn't have a local newspaper to distribute His information. God often used prophets to spread His word. Read about the information God gave Habakkuk in Habakkuk 1:1–3:19.

Questions to Discuss: Why was Habakkuk distraught? Do you always understand the ways of the Lord? How can you have peace, even when things do not seem to be going your way?

Related Activity: Read the newspaper together.

Curriculum Connection: Using the table of contents as a guide, find the parts and sections of your newspaper. Describe the different kinds of articles used in a newspaper. What is an obituary? An editorial? An advertisement?

Verse to Memorize: Philippians 4:7—"And the peace of God, which transcends all understanding, will guard your hearts and your minds in Christ Jesus."

Prayer Suggestion: Thank God for the peace He gives you through Jesus.

October 12
National Dessert Month

What is your favorite dessert? Do you like pie, cake, or cobbler the best?
Read about Ezekiel's "dessert" in Ezekiel 3:2-3.

Questions to Discuss: How can God's words "taste sweet"? Is God's word ever "hard to swallow?" What was God telling Ezekiel?

Related Activity: Make an edible sweet scroll. Use two pretzel rods for the handles of the scroll. Peel the paper from two square sheets of pressed fruit. Working on waxed paper, stick the two squares together, forming one long sheet. Place a pretzel rod at either end. Roll the pressed fruit around the pretzel. Make the first roll tight so the fruit will stick. Roll the remaining fruit loosely, so that the scroll can be rolled and unrolled. Save the snack until prayer time.

Curriculum Connection: Find out how sugar is made.

Verse to Remember: Psalm 19:9-10—"The fear of the Lord is pure, enduring forever. The ordinances of the Lord are sure and altogether righteous. They are more precious than gold, than much pure gold; they are sweeter than honey, than honey from the comb."

Prayer Suggestion: Hold your dessert scrolls in your hands. Give thanks to God for the words in the scripture, then snack.

October 13
Clergy Appreciation Day

Do you ever wonder what Jesus did before He officially began His ministry? Close your eyes and picture Jesus' family. Think about what Jesus and His family did each day. Do you think He studied the scriptures often? Do you think He talked to God a lot? Do you think He spent a lot of time helping His family? Read Matthew 4:12-17 to find out how Jesus publicly began the work of His Father.

Questions to Discuss: How did Jesus begin His public ministry? What was the very first theme He "preached" on? Does your pastor encourage you to "Repent, for the kingdom of heaven is near"?

Related Activity: Write your pastor a thank-you note. Thank him for sharing the word of God and for pastoring your church.

Curriculum Connection: Does your church sponsor any missionaries? Find out who they are and where they live. Send them a word of encouragement.

Verse to Memorize: Romans 1:16—"I am not ashamed of the gospel, because it is the power of God for the salvation of everyone who believes, first for the Jew, then for the Gentile."

Prayer Suggestion: Pray for the leaders of your church. Use a church bulletin or newsletter, and call the name of each person.

October 14
Columbus Day

Christopher Columbus, familiar with sea travel by the time he was a young adult, set sail for the Indies in 1492. He no doubt looked to the sky for signs of imminent weather during his voyage. Columbus never found the sea route to Asia, but he did land on and explore the Americas that we know today. Columbus Day is now celebrated on the second Monday in October each year. Read Matthew 16:1–4 to see what Jesus said about interpreting weather signs.

Questions to Discuss: Why did the Pharisees and Sadducees want another sign from Jesus? Do you need a "sign" from God to believe he exists? How does your faith help you believe the things you cannot see?

Related Activity: Sing this song to the tune of "My Bonnie Lies Over the Ocean": "Columbus sailed over the ocean. Columbus sailed over the sea. Columbus sailed over the ocean. To find a new country for me."

Curriculum Connection: Read more about Christopher Columbus. What were the names of his ships? How many voyages west did he make?

Verse to Memorize: Hebrews 11:6—"And without faith it is impossible to please God, because anyone who comes to him must believe that he exists and that he rewards those who earnestly seek him."

Prayer Suggestion: Sing this prayer to the tune of "My Bonnie": "God, help me have faith when I can see. God, help me have faith when I can't. God, help me have faith in you always. God, give me a strong faith in thee."

October 15
Mushroom Day

Because mushrooms lack chlorophyll, they do not use sunlight to produce the food they need. Mushrooms can grow quite well in the darkness. Paul talks about the darkness of sin in 2 Corinthians 4:1-15.

Questions to Discuss: How does God use His light to dispel the darkness of sin? How can you let God's light shine in your heart?

Related Activity: Make mushroom gravy to go with your meal today.

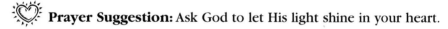

Curriculum Connection: Read about the mushroom. How does it get its food? What is a fairy ring? Where do most mushrooms live?

Verse to Memorize: 2 Corinthians 4:6— "For God, who said, 'Let light shine out of darkness,' made his light shine in our hearts to give us the light of the knowledge of the glory of God in the face of Christ."

Prayer Suggestion: Ask God to let His light shine in your heart.

October 16
Dictionary Day

Faith is defined in the dictionary as "belief that does not rest on logical proof or material evidence." Hebrews 11:1–40 cites many examples of faith, as evidenced in the Old Testament. Read these verses, then answer the questions.

Questions to Discuss: Give examples of faithful people from this passage. How did they exhibit faith in God? How do you exhibit your faith?

Related Activity: Make a "faith" dictionary. Cite examples of faithful people in your home, church, and community. Follow the writing style of today's passage.

Curriculum Connection: Work with your dictionary. Practice using guide words; study the pronunciation key; find out how words are divided into syllables, and look for the parts of speech of entry words.

Verse to Memorize: Hebrews 11:1— "Now faith is being sure of what we hope for and certain of what we do not see."

Prayer Suggestion: Pray for the people you listed in your faith dictionary. Thank God for their examples of faith.

October 17
National Clock Month

When God sent the Plague of Darkness, Egypt was completely dark for three days. Without modern-day clocks, those living there had no way of knowing whether it was day or night. Read Exodus 10:21-29.

Questions to Discuss: How do you think the people in Egypt felt to be in darkness for three days? Have you ever been without electricity in your house and had to be in the dark? How did it feel?

Related Activity: Clock Month is held each October—the month that Daylight Savings Time ends and Standard Time resumes. Check to see how many timepieces you have in your house. Don't forget to count alarm clock radios and watches. Do you feel blessed to spend time with your family?

Curriculum Connection: Practice telling time.

Verse to Memorize: John 1:1-4—"In the beginning was the Word, and the Word was with God, and the Word was God. He was with God in the beginning. Through him all things were made; without him nothing was made that has been made. In him was life, and that life was the light of men."

Prayer Suggestion: Thank God for the time spent with your family.

October 18
National Popcorn Poppin' Month

What's white and fluffy, crunchy, and often buttery and salty? You guessed it—popcorn. Read what Jesus says about "being salty" in Matthew 5:13-16.

Questions to Discuss: How is a Christian "the salt of the earth"? How can you add more "flavor" to the life of those around you?

Related Activity: Eat popcorn. Try the unsalted, no-fat variety, and compare the taste.

Curriculum Connection: Using the word *pop* as an example, talk about the rule for adding suffixes to short-vowel, one-syllable words that end in a consonant.

Verse to Memorize: Matthew 5:13— "You are the salt of the earth."

Prayer Suggestion: Ask God to help you "bring flavor" to those around you.

October 19
Sweetest Day

During America's Great Depression, a man from Cleveland organized many friends and neighbors to distribute, on the third Saturday in October, small gifts to the city's orphans and shut-ins to show them that they were indeed remembered. The practice caught on, and the day became known as Sweetest Day. Show your love to someone this Sweetest Day.
Read the passage on love, as contained in 1 Corinthians 13:1–13.

Questions to Discuss: What does *love* mean to you? What is something special that you love about each person in your family?

Related Activity: Write and illustrate a "love is . . ." book. Have each person make several pages. Put all the pages together to make a Family Love Book.

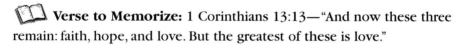

Curriculum Connection: Discuss figurative language as used in poetry and other forms of literature. What is a simile? What is a metaphor?

Verse to Memorize: 1 Corinthians 13:13—"And now these three remain: faith, hope, and love. But the greatest of these is love."

Prayer Suggestion: Thank God for the love of your family.

October 20
Comic Strip Anniversary

Do you like to read comic strips? Do you have any comic books? This week in 1896, the first comic strip appeared in a New York newspaper. It was a big hit, and comics have been in newspapers since that day. Ecclesiastes 11:7-10 encourages one to live life to the fullest ("be happy while you are young"), but do not forget your Creator. Reading comic strips can keep you young at heart, but always remember your Creator.

Questions to Discuss: What do you like to do for fun by yourself? With a friend? With your family?

Related Activity: Draw a comic strip. Decide if you want to work together as a family on one comic strip or if each person will draw his or her own and then share projects.

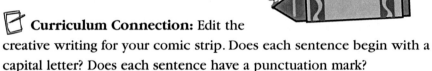

Curriculum Connection: Edit the creative writing for your comic strip. Does each sentence begin with a capital letter? Does each sentence have a punctuation mark?

Verse to Memorize: Ecclesiastes 11:8a—"However many years a man may live, let him enjoy them all."

Prayer Suggestion: Pray for comic strip artists, circus entertainers, and others who make a living entertaining others.

October 21
Hunger Awareness Month

Joseph had been imprisoned falsely for two years. Using his God-given gift of dream interpretation, Joseph was able to earn his release. Joseph was given a position of authority. That very position saved his family from starvation during a terrible famine in the land. Read this story in Genesis 41:1–56.

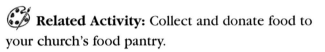 **Questions to Discuss:** How did God use Joseph's position to save his family from the famine? Who did Joseph credit for his dream-interpreting abilities? Who helps you do things that seem difficult or next-to-impossible?

 Related Activity: Collect and donate food to your church's food pantry.

Curriculum Connection: Find pertinent statistics on the homeless in your state or community. Where are the nearest shelters and food kitchens?

Verse to Memorize: Philippians 4:12b–13—"I have learned the secret of being content in any and every situation, whether well fed or hungry, whether living in plenty or in want. I can do everything through him who gives me strength."

Prayer Suggestion: Pray for those who are hungry.

October 22
Reptile Awareness Day

Moses wanted to obey God, but he quickly reminded God, as if God did not already know, that he had a speech problem. Moses did not think God's plan would work. But God had already worked everything out. God intended for Aaron (Moses' brother) to speak for him. Find out more of God's wonders in Exodus 6:26-7:13.

Questions to Discuss: What is your favorite reptile? What is your least favorite reptile? How do you feel about snakes?

Related Activity: Use clay to make snakes. Paint them when you are done and allow them to dry.

Curriculum Connection: What is a reptile? Explain the differences between reptiles and amphibians.

Verse to Memorize: Job 37:14b—"Stop and consider God's wonders."

Prayer Suggestion: Close your eyes and, in silence, meditate on God's wonders. Try not to let your mind think of anything but the wonders of God. After three to five minutes, thank God for His wonders.

October 23
World Rain Forest Week

A tropical rain forest is a forest of tall trees in a region that has warm weather most of the year and receives large amounts of rainfall. Many of the world's rain forests are diminishing, as trees are cut and land is cleared. Read Hebrews 6:1-12 to see how the writer compares a Christian to land that receives much water.

Questions to Discuss: What happens to land that drinks in a lot of rain? What happens when you "drink in the love of God?" How can you let your life be like a rain forest instead of a desert?

Related Activity: Using construction paper, turn a shoebox into a rain forest. Be sure to show the distinct canopies of a rain forest.

Curriculum Connection: Show on a map where the rain forests of the world are located.

Verse to Memorize: 1 Timothy 6:18— "Command them to do good, to be rich in good deeds, and to be generous and willing to share."

Prayer Suggestion: Thank God for the beauty of His rain forests. Ask God to help you let others see Jesus in you through your good works.

October 24
Cookbook Month

Read Genesis 40:1–23. Do you think Pharaoh's baker used a cookbook?
How many cookbooks do you have at home?

Questions to Discuss: What do you think the cupbearer and baker did to offend Pharaoh? What do you do when you offend someone? What do you do when you offend God?

Related Activity: Find a new recipe in a cookbook. Work together to prepare the recipe.

Curriculum Connection: Look at a cookbook to see how recipes are categorized. Practice using an index by looking in the back of the cookbook.

Verse to Memorize: Acts 13:38— "Therefore, my brothers, I want you to know that through Jesus the forgiveness of sins is proclaimed to you."

Prayer Suggestion: Thank God for the forgiveness of sins.

October 25
National Cleaner Air Week

Had you lived in Egypt during the time the Israelites were kept as slaves, and had you greatly disliked creepy-crawly insects, you would have been in for a nightmare. Pharaoh's hardened heart caused great plagues on his people, three of which involved the air being filled with six-legged animals. Read Exodus 8:16–32, 10:1–20 to find out which insects God sent to Egypt in large numbers.

Questions to Discuss: Re-read verses 30 and 31. What do you think Moses said to God? Does God answer your prayers?

Related Activity: Sit outside and take a couple of deep breaths of fresh air. Talk about your blessings from God.

Curriculum Connection: What gas do we inhale? What gas do we exhale? Why do some areas of the country have poorer air quality than others?

Verse to Memorize: Mark 11:24— "Therefore I tell you, whatever you ask for in prayer, believe that you have received it, and it will be yours."

Prayer Suggestion: Thank God for clean air to breathe.

October 26
Make-a-Difference Day

Usually falling on the third or fourth Saturday in October, this day is set aside as a day for community service. Read Matthew 25:31-46 to see how Jesus feels about community service.

Questions to Discuss: What have you done for someone today?

Related Activity: Using a box of detergent, put one laundry cup's worth of detergent in individual bags. Deliver to a homeless shelter.

Curriculum Connection: Do a report on someone who has made a difference in your life. Thank God for that person.

Verse to Memorize: Matthew 25:40—"The King will reply: I tell you the truth, whatever you did for one of the least of these brothers of mine, you did for me."

Prayer Suggestion: Holding a bag of detergent in your hand, try to imagine the face of the person who might use it to wash his or her few articles of clothing. Pray for that person.

October 27
NIV of the Bible Week

The New International Version (NIV) of the Bible was first
published on October 27, 1978, by Zondervan Publishers.
Do you have an NIV Bible? Read Hebrews 12:1-12.

Questions to Discuss: Who is the author of the Bible? Do you
know someone who does not have a Bible?

Related Activity: Find something new in an NIV Bible that you have
not looked at before—a new map, a new chart, a new table in the back.
Learn something new from that part of the Bible.

Curriculum Connection: Show these divisions
of the books of the Bible: Law, History, Poetry, Major
Prophets, Minor Prophets, Gospels, Paul's Letters,
General Letters, Prophecy.

Verse to Memorize: Hebrews 12:2—"Let us
fix our eyes on Jesus, the author and perfector of our
faith, who for the joy set before him endured the
cross, scorning its shame, and sat down at the right hand of the
throne of God."

Prayer Suggestion: Hold your Bible in your lap, and give thanks to
God for His word.

October 28
Statue of Liberty Day

The people of France gave the Statue of Liberty to the United States in 1884 as an expression of friendship and of belief in the liberty of both countries. Read Ruth 4:1–22 to see what Boaz did for Naomi and Ruth as an expression of friendship and love.

Questions to Discuss: How did Boaz "save" Naomi and Ruth? Why was he called a kinsman-redeemer? Who is your redeemer?

Related Activity: Play a statue game. Freeze in silly statue-like positions and judge each other.

Curriculum Connection: Read about the history of the Statue of Liberty. Where does she stand? What is she made of? How many people visit this American symbol per year?

Verse to Memorize: 1 Timothy 4:10b— "That we have put our hope in the living God, who is the Savior of all men, and especially of those who believe."

Prayer Suggestion: Give thanks to God for Jesus, our Redeemer.

October 29
National Caramel Month

Read Psalm 119:103. There are many references to God's word being sweet throughout the Bible. Use a concordance to find other, similar passages.

Questions to Discuss: What is your favorite candy? Describe its taste to your family. Describe how you feel when you read the words of the Scripture.

Related Activity: Place individually wrapped caramels on the Bible, and put it in the center of the table.

Curriculum Connection: Find a recipe for caramel apples. Give a demonstration on how to make them.

Verse to Memorize: Psalm 119:103—"How sweet are your words to my taste, sweeter than honey to my mouth!"

Prayer Suggestion: Sit at the table with the caramel-topped Bible still in the center. Give God praise with this rhyming prayer: "Thank you, Lord, for your words so sweet. Let your word be my favorite treat!" Then snack on the caramel candies.

October 30
National Pizza Month

The origin of pizza is not clear, though there are several theories floating about. Most theories give credit to Italy originally, but how it came to America is not known. Many believe Italian immigrants brought pizza to New York. At any rate, there is probably not a kid around who has not thought about changing the words to "Give us this day our daily pizza." But that's not what Jesus said at all. Read for yourself in Matthew 6:5-15 and see how Jesus taught His disciples to pray.

Questions to Discuss: Why did Jesus tell His disciples to pray behind closed doors? Did Jesus mean that He does not like long prayers? How often do you pray?

Related Activity: Go out for pizza, of course.

Curriculum Connection: Talk about graphs: pie graphs, bar graphs, pictographs.

Verse to Memorize:
Matthew 6:9-13—"Our Father in heaven, hallowed be your name, your kingdom come, your will be done on earth as it is in heaven. Give us today our daily bread. Forgive us our debts, as we also have forgiven our debtors. And lead us not into temptation, but deliver us from the evil one."

Prayer Suggestion: Hold hands in a circle and say the Lord's prayer, as written here.

October 31
Reformation Day

On October 31, 1517, Martin Luther, a monk and professor of theology, wrote his Ninety-Five Theses and, according to tradition, nailed them to the door of a church in Germany. This paper listed a series of statements that attacked much that was going on in the Catholic Church. He felt the need for reform within the church, but his ideas were met with great resistance. Read about Peter in Acts 12:1–25. His words and actions were met with great resistance during his time also.

Questions to Discuss: Why was Peter put in prison? What did the church do while he was in jail? What happened to Peter? Do you remember to pray when you are faced with difficulties?

Related Activity: Make a list of things you want to "reform" or change in your life.

Curriculum Connection: Write a report on Martin Luther.

Verse to Memorize: James 5:16b—"The prayer of a righteous man is powerful and effective."

Prayer Suggestion: Pray specifically for the items of change on your list.

November

November 1
Prime Meridian Day

On November 1, 1884, delegates from twenty-five nations met in Washington, D.C., to establish time zones for the world. Every fifteen degrees of longitude equals one hour. Read Matthew 8:5-13. Jesus says that people from all "time zones" will be in the Kingdom of Heaven.

Questions to Discuss: What does Jesus mean when He says, "many will come from the east and west?" How did the centurion exhibit faith? How do you show your faith to others?

Related Activity: Trace the outlines of the continents. Enlarge the outlines and place them on a sheet of poster-board. Toss a penny onto the map. Name the continent and, if possible, the country where your penny lands.

Curriculum Connection: Locate the Prime Meridian on a globe. Find the lines of longitude. What line are you closest to?

Verse to Memorize: Proverbs 28:20a—"A faithful man will be richly blessed."

Prayer Suggestion: Ask God to strengthen your faith.

November 2
Sandwich Day

John Montague, Fourth Earl of Sandwich, was said to have invented the sandwich. His birthday is now celebrated as Sandwich Day. Read what John says about bread in John 6:25-59.

Questions to Discuss: What is your favorite sandwich? How is Jesus the "bread of life"?

Related Activity: Make a sandwich. Cut the bread and ingredients with a heart-shaped cookie cutter.

Curriculum Connection: Which islands were originally named Sandwich Islands? Read about Captain James Cook.

Verse to Memorize: John 6:35—"Then Jesus declared, 'I am the bread of life. He who comes to me will never go hungry, and he who believes in me will never be thirsty.'"

Prayer Suggestion: Thank God for the words and wonders of the New Testament.

November 3
National Religious Books Week

*John, in 1 John 1:1-10, has a message to proclaim: God is light;
Jesus, the Son of the Light, purifies us from all sin. John's message
may have been written many years ago, but the Christian
books still proclaim the same message.*

Questions to Discuss: What is the underlying message proclaimed by every Christian book? Do you have a Christian book you could share with another person?

Related Activity: Visit a Christian bookstore. Choose a new book or new author to read.

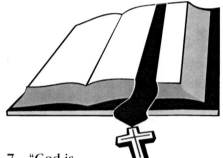

Curriculum Connection: Find out about the many genres of literature available on the market.

Verse to Memorize: 1 John 1:5b, 7—"God is light; in him there is no darkness at all. But if we walk in the light, as he is in the light, we have fellowship with one another, and the blood of Jesus, his Son, purifies us from all sin."

Prayer Suggestion: Thank God for Christian authors. Pray for their writing that they might proclaim the message of Jesus to many.

November 4
National Chemistry Week

Read about God's amazing display of chemistry that only He could perform. Read Exodus 3:1–22.

Questions to Discuss: Why was Moses surprised by the burning bush? Who spoke to Moses from the burning bush? In what ways does God speak to you?

Related Activity: Tear red, yellow, and orange tissue paper into strips. Place them on a small plant to see what Moses' burning bush might have looked like.

Curriculum Connection: Look at the periodic table of elements.

Verse to Memorize: Exodus 3:12a—"And God said, 'I will be with you.'"

Prayer Suggestion: Praise the Lord for being your constant companion.

November 5
General Election Day

The first Tuesday after the first Monday in November of each year is Election Day. God has words to say about elected officials. See Romans 13:1-7.

Questions to Discuss: Why does God want you to support elected officials? How can you support them through your prayers?

Related Activity: Watch the election results. Make a list of governing authorities: local, state, and national.

Curriculum Connection: What are the three branches of the U.S. government?

Verse to Memorize: Romans 13:1— "Everyone must submit himself to the governing authorities, for there is no authority except that which God has established. The authorities that exist have been established by God."

Prayer Suggestion: Pray for each person on your list of government officials.

November 6
Saxophone Day

God, in mighty, marvelous ways, led His people out of Egypt. As if that were not enough of a display of His powers, God parted the Red Sea for all the Israelites to pass through safely. These miracles brought great shouts of praise, singing, instrument playing, and dancing. Read about this worship of the Lord in Exodus 15:1-27.

Questions to Discuss: Why were the Israelites singing? What musical instrument did Miriam use to praise God? How do you like to praise God?

Related Activity: Sing a hymn of praise to God.

Curriculum Connection: What are some different kinds of music? Discuss jazz, rhythm and blues, classical, pop, country, gospel.

Verse to Memorize: Psalm 95:1-2—"Come, let us sing for joy to the Lord, let us shout aloud to the Rock of our salvation. Let us come before him with thanksgiving and extol him with music and song."

Prayer Suggestion: Praise God with music. Clang on pots, play instruments, shake jars of rice, create other joyful noisemakers.

November 7
Cat Week

Over fifty-five million cats live as pets in American homes.
Find out who all those cats belong to by reading Psalm 50:11.

Questions to Discuss: Why does everything belong to God? Do you have a pet cat? Do you know someone who has a pet cat?

Related Activity: Act out the story of the "Three Little Kittens."

Curriculum Connection: Find the meanings of these words: *nocturnal, diurnal.*

Verse to Memorize: Psalm 50:11—"I know every bird in the mountains, and the creatures of the field are mine."

Prayer Suggestion: Pray for cat owners.

November 8
X-Ray Day

November 8, 1895, physicist Wilhelm Conrad Röntgen discovered X-rays, changing physics and medicine forever. There were no medical personnel capable of taking care of the Egyptians during the plague of the boils. Read Exodus 9:8-12.

Questions to Discuss: Have you ever had an X-ray? How does God use others to heal you physically? How did God use Jesus to heal you spiritually?

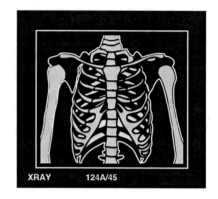

Related Activity: Draw a picture of an X-ray fish.

Curriculum Connection: Learn the names of the major bones in your body.

Verse to Memorize: Isaiah 53:5-6—"But he was pierced for our transgressions, he was crushed for our iniquities; the punishment that brought us peace was upon him, and by his wounds we are healed. We all, like sheep, have gone astray, each of us has turned to his own way; and the Lord has laid on him the iniquity of us all."

Prayer Suggestion: Pray for X-ray technicians and hospital personnel. Thank God for His healing powers, physical as well as spiritual.

November 9
National Parents-as-Teachers Day

Parents, today is your day! Read Proverbs 1:8 and celebrate the day.

Questions to Discuss: What do you like best about homeschooling? How are you obeying God when you are a good student or good teacher?

Related Activity: Parents, write a letter to your children, praising their work as a student. Children, write a thank-you note to your parents for training you in the ways of God and for the love they demonstrate by spending so much time with you each day.

Curriculum Connection: Read a home-schooling magazine together.

Verse to Memorize: Proverbs 22:6—"Train a child in the way he should go and when he is old he will not turn from it."

Prayer Suggestion: Children, place your hands on your parents' shoulders. Ask God to bless their teaching, as well as their lives. Give thanks for godly parents who love you.

November 10
National Fig Week

Figs are mentioned often in the Bible and must have been very prevalent. A couple of Jesus' parables deal specifically with the fig tree. Read Genesis 4:1-16. Do you think Cain grew figs?

 Questions to Discuss: What did Abel offer God? What did Cain offer God? Why did God favor Abel's offering but not Cain's? Do you always give God your best?

 Related Activity: Eat dried figs.

Curriculum Connection: Find the state tree for each of the fifty states. What is your state's tree?

Verse to Memorize: Romans 12:1—"Therefore, I urge you, brothers, in view of God's mercy, to offer your bodies as living sacrifices, holy and pleasing to God—this is your spiritual act of worship."

Prayer Suggestion: Ask God to help you always give him your best.

November 11
Veterans' Day

Veterans' Day has been celebrated on November 11 since 1926, except for a short time when it was celebrated on the fourth Monday in October. This day honors soldiers of all wars. Samson was a soldier and fought the Philistines. Read more about him in Judges 13:1-7, 24; 16:4-31.

Questions to Discuss: What were God's intentions for Samson's life? Why was Samson so strong? Why did Samson lose his strength?

Related Activity: Visit a veterans' hospital or write a letter to a veteran, thanking him or her for playing a role in making you free.

Curriculum Connection: Read about the U.S. Navy, Army, Air Force, Marines.

Verse to Memorize: Psalm 28:7—"The Lord is my strength and my shield; my heart trusts in him, and I am helped. My heart leaps for joy and I will give thanks to him in song."

Prayer Suggestion: Pray for veterans of the past and for the military currently serving today.

November 12
Harvest Month

Celebrate the goodness of God's bounty. Joseph and his brothers should have been celebrating the bounty of harvest time, but instead his brothers were scheming and planning sinful acts as a result of their jealousy of Joseph. Read Genesis 37:5-10.

Questions to Discuss: What did the sheaves of grain represent in Joseph's dream? What did the sun, moon, and eleven stars represent? Did Joseph's brothers have any idea of what God had in mind for Joseph? What plans do you think God has for your life?

Related Activity: Joseph and his brothers were harvesting grain from the fields. Make a party mix, using a variety of grain cereals. Heat the oven to two hundred fifty degrees. Melt six tablespoons margarine in a large roasting pan. Stir in one and one-half teaspoons seasoned salt, three-quarters teaspoon garlic powder, one-half teaspoon onion powder. In another bowl, stir together three cups of corn cereal, three cups of rice cereal, three cups of wheat cereal, and three cups of pretzels. Combine all ingredients, stirring gently to coat. Bake one hour, stirring every fifteen minutes. Spread on paper towels to cool.

Curriculum Connection: Name the agricultural products your state produces.

Verse to Memorize: 1 John 2:17b—"But the man who does the will of God lives forever."

Prayer Suggestion: Ask God to prepare your life to do His will.

November 13
Accountants' Day

By definition, an accountant is a person who "keeps and inspects the financial records of a person or business." Accountants' Day honors those who are responsible for others' financial business. In Genesis 42:1-38, Joseph's brothers are responsible for the intended destruction of their brother. Fortunately for Joseph, God had other plans in mind for his life.

Questions to Discuss: Why does Reuben say that they must give an accounting for Joseph's blood? How should you give an accounting for Jesus' blood that was spilled for you?

Related Activity: Eat chocolate covered coins, in honor of Accountants' Day.

Curriculum Connection: Discuss the proper way to write a check.

Verse to Memorize: 1 Peter 1:18-19—"For you know that it was not with perishable things such as silver or gold that you were redeemed from the empty way of life handed down to you from your forefathers, but with the precious blood of Christ, a lamb without blemish or defect."

Prayer Suggestion: Pray for accountants.

November 14
National Teddy Bear Day

How many stuffed animals do you have at home? How many of those animals are teddy bears? Do you remember when you got your first teddy bear? Young Samuel likely did not own a teddy bear, but he may have had other childhood toys. Read to see what you think he may have taken with him to the house of the Lord. Read 1 Samuel 1:1-28.

Questions to Discuss: How did God answer Hannah's prayer? How did Hannah show her thanksgiving to God for the birth of her son? How do you show your thanks to God?

Related Activity: Gather your stuffed animals and bears. Donate some of your like-new stuffed animals to a women's shelter or children's home for young boys like Samuel.

Curriculum Connection: Read about the president for whom, supposedly, the teddy bear was named. What is the other widely held theory about how the bear got its name?

Verse to Memorize: 1 Samuel 2:2—"There is no one holy like the Lord; there is no one besides you; there is no Rock like our God."

Prayer Suggestion: Give thanks to God for your toys and material blessings.

November 15
National Geography
Awareness Week

Did Moses have a map to help him find his way? How did Moses know where God wanted him to go? Moses probably had no idea of much of the geography surrounding him. Moses followed God's lead. Read Exodus 13:17–14:31 to see what guided Moses.

Questions to Discuss: How did the Israelites escape from the Egyptians? Describe God's miracle of parting the waters. How amazed do you think the Israelites were at this wonder? Do you marvel at God's wonders? Tell about a recent wonder of God in your life.

Related Activity: Play Follow-the-Leader. End your game at two blue towels or sheets. "Part" the water and walk through on "dry" ground. Try to imagine how the Israelites felt.

Curriculum Connection: Explain these terms: *glacier, volcano, lake, plain, bay, peninsula, mountain, isthmus.*

Verse to Memorize: Psalm 40:5—"Many, O Lord my God, are the wonders you have done. The things you planned for us no one can recount to you; were I to speak and tell of them, they would be too many to declare."

Prayer Suggestion: Thank God for the wonders of the long-ago past and the wonders He has performed in your life.

November 16
Doll Collection Month

Do you have a collection? This month celebrates those who collect dolls. Many people have quite an extensive doll collection, and sometimes these are quite valuable. God gives warnings about placing too much value on material goods. Read His words in Matthew 6:19-21.

Questions to Discuss: What material possession that you own is most important to you? Why? How can you make sure that your salvation in Jesus and eternal life in heaven is the most important treasure you have?

Related Activity: Make a treasure box. Decorate a shoebox. From time to time, add notes about God, Jesus, the Bible, answers to prayer, and things you look forward to about heaven.

Curriculum Connection: Review these terms: *addends, sum, difference, factor, product, dividend, divisor.*

Verse to Memorize: Matthew 6:21—"For wherever your treasure is, there your heart will be also."

Prayer Suggestion: Ask God to help you keep your material wealth and possessions in perspective, always placing eternity in heaven at the top of your list.

November 17
Homemade Bread Day

Can you imagine having every meal prepared for you? Can you imagine waking up to find breakfast already on the table? Can you imagine walking outside and finding bread for lunch, already there, just waiting for you to collect it? And dinner is the same way; you never have to prepare a meal. How do you think you would feel? Would you grumble or would you praise God? Read Exodus 16:1–35 to see what the Israelites did.

 Questions to Discuss: How did God provide food for the Israelites? How does God take care of your needs? Do you remember to thank God, or do you grumble and complain?

Related Activity: Bake homemade bread.

Curriculum Connection: Starting with the word *homemade,* review some compound words. How many compound words can you think of?

 Verse to Memorize: Philippians 4:19—"And my God will meet all your needs according to his glorious riches in Christ Jesus."

Prayer Suggestion: Thank God for providing for your needs.

November 18
Adding Machine Day

The first accurate adding machine was patented in 1887.
How do you think Matthew, the tax collector, kept up with his
figures and money without an adding machine?
Read Matthew 9:9-13 to see what he traded his profession for.

Questions to Discuss: Explain what Jesus meant when He said, "It is not the healthy who need a doctor, but the sick." For what "illnesses" do you need Jesus?

Related Activity: Use a calculator or an adding machine to do your math work for today.

Curriculum Connection: How do you think Matthew wrote numbers for his tax purposes? Practice writing numbers in expanded notation.

Verse to Memorize: Matthew 9:12-13—"On hearing this, Jesus said, 'It is not the healthy who need a doctor but the sick. But go and learn what this means: I desire mercy, not sacrifice. For I have not come to call the righteous, but sinners.'"

Prayer Suggestion: Give thanks to God that Jesus came for the sinners.

November 19
Gettysburg Anniversary

President Abraham Lincoln gave a stirring speech at the site of the Battle of Gettysburg. His speech was in part to dedicate the site as a cemetery for those who had died during this Civil War battle. He also used the opportunity to remind the Northern states of the purpose of the battle. He believed that all men were created equal. He wanted freedom for all people in the United States. Read about another type of slavery in Romans 6:1-23.

Questions to Discuss: How can you be a slave to sin? In contrast, how can you be a slave to righteousness?

Related Activity: Write a Family Address, explaining why you believe in Jesus and why He is Lord of your life.

Curriculum Connection: Read the Gettysburg Address.

Verse to Memorize: Romans 6:12, 23—"Therefore do not let sin reign in your mortal body so that you obey its evil desires. For the wages of sin is death, but the gift of God is eternal life in Christ Jesus our Lord."

Prayer Suggestion: Thank God for the freedom that blesses your country. Ask God to help you stay free from sin.

November 20
American Education Week

Solomon was a brilliant man. God granted him a wealth of wisdom.
God wants you to use the wisdom He gave you. This week reminds
you to treasure and appreciate your education and to do all that
you can do to learn as much as God wants you to learn.
Read 1 Kings 4:29-34 about Solomon's wisdom.

Questions to Discuss: How "smart" was Solomon? What are some of the things Solomon knew? What else do you think he knew? Where did Solomon get his wisdom? How does God want you to use the mind and wisdom He gave you?

Related Activity: Choose something that is not on your lesson plans, and learn about that subject today.

Curriculum Connection: Read about the early education of the Pilgrim children.

Verse to Memorize: Proverbs 1:7a—"The fear of the Lord is the beginning of knowledge."

Prayer Suggestion: Thank God for the wisdom that He has given you.

November 21
World Hello Day

This day was started to encourage people to make the world a friendlier place. Founders hoped that by greeting people in a warm and friendly manner on this day, the world would be brighter and happier. Read Matthew 28:16–20 to see what would make Jesus happy.

Questions to Discuss: Does God want you to keep the good news of Jesus a secret? Who does God want you to tell about Jesus?

Related Activity: Find ten people to say hello to today via phone, e-mail, or in person. Tell them about Jesus. Then the world really will be a happier place.

Curriculum Connection: Name the continents of the world.

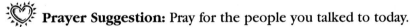

Verse to Memorize: Matthew 28:19—"Therefore go and make disciples of all nations, baptizing them in the name of the Father and of the Son and of the Holy Spirit."

Prayer Suggestion: Pray for the people you talked to today.

November 22
Aviation History Month

This month commemorates the aviation experiments of the Montgolfier brothers. Their experiments and work led to the development of the first hot air balloon and, ultimately, to aviation in general. Read about Elijah's "aviation history" in 2 Kings 2:1-18.

Questions to Discuss: Have you ever flown in an airplane? How do you think it would have felt to fly in a chariot of fire? Why do you think God took Elijah to heaven this way?

Related Activity: Make paper airplanes and have a plane race.

Curriculum Connection: Read about another pair of brothers: Wilbur and Orville Wright.

Verse to Memorize: Psalm 78:3-4—"What we have heard and known, what our fathers have told us. We will not hide them from their children; we will tell the next generation the praiseworthy deeds of the Lord, his power and the wonders he has done."

Prayer Suggestion: Thank God for the miracles and wonders of the Old Testament.

November 23
Pencil Sharpener Week

J. L. Love patented the first pencil sharpener in 1897. Where would you be without the pencil sharpener? Read how God does not need a pencil sharpener, in Daniel 5:1-31, to make His messages known.

Questions to Discuss: How did God use Daniel's prophetic abilities to promote Daniel's position with the King?

Related Activity: Sharpen all the pencils in your house.

Curriculum Connection: Practice doing long division with a sharpened pencil.

Verse to Memorize: Acts 10:43—"All the prophets testify about him that everyone who believes in him receives forgiveness of sins through his name."

Prayer Suggestion: Thank God for the prophets in the Bible who told us much about God.

November 24
National Bible Week

*Crowds of people followed Jesus practically everywhere He went.
He had great compassion for the people, their illnesses and diseases,
their grief and sadness, their poverty and wealth, their young and old.
Jesus said that the "harvest is plentiful but the workers are few" in
Matthew 9:35–38. There are so many people who need to hear about
Jesus and the Bible, but few people are willing to boldly proclaim the news.
Take the opportunity this week to share Christ with someone.*

 Questions to Discuss: What were Jesus' instructions to His disciples? Do you think those instructions still apply to you today? Who can you tell about the Bible this week?

Related Activity: Purchase a new Bible. Give it to someone who needs a Bible or donate it to a homeless or women's shelter.

Curriculum Connection: Learn to say all sixty-six books of the Bible in order.

Verse to Memorize: Matthew 9:37–38—"Then he said to his disciples, 'The harvest is plentiful but the workers are few. Ask the Lord of the harvest, therefore, to send out workers into his harvest field.'"

Prayer Suggestion: Thank God for His word—your Bible.

November 25
National Farm-City Week

Since a 1959 presidential proclamation, Farm-City Week is celebrated the week ending in Thanksgiving. The purpose of the week is to acknowledge and celebrate the partnership between the farm and the city. Read Genesis 43:1–47:11 and Acts 7:8–15 to see why Joseph's family left their "farm" home to journey to the "city" of Egypt.

Questions to Discuss: Why did Joseph's brothers go to the city for a second time? How did Joseph feel when he saw Benjamin? How did Joseph reveal himself to his brothers? How did the brothers expect Joseph to feel about them? Had Joseph forgiven his brothers?

Related Activity: If you live in the city, take a drive to the country and vice versa. Discuss what you like best about a large city and a rural community.

Curriculum Connection: Talk about opposites like *farm* and *city*. See how many opposite pairs you can name.

Verse to Memorize: Psalm 103:2–5—"Praise the Lord, O my soul, and forget not all his benefits—who forgives all your sins and heals all your diseases, who redeems your life from the pit and crowns you with love and compassion, who satisfies your desires with good things so that your youth is renewed like the eagle's."

Prayer Suggestion: Thank God for the beauty of your home, whether it's in the city or in the country.

November 26
National Game-and-Puzzle Week

Have you played a game with your family this week? Have you put together a puzzle? This week is set aside to spend quality, fun, family time. Read also about some men in the New Testament who were "puzzled" over a particular event. Read Acts 5:12-42.

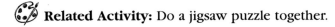 **Questions to Discuss:** Why were the apostles put in jail? Why were the guards puzzled when they checked on the prisoners? Why did the apostles rejoice in their persecution? Have you ever suffered for being a Christian?

Related Activity: Do a jigsaw puzzle together.

Curriculum Connection: Use a thesaurus to complete a crossword puzzle.

Verse to Memorize: 1 Peter 4:13— "But rejoice that you participate in the sufferings of Christ, so that you may be overjoyed when his glory is revealed."

Prayer Suggestion: Pray for those who are persecuted for being a Christian.

November 27
Thanksgiving

Thanksgiving is a day set aside each year for giving thanks to God for the blessings He has bestowed on His people throughout the year. Early celebrations involved the first settlers in America. Reportedly, the very first Thanksgiving to be observed in America, in 1619, was completely religious and did not involve the feasts of Thanksgiving like the ones we have today. The first New England Thanksgiving, held two years later, was a celebration of the harvest and lasted for three days. Read about having a heart "overflowing with Thanksgiving" in Colossians 2:6-7.

Questions to Discuss: Share what you are thankful for about each person in your family. For example, Dad's provision for the family, a helpful spirit in a child, and so on.

Related Activity: Make turkey rolls for each person in the family. Place a roll in a small basket. (Most craft stores carry small, very inexpensive baskets.) Write things you are thankful for on construction-paper feathers. Place them behind the roll like feathers. On a plastic spoon, glue on construction paper turkey facial features. Stand the spoon "head" in front of the roll, inside the basket. Place the rolls as place markers at the table.

Curriculum Connection: Read about the early Thanksgiving celebrations. What did the families likely eat for their meal?

Verse to Memorize: 1 Thessalonians 5:16-18—"Be joyful always; pray continually; give thanks in all circumstances, for this is God's will for you in Christ Jesus."

Prayer Suggestion: Thank God for your many blessings; name them specifically.

November 28
National Philanthropy Day

Philanthropy: the love of mankind; the effort to improve the well-being of mankind. National Philanthropy Day, held since 1986, seeks to recognize those who have enriched the world and encourage people nationwide to enrich the lives of others through giving and volunteer efforts. Although the official holiday is relatively new, in James 2:14-26 James advocates this same spirit.

Questions to Discuss: How do you feel when you do a good deed for someone? How do you think God feels?

Related Activity: Make a list of good deeds that you want to do for the next year. Choose at least one project per month. Carry out a good deed for someone today.

Curriculum Connection: Look in your phone book to find the service organizations available in your area. Choose one to donate your services or tangible goods to in the upcoming year.

Verse to Memorize: 1 John 3:18—"Dear children, let us not love with words or tongue but with actions and in truth."

Prayer Suggestion: Ask God to help you show the love of Jesus by your actions toward others.

November 29
Peanut Butter Lovers' Month

In Romans 14:1–23, Paul talks about not looking down on someone because of what they eat or do not eat. Most people have probably tried peanut butter in one form or another. Have you ever made homemade peanut butter? Put roasted, salted peanuts in a food chopper. Process until the nuts turn into peanut butter. Taste. Does it taste like the kind you buy in the store?

Questions to Discuss: Do you agree on everything with all of your Christian friends? Do you like all the same foods as your family members?

Related Activity: Make peanut butter cookies as a family.

Curriculum Connection: Find other uses for the peanut.

Verse to Memorize: Romans 14:17–18—"For the kingdom of God is not a matter of eating and drinking, but of righteousness, peace and joy in the Holy Spirit, because anyone who serves Christ in this way is pleasing to God and approved by men."

Prayer Suggestion: Ask God to help you not quibble about trivial details in your spiritual life but rather dwell on the assurance of your salvation in Jesus Christ.

November 30
International Drum Month

Did you know that some cultures have used drums in the past to communicate with others over long distances? Do you think you could get a message to someone by using a drum? Read Psalm 81:1-2 to see how the psalmist likes to communicate with God.

Questions to Discuss: How do you like to praise God? How is that different from another family member?

Related Activity: Use wooden spoons to bang on bowls, oatmeal boxes, kitchen pots, and so on. Have an all-drum band to praise God.

Curriculum Connection: Learn about the different kinds of drums. What are tympani? What are bongo drums?

Verse to Memorize: Psalm 104:33-34—"I will sing to the Lord all my life; I will sing praise to my God as long as I live. May my meditation be pleasing to him, as I rejoice in the Lord."

Prayer Suggestion: After the "noisy" praise time, have family meditation in which each person silently meditates on the goodness of God.

December

December 1
Advent

Most Christians think of Advent as falling on the four Sundays before Christmas. However, due to the popularity of commercial Advent calendars, many think Advent lasts from December 1 to December 24. Regardless of the calendar dates, Advent is a time of joyful preparation for Christmas— the birth of the Lord and Savior. Read Luke 1:39-56.

Questions to Discuss: What will you do to prepare for Christmas? How should you prepare daily for Jesus' second coming?

Related Activity: Decorate a grapevine wreath with ribbons and bows. Add the candles and discuss the meaning of each candle.

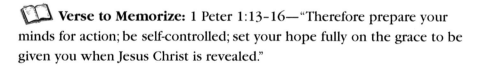

Curriculum Connection: Find out how Jesus' birth is celebrated in other Christian parts of the world.

Verse to Memorize: 1 Peter 1:13-16—"Therefore prepare your minds for action; be self-controlled; set your hope fully on the grace to be given you when Jesus Christ is revealed."

Prayer Suggestion: Ask God to prepare your heart and mind for the coming season, to avoid the commercialism of this blessed holiday, and to remember the true meaning of Christmas.

December 2
Rosa Parks Day

*Rosa Parks, an African-American seamstress, was arrested in 1955
for refusing to give up her seat to a white passenger on a bus in
Montgomery, Alabama. Her arrest led to a yearlong boycott of the
public transportation system in Montgomery. The success of the
boycott sparked a nationwide effort to bring about equality for all races.
Read 1 John 2:1–11 to see how John says to treat others.*

Questions to Discuss: How would it feel to be required to sit in the back of a bus or plane because of your skin color? How does God want you to treat all people, regardless of skin color?

Related Activity: Go for a bus ride or set up chairs in your house to resemble a bus; take a pretend ride.

Curriculum Connection: Pretend to be Rosa Parks. Write an autobiographical article for a magazine about your experience.

Verse to Memorize: Galatians 3:26–27—"You are all sons of God through faith in Christ Jesus, for all of you who were baptized into Christ have clothed yourselves with Christ."

Prayer Suggestion: Ask God to help you love your fellow man, regardless of skin color, hair color, eye color, or whatever differences you may have.

December 3
Cookie-Cutter Week

This week is set aside to celebrate the joy of Christmas baking. What does it mean to say, "cut from the same pattern"? Read Romans 12:1–8 to see what Paul says about being the same "pattern" as the rest of the world.

Questions to Discuss: How can you be a living sacrifice to God? How can you, as a Christian, be different from those of this world who are not Christians?

Related Activity: Make gingerbread cookies to look like your family.

Curriculum Connection: Read the story of "The Gingerbread Boy." Who are the main characters? What is the setting of the story?

Verse to Memorize: Colossians 3:1–2— "Since, then, you have been raised with Christ, set your hearts on things above, where Christ is seated at the right hand of God. Set your minds on things above, not on earthly things."

Prayer Suggestion: Hold a cookie cutter in your hand. Make sure that each person in the family has a very different cookie cutter. Ask God to help you, as a Christian, to be different—to avoid giving in to sinful desires.

338

December 4
Basketball Season

Do you think Zacchaeus would have made a very good basketball player? In a regulation basketball game, the backboard with the net is ten feet above the ground. Read Luke 19:1-10 to help you decide if Zacchaeus could have played.

Questions to Discuss: What do you think Zacchaeus had heard about Jesus? Why do you think Jesus needed to stay at Zacchaeus' house?

Related Activity: Play basketball as a family.

Curriculum Connection: Learn the rules of basketball.

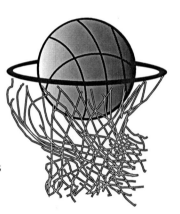

Verse to Memorize: Luke 19:10—"For the son of Man came to seek and to save what was lost."

Prayer Suggestion: Thank God for sending Jesus to "seek and save" you.

December 5
Harriet Tubman Day

Harriet Tubman was sometimes referred to as the Moses of her day.
Read Exodus 4:1–31 to find out about the original Moses.

Questions to Discuss: Why was God angry with Moses when Moses asked God to send someone else? How did God use Aaron to overcome Moses' shortcoming? Do you have a weakness that you believe hinders your work for God? How can you do God's will, despite that disability?

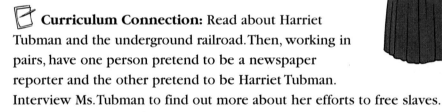

Related Activity: Harriet Tubman was the most famous leader of the "underground railroad." Sing this song to the tune of "I've Been Working on the Railroad": "God can work through every weakness. Let God have His way. God can work through every weakness. Just try it; start today. Can't you hear the Lord; He's calling. God's got an awesome job for you. Can't you hear the Lord; He's pleading. He will see you through. Jesus has the power; Jesus has the power; Jesus has the power to work through you. Jesus has the power; Jesus has the power; He will see you through."

Curriculum Connection: Read about Harriet Tubman and the underground railroad. Then, working in pairs, have one person pretend to be a newspaper reporter and the other pretend to be Harriet Tubman. Interview Ms. Tubman to find out more about her efforts to free slaves.

Verse to Memorize: 2 Corinthians 12:9—"But he said to me, 'My grace is sufficient for you, for my power is made perfect in weakness.' Therefore I will boast all the more gladly about my weaknesses, so that Christ's power may rest on me."

Prayer Suggestion: Ask God to help you accept your weaknesses and depend on the power of Jesus to help you do God's will.

December 6
St. Nicholas Day

Not much is known about Nicholas, the son of wealthy parents. He became Bishop of Myra in Asia Minor and was well known as a protector of innocent people. During the Roman persecution, Nicholas was imprisoned for this faith but later freed. At the Council of Nicaea, Nicholas defended Christ's divinity. Stories abound about St. Nicholas. A more prevalent one involves twelfth-century French nuns distributing candy to children on St. Nicholas day. Legend began that St. Nicholas himself, now passed away, left the gifts. The custom caught on in other countries and took on various names and traditions. Although the majority of the stories about St. Nicholas were untrue, the fact remains that he was a loving, giving man of God. Read in 2 Corinthians 9:6–15 what Paul says about giving.

Questions to Discuss: How do you feel when you give someone a gift? What kinds of gifts can you give that do not cost any money? What kinds of homemade gifts or crafts can you give?

Related Activity: Make a list of family and friends whom you plan to buy or make Christmas presents for. Decide what you will make or buy for those people.

Curriculum Connection: Find out more about Saint Nicholas. How did his life influence the legend of Santa Claus?

Verse to Memorize: 2 Corinthians 9:7—"Each man should give what he has decided in his heart to give, not reluctantly or under compulsion, for God loves a cheerful giver."

Prayer Suggestion: Pray for each person on your list.

December 7
Anniversary of First
Symphony Orchestra

The first orchestras in the United States formed in the late 1700s. Read in Daniel 3:1-30 about a "symphony" involving lots of musical instruments.

Questions to Discuss: What were the people supposed to do when they heard all the musical instruments? Why didn't Shadrach, Meshach, and Abednego obey the King? Do you think you would stand up for God, even if it meant you might be persecuted?

Related Activity: Listen to music, preferably instrumental Christmas carols.

Curriculum Connection: What four main groups are the musicians in a symphony divided into? What is a conductor? What cities host large orchestras today?

Verse to Memorize: James 1:12—"Blessed is the man who perseveres under trial, because when he has stood the test, he will receive the crown of life that God has promised to those who love him."

Prayer Suggestion: Ask God to help you pass your test, just as Shadrach, Meshach, and Abednego did.

December 8
Cotton Gin Anniversary

A cotton gin is a piece of machinery that removes the seeds from cotton fibers. Although some forms of cotton gins were used in ancient times, Eli Whitney is credited with inventing the modern-day cotton gin on this day in 1793. Read Acts 9:32-43 to find out about another person who had a part in the "clothing industry."

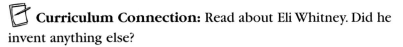

Questions to Discuss: What kinds of good things do you think Dorcas did? How do you think she helped the poor? What kinds of good things do you do? How can you do those things for God rather than man?

Related Activity: Using cotton material, sew two large pieces together to make a small blanket. Have each person dip his or her hand in fabric paint, then press the print onto the blanket. Talk about today's verse as you work.

Curriculum Connection: Read about Eli Whitney. Did he invent anything else?

Verse to Memorize: 1 Thessalonians 5:12a—"Now we ask you, brothers, to respect those who work hard among you."

Prayer Suggestion: Hold hands in a circle and pray for the person on your left and on your right.

December 9
Christmas Card Day

Do you send Christmas cards to your friends and family members? Many, many people send holiday greetings to loved ones across the world during this time of year. The post office recommends sending your cards and packages early to avoid late deliveries. Read 1 Corinthians 1:18 to see what message you will be sending to your friends this season.

 Questions to Discuss: What is the message of the cross?

Related Activity: Send out Christmas cards. Make sure you tell the message of the cross in your cards. For an added treat, use new twist-ties to make crosses. Form a cross from two twist-ties. Form a loop at the very top of the cross; add a ribbon hanger.

Curriculum Connection: Learn the proper way to address an envelope. Where does the return address go?

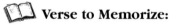

Verse to Memorize:
Ephesians 2:4–5—"But because of his great love for us, God, who is rich in mercy, made us alive with Christ even when we were dead in transgressions—it is by grace you have been saved."

Prayer Suggestion: After addressing Christmas cards and envelopes, pray specifically for each family.

December 10
Nobel Prize Day

The Nobel Prize is awarded each year in December to people, regardless of nationality, who have made valuable contributions to the "good of humanity." Read about Jesus' love of mankind in Titus 3:3-8.

Questions to Discuss: Why would Jesus deserve the Nobel Prize?

Related Activity: Make a trophy for Jesus.

Curriculum Connection: Read about some of the recipients of the Nobel Prize and their contributions.

Verse to Memorize: Titus 3:5-7—"He saved us, not because of righteous things we had done, but because of his mercy. He saved us through the washing of rebirth and renewal by the Holy Spirit, whom he poured out on us generously through Jesus Christ our Savior so that, having been justified by his grace, we might become heirs having the hope of eternal life."

Prayer Suggestion: Give thanks to God for Jesus, the Savior of mankind.

December 11
First Reindeer in United States

Reindeer have been domesticated in Lapland and North Siberia for centuries. Domesticated reindeer were introduced into Alaska from Siberia during this month in the early 1890s. Read about another herd of animals in John 10:1-18.

Questions to Discuss: How does a shepherd feel about his sheep? How do you think the sheep feel about the shepherd? How is that like your relationship to Christ?

Related Activity: Have a reindeer relay. Pair two members of the family; have them stand with their hands and feet on the ground. On "go," have the two contestants run, on all fours, to the finish line. The first "reindeer" to cross the line is the winner.

Curriculum Connection: Name other animals in the deer family.

Verse to Memorize: John 10:14-15—"I am the good shepherd; I know my sheep and my sheep know me—just as the Father knows me and I know the Father—and I lay down my life for the sheep."

Prayer Suggestion: Give thanks to Jesus for being your Good Shepherd.

December 12
Poinsettia Day

This day is named for the man who introduced this Christmas plant into the United States: Joel Roberts Poinsett. Read Isaiah 40:8, then answer the questions that follow.

Questions to Discuss: How long is forever? Will your Christmas poinsettia last forever? How long does God say His word will last?

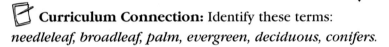

Related Activity: Use chalk to draw a poinsettia on paper. Write the memory verse, and hang your picture in your room.

Curriculum Connection: Identify these terms: *needleleaf, broadleaf, palm, evergreen, deciduous, conifers.*

Verse to Memorize: 1 Peter 1:25a—"But the word of the Lord stands forever."

Prayer Suggestion: Thank God that even though poinsettias, Christmas cacti, and Christmas trees will eventually die, the word of the Lord endures forever.

347

December 13
One-Way Street Birthday

The first one-way street was created this week in New York City in 1791. One-way streets were designed to alleviate traffic problems and encourage safety for motorists. God wants us to feel safe, too. Read Psalm 4:6–8.

Questions to Discuss: How does God help you feel safe? What do you do when you are frightened?

Related Activity: Make a street sign that says, "Thank you, Jesus, for keeping me safe!"

Curriculum Connection: Using a driver's manual, study street and road signs.

Verse to Memorize: John 14:6— "Jesus answered, 'I am the way and the truth and the life. No one comes to the Father except through me.'"

Prayer Suggestion: Ask God to help you remember each time you see a one-way sign to trust in Jesus and help you obey His signals.

December 14
Aardvark Week

An aardvark is an African mammal that lives in the ground. The aardvark's favorite foods are ants and termites. Would you like to eat ants? What about termites? Read about the ant in Proverbs 6:6–11.

Questions to Discuss: What is a sluggard? Why is the sluggard told to regard the ant? How can you keep from being a sluggard?

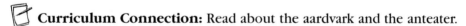

Related Activity: Often ants can be seen following one another in a line. Play an ant follow-the-leader game. For each family member, use a three-inch-wide strip of ribbon or cloth. To determine the length, have each person crouch on hands and knees on the floor. The ribbon should stretch across the person's back and almost touch the floor on each side. Tie one sock to each end of the ribbon; pin the ribbon to the "ant's" clothing to resemble three pair of legs on each side. Choose a family member to be the leader; have the rest of the "ants" crawl behind the leader.

Curriculum Connection: Read about the aardvark and the anteater.

Verse to Memorize: Romans 12:11—"Never be lacking in zeal, but keep your spiritual fervor, serving the Lord."

Prayer Suggestion: Ask God to guard you from laziness and to help you have "zeal for serving the Lord."

December 15
First Ping-Pong Tournament

The first world championship tournament was held in London in 1927. Ping-Pong is also known as table tennis. Players stand on either side of a table; using a small paddle, they bounce a ball back and forth across the table. In Genesis 32:22-32, Jacob wrestles with an angel of God. He wrestles all night, going back and forth with the man. Someone watching may have thought they were watching an endless Ping-Pong match. Read to find out the story.

Questions to Discuss: How do you think Jacob knew he was wrestling with an angel of God? Close your eyes, and try to imagine the splendor of God's face.

Related Activity: Play with Ping-Pong balls.

Curriculum Connection: Learn the rules of Ping-Pong.

Verse to Memorize: John 14:9b, 11a—"Anyone who has seen me has seen the Father. Believe me when I say that I am in the Father and the Father is in me."

Prayer Suggestion: Say your prayers while bouncing Ping-Pong balls. Bounce a ball to Mom; say, "God bless Mommy." Keep bouncing until you have prayed for everyone in the family.

December 16
Audubon's Bird Count Day

Every year, thousands of volunteers participate in an all-day census of early-winter bird populations. The bird count was named for John James Audubon, one of the first persons to study and paint the North American birds. Read in Genesis 1:20–23 about the Creator of these beautiful creatures Mr. Audubon loved.

Questions to Discuss: What is your favorite bird? What do you think of when you see birds flying in the sky? How can you let each bird you see remind you of God's awesome powers?

Related Activity: Have a family birdwatch time. Sit outside for thirty or more minutes (if it is really cold, just watch from a window), and make a list of all the birds you see.

Curriculum Connection: Read to find out why some birds migrate. Make a list of migratory birds.

Verse to Memorize: Genesis 2:1—"Thus the heavens and the earth were completed in all their vast array."

Prayer Suggestion: Thank God for the magnificent birds He created.

December 17
Boston Tea Party Anniversary

The Boston Tea Party was a raid conducted by American colonists on three British ships in the Boston Harbor. The colonists emptied over three hundred chests of tea into the harbor rather than pay a British tax on tea. The response to the act unified the colonists and brought them closer to an independence movement. Read about an equally exciting event involving a beverage (not tea, just water) in Genesis 24:1-66.

Questions to Discuss: How was Abraham's servant going to select a wife for Isaac? What happened, even before the servant finished praying? Do you think God knows your prayer requests, even before you ask? If so, why does God want you to pray?

Related Activity: Have a tea party.

Curriculum Connection: Read about the Boston Tea Party and the chain of events that occurred next.

Verse to Memorize: Matthew 6:8b—"For your Father knows what you need before you ask him."

Prayer Suggestion: Give thanks to God for knowing what is in your heart.

352

December 18
North Pole Day

American explorer Robert E. Peary led the first expedition credited with reaching the North Pole in 1909. With this new discovery, many probably thought they "had" the whole world now. Read what Jesus says about "gaining the world" in Matthew 16:21-28.

Questions to Discuss: What does it mean to "deny himself"? Are there things in this world that you need to deny in order to make Jesus first in your life?

Related Activity: Four Eskimos made the trip with Peary. The Eskimo name for shelter is *igloo*. Make an edible igloo. Frost a cupcake completely, top and sides, and place it on a small plate. Score it with a fork to resemble ice blocks. Place a large marshmallow in front for the entrance. Sprinkle coconut around the igloo for snow.

Curriculum Connection: Find out more about the discovery of the North Pole. What exactly is the North Pole?

Verse to Memorize: Matthew 16:24-26a— "Then Jesus said to his disciples, 'If anyone would come after me, he must deny himself and take up his cross and follow me. For whoever wants to save his life will lose it, but whoever loses his life for me will find it. What good will it be for a man if he gains the whole world, yet forfeits his soul?'"

Prayer Suggestion: Pray for people who live in places with extreme temperatures.

December 19
Giant Panda Anniversary

Supposedly, the first Westerner—a French missionary and naturalist—to describe a giant panda wrote of a "fine skin of the famous white and black bear" in 1869. Years later, in 1934, the first giant panda cub appeared at a Chicago zoo. Americans fell in love with this adorable creature. Other zoos also purchased pandas. The anniversary of the first giant pandas in the National Zoo in Washington, D.C., is celebrated each December. Giant pandas typically do a lot of sitting upright and eating bamboo. The panda is not an unusually active animal. Read Paul's words of advice about too much inactivity, as found in 2 Thessalonians 3:6-14.

Questions to Discuss: What can happen when you have too much idle time on your hands? What can you do when you are feeling bored or idle? What did Paul encourage the Thessalonians to do to keep busy?

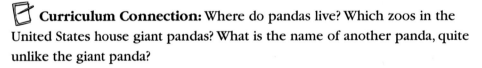

Related Activity: Make a panda face. Dip a chocolate sandwich cookie in melted white chocolate. Place on waxed paper for the chocolate to harden. When the chocolate is firm, use frosting to attach two miniature chocolate sandwich cookies on the top for ears. Then add chocolate chips for eyes and nose.

Curriculum Connection: Where do pandas live? Which zoos in the United States house giant pandas? What is the name of another panda, quite unlike the giant panda?

Verse to Memorize: 2 Thessalonians 3:13b—"Never tire of doing what is right."

Prayer Suggestion: Ask God to keep your hands and minds occupied doing His will.

December 20
Flashlight Day

The winter solstice occurs on the shortest day of the year and indicates the beginning of winter. Because this day has the least amount of sunlight, it is celebrated as Flashlight Day. Read John 8:12-30 and find out about another Light.

Questions to Discuss: What kind of light does Jesus give? Describe the comfort you feel, knowing Jesus as your light in the darkness. How can you let others see the light of Jesus in you?

Related Activity: Give each person a flashlight, and turn off the lights. Sit on the floor and sing this song to the tune of "This Little Light of Mine": "Jesus is the light of mine. I'm going to let Him shine. Jesus is the light of mine. I'm going to let Him shine. Jesus is the light of mine. I'm going to let Him shine. Let Him shine, all the time, let Him shine."

Curriculum Connection: Find areas on the map that have almost total darkness, day and night, during the winter.

Verse to Memorize: John 8:12—"When Jesus spoke again to the people, he said, 'I am the light of the world. Whoever follows me will never walk in darkness, but will have the light of life.'"

Prayer Suggestion: In darkness, with a flashlight, pray: "Thank you for your light, so bright. Lead me, Jesus, day and night."

December 21
Winter

Job says, in Job 37:1-24, that his heart pounds at the very sight of God's awesome marvels. Job points out that at the very word of God, snow falls to the earth. God's breath can cause the ice to cover the land. Job marvels at many more of God's displays of power. Read Job's appreciation of God's hand in nature, specifically looking for parts that involve winter.

Questions to Discuss: What do you like best about winter? What do you like least about winter? What part of winter reminds you of God the most?

Related Activity: Use doilies to make snowflakes. Fold a doily in half several times. Cut designs carefully, without cutting the fold completely. Unfold your doily for a lacy, unique snowflake. Write blessings from the year on each snowflake and decorate your room for winter.

Curriculum Connection: Chart the temperature for today in the United States. Where is it the warmest? Coldest? Who has the most snow? And what is your high and low temperature for the day?

Verse to Memorize: Job 37:5—"God's voice thunders in marvelous ways; he does great things beyond our understanding."

Prayer Suggestion: Thank God for the beauty of winter.

December 22
Forefathers' Day

The group of people who left England in search of a new home have, for years, been called Pilgrims. However, for more than two hundred years, this group of people called themselves Founders or Forefathers. The Forefathers landed at Plymouth Rock in 1620. The day became known as Forefathers' Day. Paul made a difficult journey, just like the Pilgrims. Read Acts 27:1–28:31 to see what happens to him.

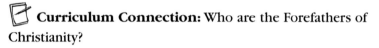

Questions to Discuss: How difficult was Paul's journey to Rome? Did Paul's trials hinder his witnessing? What do you think happened to each person accepting Jesus? Do you think they, in turn, told others about Jesus? Who have you told about Jesus today?

Related Activity: Spread a blanket on the floor. Sit on the blanket and pretend to be out to sea. Make up stories about your adventure.

Curriculum Connection: Who are the Forefathers of Christianity?

Verse to Memorize: Romans 10:13—"For everyone who calls on the name of the Lord will be saved."

Prayer Suggestion: Ask God to help you encourage others to call on the name of the Lord.

December 23
Bingo Month

Have you ever played bingo? Sometimes churches hold bingo games for senior citizens or for family fun times. Read about a time that Jesus did not approve of what was happening in the temple. Read Mark 11:15–19.

Questions to Discuss: Why was Jesus unhappy with what was taking place at the temple? How should God's house be treated? What do you like to do at your house of worship?

Related Activity: Make a JESUS game. Make the game like bingo, however, using the letters in Jesus' name to go across the top. Instead of numbers, use words to describe Jesus, such as *love, grace, peace, forgive, sinless, God's Son, cross.*

Curriculum Connection: Write the numbers from 1 to 1,000.

Verse to Memorize: Mark 11:17b—"My house will be called a house of prayer for all nations."

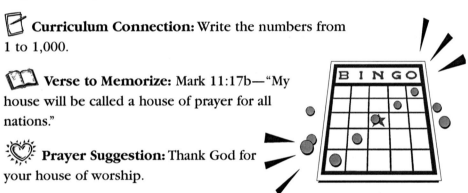

Prayer Suggestion: Thank God for your house of worship.

December 24
Happy Birthday, Street Cleaning Machine

In 1854, Philadelphia residents were amazed to see the first practical street cleaning machine in their neighborhood. Do you need a "heart" and "head" cleaning machine sometimes? In Philippians 4:8-9, Paul talks about keeping your heart and mind clean. Read to see what he says.

Questions to Discuss: What kinds of thoughts does Paul say Christians should meditate on? What kinds of thoughts do you think you should avoid?

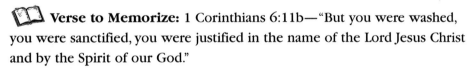

Related Activity: Clean the street where you live.

Curriculum Connection: Learn the proper way to write your street address. Learn your phone number, too.

Verse to Memorize: 1 Corinthians 6:11b—"But you were washed, you were sanctified, you were justified in the name of the Lord Jesus Christ and by the Spirit of our God."

Prayer Suggestion: Ask God to keep your thoughts clean and pure.

December 25
Christmas—Happy Birthday, Jesus

*What a special day in the life of a Christian! God's promise—
wrapped in a blanket and lying in a manger. Don't you wish you
could have been there on that glorious night?
Read Luke 2:1-7 to find out about the people who were there.*

Questions to Discuss: How do you think
Joseph felt on this special day? How did Mary
feel? Why did God send His son into the
world?

Related Activity: Wrap a doll in a
blanket. Sit in a dark, quiet room or
under a table with a blanket spread over
the top. Hold baby Jesus close to your heart.
Share aloud what Jesus means to you.

Curriculum Connection: Follow the directions to make a cake. Put
one candle in for each member of the family. Sing "Happy Birthday to Jesus."

Verse to Memorize: Luke 2:11—"Today in the town of David a
Savior has been born to you; he is Christ the Lord."

Prayer Suggestion: Take turns holding the wrapped baby and thank
God for His Precious Son, Baby Jesus.

December 26
Boxing Day

On the first working day after Christmas, Great Britain, Canada, and a few other countries celebrate Boxing Day. On this day, people treat various service people with gifts. Mail carriers, paper deliverers, and other people in the service industry receive small tokens of appreciation. In Acts 20:32–35, Paul points out Jesus' words about giving.

Questions to Discuss: What was your favorite gift to someone else yesterday? How did that person feel when he or she received your gift? What is God's special gift?

Related Activity: Give a gift to your letter carrier, landlord, or anyone you feel needs an after-Christmas treat today.

Curriculum Connection: Name the provinces in Canada.

Verse to Memorize: Acts 20:35b—"Remembering the words the Lord Jesus himself said: 'It is more blessed to give than to receive.'"

Prayer Suggestion: Give thanks for each gift you received yesterday. Pray for the person who gave you that gift.

December 27
Kwanzaa

Kwanzaa begins on December 26 and lasts seven days. A professor of Pan-African studies, M. Ron Karenga, developed the holiday in 1966. Each day of Kwanzaa is based on one of seven principles, and a particular color represents each day. Kwanzaa is an African-American holiday that comes from the traditional African festival of the harvest of the first crops. Read the psalmist's words in Psalm 85:12 about God's bountiful harvest.

Questions to Discuss: What is your favorite fresh vegetable? How can you thank God for your blessings?

Related Activity: Have a buffet of fresh vegetables.

Curriculum Connection: Read about the seven principles of Kwanzaa. Locate the countries of Africa.

Verse to Memorize: Galatians 6:9—"Let us not become weary in doing good, for at the proper time we will reap a harvest if we do not give up."

Prayer Suggestion: Stand in the kitchen, near the pantry, for today's prayer. As you pray, thank God specifically for the good foods you have in your house and for a bountiful harvest this year.

December 28
Chewing Gum Day

William Semple of Mount Vernon, Ohio, patented chewing gum on this day in 1869. Would you like to thank him for his invention? Do you like to chew gum? Chewing gum was originally made from the sap of certain trees. Did you know you were chewing on part of a tree? Read about an incident with a particular tree in Matthew 21:18-22.

Questions to Discuss: Why did Jesus expect to find fruit on the tree? Why were the disciples shocked at yet another one of Jesus' displays of power? Do you still marvel at Jesus' power?

Related Activity: Have a bubble-blowing contest.

Curriculum Connection: Talk about the numbers on a number line. Draw a number line using a stick of gum as your ruler.

Verse to Memorize: Matthew 21:22—"If you believe, you will receive whatever you ask for in prayer."

Prayer Suggestion: Thank God for answers to prayer.

December 29
Shepherds' Day

When God sent His messengers to announce the birth of His Son, He sent them first to a field of shepherds. The life of a shepherd in biblical times was hard and even dangerous. He led a difficult life, protecting and taking care of a herd of sheep, both daytime and nighttime. Shepherds were not always known as a wealthy lot of people. In fact, many were regarded as lowly. But the lowly, seemingly unimportant shepherd heard God's news first. What does that tell you about God? Read Luke 2:8-20 to see the shepherds' reaction to the news.

Questions to Discuss: Why did God choose shepherds to reveal Jesus' birth to first? How do you think the shepherds felt? How do you think they glorified God? How do you glorify God?

Related Activity: Read about the shepherd in a Bible dictionary. Talk about the items he carried with him to protect the sheep. Eat a candy cane and talk about how a shepherd used his staff.

Curriculum Connection: Give a television broadcast about what the shepherds saw. Pretend to be a television news reporter, and give a "This just in!" announcement.

Verse to Memorize: Psalm 86:12—"I will praise you, O Lord my God, with all my heart; I will glorify your name forever."

Prayer Suggestion: Pretend to be shepherds. Pray the words that the shepherds in the Bible might have said on that glorious night.

December 30
Make-Up-Your-Mind Day

This day gives procrastinators just one more day to make up their minds before the New Year starts. Is there anything that you need to decide before the closing of another year? Read about the most important decision a person can make in John 3:1-22.

Questions to Discuss: Have you made up your mind about Jesus? Do you know someone who needs to decide to follow Jesus? Can you talk to that person today?

Related Activity: Play Twenty Questions, using something or someone from the Bible. Make up your mind about the answer before the twenty questions are up.

Curriculum Connection: Practice telling time using seconds, minutes, and hours. How many minutes are left in this year? How many hours?

Verse to Memorize: John 3:3,18—"In reply Jesus declared, 'I tell you the truth, no one can see the kingdom of God unless he is born again.' Whoever believes in him is not condemned, but whoever does not believe stands condemned already because he has not believed in the name of God's one and only Son."

Prayer Suggestion: If you have not made a decision about Jesus, ask God to help you make up your mind in the new year. If you have made up your mind, give thanks for your salvation.

December 31
New Year's Eve

According to the calendar, one minute after midnight tonight starts a brand new year. Are you ready for a new year? Read about a young man who had trouble staying up until midnight, which led to a disastrous fall. Read Acts 20:7–12.

Questions to Discuss: Why do you think Eutychus had a difficult time staying awake? What do you think Paul was talking about? Do you plan to stay up until midnight tonight?

Related Activity: Write your blessings for the year on small sheets of colored paper. Fold the paper into even tinier pieces of paper. Let each person write twenty or more blessings. At the stroke of midnight (in whatever time zone you choose to celebrate), throw the paper in the air like confetti. Spend the first part of the new year re-reading all of the blessings of the previous year.

Curriculum Connection: Count backwards from one hundred.

Verse to Memorize: 2 Corinthians 5:17—"Therefore, if anyone is in Christ, he is a new creation, the old has gone, the new has come."

Prayer Suggestion: Thank God for the blessings He gave you in the current year. Pray for His peace and guidance in the new year.

Bible Story Index

A

Acts 1:7-11, 145
Acts 1:12-2:41, 155
Acts 2:42-47, 280
Acts 3:1-16, 231
Acts 3:19-26, 107
Acts 4:1-22, 275
Acts 5:1-11, 233
Acts 5:12-42, 331
Acts 6:1-15, 149
Acts 7:8-15, 330
Acts 7:48-8:1, 149
Acts 8:1b-8, 63
Acts 8:26-40, 118
Acts 9:1-31, 4
Acts 9:32-43, 343
Acts 10:9-16, 47
Acts 10:21-48, 15
Acts 11:19-30, 63
Acts 12:1-25, 305
Acts 13:1-14:28, 187
Acts 14:8-10, 60
Acts 16:16-40, 121
Acts 17:24-28, 218
Acts 18:1-11, 120
Acts 18:24-28, 120
Acts 20:7-12, 366
Acts 20:32-35, 361
Acts 27:1-28:31, 357

C

1 Chronicles 4:13-23, 27
2 Chronicles 26:1-23, 214
Colossians 2:6-7, 332
1 Corinthians 1:18, 344
1 Corinthians 2:14-16a, 158
1 Corinthians 5:6-8, 115
1 Corinthians 9:24-27, 163
1 Corinthians 11:17-34, 280
1 Corinthians 12:1-31, 74
1 Corinthians 13:1-13, 293
1 Corinthians 15:1-58, 255

1 Corinthians 15:20-28, 119
1 Corinthians 16:15-18, 156
2 Corinthians 3:1-3, 7
2 Corinthians 4:1-15, 289
2 Corinthians 5:1-10, 132
2 Corinthians 9:6-15, 341

D

Daniel 1:1-21, 83
Daniel 3:1-30, 342
Daniel 5:1-31, 328
Daniel 6:1-23, 64
Deuteronomy 6:1-25, 31
Deuteronomy 27:1-10, 41
Deuteronomy 34:1-12, 251

E

Ecclesiastes 2:9-11, 21
Ecclesiastes 7:1a, 198
Ecclesiastes 8:8a, 68
Ecclesiastes 11:1, 153
Ecclesiastes 11:7-10, 294
Ecclesiastes 12:9-14, 62
Ephesians 1:1-14, 190
Ephesians 3:14-19, 99
Ephesians 4:17-5:2, 1
Ephesians 5:1-20, 101
Ephesians 6:10-18, 35
Esther 2:1-18, 178
Esther 2:19-9:32, 66
Exodus 1:1-22, 203
Exodus 2:1-10, 72
Exodus 3:1-22, 309
Exodus 4:1-31, 340
Exodus 5:1-6:1, 203
Exodus 6:2-12, 16
Exodus 6:26-7:13, 296
Exodus 7:14-24, 264
Exodus 8:1-15, 262
Exodus 8:16-32, 299
Exodus 9:1-7, 240
Exodus 9:8-12, 313
Exodus 9:13-35, 228

Exodus 10:1-20, 299
Exodus 10:21-29, 291
Exodus 11:1-10, 130
Exodus 12:1-16, 97
Exodus 12:17-20, 115
Exodus 12:21-29, 97
Exodus 12:31-40, 32
Exodus 12:37-39, 115
Exodus 12:43-50, 97
Exodus 13:1-16, 186
Exodus 13:17-14:31, 320
Exodus 15:1-27, 311
Exodus 16:1-35, 322
Exodus 17:1-7, 243
Exodus 20:1-17, 23
Exodus 25:10-22, 140
Exodus 31:1-11, 67
Exodus 31:18, 23
Exodus 32:1-14, 179
Ezekiel 3:2-3, 286
Ezra 1:1-8, 70
Ezra 3:7-13, 70
Ezra 6:13-18, 70

G

Galatians 3:26-4:7, 52
Galatians 6:7-10, 81
Genesis 1:1, 114
Genesis 1:9-10, 108
Genesis 1:11-13, 43
Genesis 1:13, 108
Genesis 1:14-19, 202
Genesis 1:20-23, 108, 351
Genesis 1:24-31, 112
Genesis 2:4-15, 100
Genesis 2:15-17, 177
Genesis 3:1-24, 138
Genesis 4:1-16, 315
Genesis 6:1-7:24, 86
Genesis 8:1-21, 180
Genesis 8:22, 34
Genesis 11:1-9, 213
Genesis 12:1-9, 152

Genesis 13:1-14:24, 199
Genesis 18:1-15, 94
Genesis 18:16-19:29, 181
Genesis 21:1-7, 183
Genesis 21:8-21, 30
Genesis 22:1-19, 247
Genesis 24:1-66, 352
Genesis 25:27-34, 25
Genesis 27:1-28:5, 252
Genesis 28:10-22, 75
Genesis 29:1-14a, 22
Genesis 29:14b-30, 253
Genesis 32:1-21, 175
Genesis 32:22-32, 350
Genesis 33:1-20, 175
Genesis 37:1-4, 284
Genesis 37:5-10, 317
Genesis 37:12-36, 171
Genesis 40:1-23, 298
Genesis 41:1-56, 295
Genesis 42:1-38, 318
Genesis 43:1-47:11, 330
Genesis 43:11, 84

H

Habakkuk 1:1-3:19, 285
Hebrews 4:9-11, 88
Hebrews 5:11-14, 164
Hebrews 6:1-12, 297
Hebrews 10:1-18, 185
Hebrews 11:1-40, 290
Hebrews 12:1-12, 301

I

Isaiah 6:1-13, 195
Isaiah 35:8-9, 136
Isaiah 40:3-5, 109
Isaiah 40:8, 347
Isaiah 40:12, 196
Isaiah 40:22, 79
Isaiah 40:27-31, 172
Isaiah 52:7, 2

J

James 2:14-26, 333
James 2:20-24, 247
James 3:1-12, 245
James 5:7-11, 267
Jeremiah 10:12-13, 36
Jeremiah 18:1-12, 76
Jeremiah 19:1-15, 76
Jeremiah 31:35, 82

Job 1:1-2:13, 244
Job 9:8-9, 131
Job 37:1-24, 356
Job 38:1-42:17, 244
Joel 2:1-3:21, 273
John 2:1-11, 42
John 3:1-22, 365
John 3:16-21, 168
John 4:1-30, 241
John 4:31-34, 150
John 4:39-42, 241
John 5:1-15, 205
John 6:25-59, 307
John 7:1-13, 283
John 7:37-39, 283
John 8:1-11, 58
John 8:12-30, 355
John 9:1-41, 116
John 10:1-18, 346
John 11:1-44, 236
John 12:1-8, 143
John 12:12-19, 98
John 13:1-17, 29
John 13:33-36, 102
John 14:1-4, 278
John 14:5-31, 77
John 15:1-8, 139
John 15:9-17, 221
John 16:5-16, 155
John 19:31-37, 97
John 20:19-31, 146
John 21:1-14, 246
John 21:15-24, 225
John 21:25, 96
1 John 1:1-10, 308
1 John 2:1-11, 337
1 John 4:7-21, 45
Jonah 1:1-2:10, 232
Jonah 3:1-4:11, 141
Joshua 1:1-18, 159
Joshua 2:1-24, 182
Joshua 3:1-4:24, 184
Joshua 5:13-6:27, 46
Joshua 23:1-24:33, 230
Judges 7:1-5, 3
Judges 13:1-7, 316
Judges 13:24, 316
Judges 16:4-31, 316

K

1 Kings 3:1-28, 49
1 Kings 4:29-34, 325
1 Kings 6:1-38, 91

1 Kings 10:1-13, 127
1 Kings 17:1-6, 37
1 Kings 17:7-24, 57
1 Kings 18:1-46, 282
1 Kings 19:1-18, 276
1 Kings 19:19-21, 9
1 Kings 21:1-28, 210
2 Kings 2:1-18, 327
2 Kings 4:8-17, 208
2 Kings 4:15-37, 281
2 Kings 4:42-44, 256
2 Kings 5:1-16, 12

L

Leviticus 16:1-34, 274
Leviticus 23:6-8, 115
Leviticus 23:9-14, 119
Leviticus 23:15-22, 154
Leviticus 23:23-25, 273
Leviticus 23:33-43, 283
Luke 1:5-25, 71
Luke 1:26-38, 85
Luke 1:39-56, 336
Luke 1:57-66, 71
Luke 2:1-7, 360
Luke 2:8-20, 364
Luke 2:21-40, 217
Luke 2:22, 33
Luke 2:41-52, 266
Luke 4:1-13, 192
Luke 7:36-50, 65
Luke 8:40-56, 204
Luke 10:17-20, 151
Luke 10:25-37, 48
Luke 10:29-37, 268
Luke 10:38-42, 169
Luke 12:1-12, 248
Luke 13:31-35, 148
Luke 14:15-23, 73
Luke 15:3-7, 28
Luke 15:8-10, 110
Luke 15:11-32, 61
Luke 16:19-31, 224
Luke 17:11-19, 11
Luke 18:1-8, 226
Luke 19:1-10, 339
Luke 20:20-26, 106
Luke 21:1-4, 215
Luke 24:1-12, 105
Luke 24:13-35, 216

M

Mark 2:1-12, 90
Mark 2:23-28, 167
Mark 4:21-23, 222
Mark 4:30-34, 237
Mark 6:14-29, 124
Mark 6:30-44, 93
Mark 7:1-23, 160
Mark 7:24-30, 272
Mark 11:15-19, 358
Mark 16:14-18, 166
Mark 16:19-20, 145
Matthew 1:18-25, 209
Matthew 2:1-12, 6
Matthew 2:13-23, 144
Matthew 3:1-12, 176
Matthew 3:13-17, 242
Matthew 4:1-11, 59
Matthew 4:12-17, 287
Matthew 4:18-22, 157
Matthew 4:23-25, 142
Matthew 5:1-12, 239
Matthew 5:13-16, 292
Matthew 5:17-20, 162
Matthew 6:1-4, 229
Matthew 6:5-15, 304
Matthew 6:19-21, 321
Matthew 6:24, 223
Matthew 6:28-34, 174
Matthew 7:1-5, 51
Matthew 7:7-8, 188
Matthew 7:24-27, 19
Matthew 8:5-13, 306
Matthew 8:18-22, 269
Matthew 8:23-27, 260
Matthew 9:9-13, 323
Matthew 9:35-38, 329
Matthew 10:1-42, 263
Matthew 11:1-19, 270
Matthew 11:25-30, 227
Matthew 12:33-37, 53
Matthew 13:24-30, 26
Matthew 13:36-43, 26
Matthew 13:53-58, 135
Matthew 14:1-5, 124
Matthew 14:22-33, 133
Matthew 15:21-28, 18
Matthew 15:29-39, 194
Matthew 16:1-4, 288
Matthew 16:21-28, 353
Matthew 17:1-13, 189
Matthew 17:24-27, 170

Matthew 19:13-15, 161
Matthew 19:16-22, 23
Matthew 20:1-16, 207
Matthew 21:18-22, 363
Matthew 22:34-40, 268
Matthew 24:36-51, 249
Matthew 25:1-13, 92
Matthew 25:14-30, 279
Matthew 25:31-46, 300
Matthew 26:17-46, 102
Matthew 26:47-27:61, 103
Matthew 27:62-66, 104
Matthew 28:16-20, 326

N

Numbers 13:1-14:38, 257
Numbers 22:1-23:12, 128

P

1 Peter 1:13-16, 39
1 Peter 1:17-21, 97
1 Peter 2:1, 14
Philippians 3:12-4:1, 258
Philippians 4:8-9, 359
Proverbs 1:8, 314
Proverbs 6:6-11, 349
Proverbs 10:26, 69
Proverbs 12:25, 40
Proverbs 15:17, 55
Proverbs 16:24, 54
Proverbs 17:6, 259
Proverbs 20:12, 116
Proverbs 30:4, 89
Proverbs 31:10-31, 134
Psalm 4:6-8, 348
Psalm 8:1-9, 5
Psalm 19:1-4, 50
Psalm 23:1-6, 111
Psalm 24:1-2, 277
Psalm 32:1-5, 219
Psalm 33:12-22, 125
Psalm 50:10, 193
Psalm 50:11, 312
Psalm 51:1-17, 235
Psalm 56:3-4, 113
Psalm 65:9-13, 80
Psalm 74:17, 173
Psalm 81:1-2, 335
Psalm 85:12, 362
Psalm 92:12, 98
Psalm 95:1-7, 8
Psalm 98:1-9, 56
Psalm 107:23-31, 220
Psalm 108:4-5, 201

Psalm 119:1-16, 123
Psalm 119:103, 303
Psalm 141:4, 24
Psalm 147:7-9, 197
Psalm 147:10-11, 117
Psalm 148:1-6, 211
Psalm 148:7, 200

R

Revelation 20:1-10, 78
Revelation 22:1-21, 165
Romans 3:21-30, 274
Romans 5:6-11, 212
Romans 6:1-23, 324
Romans 11:11-24, 191
Romans 12:1-8, 338
Romans 13:1-7, 310
Romans 13:14a, 261
Romans 14:1-23, 334
Romans 15:30-33, 206
Ruth 1:1-22, 250
Ruth 2:1-23, 87
Ruth 3:1-18, 122
Ruth 4:1-22, 302

S

1 Samuel 1:1-28, 319
1 Samuel 3:1-41a, 271
1 Samuel 4:1b-18, 234
1 Samuel 5:1-6:21, 234
1 Samuel 8:19-10:1, 20
1 Samuel 16:1-13, 44
1 Samuel 16:14-23, 13
1 Samuel 17:1-50, 17
1 Samuel 18:1-30, 254
1 Samuel 19:1-20:42, 238
1 Samuel 24:1-22, 95
1 Samuel 25:1-35, 10
1 Samuel 30:1-31, 129
2 Samuel 4:4, 137
2 Samuel 6:1-15, 38
2 Samuel 9:1-13, 137
2 Samuel 11:1-12:25, 265

T

1 Thessalonians 4:13-18,
  119
2 Thessalonians 3:6-14, 354
1 Timothy 5:1-16, 126
2 Timothy 4:1-8, 147
Titus 3:3-8, 345

Memory Verse Index

A

Acts 2:21, 198
Acts 4:12, 275
Acts 10:43, 328
Acts 13:38, 298
Acts 13:49, 187
Acts 16:31b, 216
Acts 17:25c, 218
Acts 20:35b, 361

C

2 Chronicles 15:7, 72
Colossians 1:13-14, 222
Colossians 2:16-17, 162
Colossians 3:1-2, 338
Colossians 3:13, 61
Colossians 3:17, 142
Colossians 3:23-24, 169
1 Corinthians 5:7, 97
1 Corinthians 5:7a, 1
1 Corinthians 6:11b, 359
1 Corinthians 10:31b, 27
1 Corinthians 10:16, 280
1 Corinthians 10:26, 82
1 Corinthians 12:13, 74
1 Corinthians 13:13, 293
1 Corinthians 15:3b-455, 255
1 Corinthians 15:51b-52, 273
2 Corinthians 1:3-4a, 264
2 Corinthians 2:15a, 158
2 Corinthians 4:6, 289
2 Corinthians 4:18, 116
2 Corinthians 5:7, 4
2 Corinthians 5:17, 366
2 Corinthians 5:20, 237
2 Corinthians 5:21, 102
2 Corinthians 6:2b, 73
2 Corinthians 7:1b, 115
2 Corinthians 9:6, 81
2 Corinthians 9:7, 341
2 Corinthians 9:15, 231
2 Corinthians 12:9, 340

D

Daniel 2:20-21a, 36
Deuteronomy 6:5, 31
Deuteronomy 27:10a, 41

E

Ecclesiastes 5:18-19, 253
Ecclesiastes 9:10a, 251
Ecclesiastes 11:8a, 294
Ephesians 1:7, 175
Ephesians 1:7-8, 190
Ephesians 2:4-5, 344
Ephesians 2:8-9, 229
Ephesians 2:10, 261
Ephesians 4:31-32, 48
Ephesians 5:6, 252
Ephesians 5:15-18, 101
Ephesians 5:19, 56
Ephesians 6:1-3, 209
Ephesians 6:10-11, 35
Ephesians 6:18a, 226
Exodus 3:12a, 309
Exodus 6:7a, 16
Exodus 9:16, 228
Exodus 20:8, 167
Exodus 20:15, 210
Exodus 29:46, 66
Ezekiel 18:32, 141
Ezekiel 33:11, 199

G

Galatians 3:9a, 60
Galatians 3:26-27, 337
Galatians 3:28, 52
Galatians 5:22-23a, 250
Galatians 6:4-5, 51
Galatians 6:9, 362
Genesis 1:12b, 43
Genesis 1:31a, 100
Genesis 2:1, 351
Genesis 18:14a, 94
Genesis 28:15a, 75

H

Hebrews 3:13a, 40, 206
Hebrews 4:15, 59
Hebrews 5:8-9, 247
Hebrews 8:12, 185
Hebrews 10:12, 145
Hebrews 10:38, 147
Hebrews 11:1, 133, 290
Hebrews 11:6, 288
Hebrews 11:7, 86
Hebrews 12:2, 301
Hebrews 12:5b-7a, 232
Hebrews 13:5, 223

I

Isaiah 6:8, 195
Isaiah 12:2a, 64
Isaiah 26:4, 19
Isaiah 40:31, 172
Isaiah 50:10, 57
Isaiah 53:5-6, 313
Isaiah 58:11, 30
Isaiah 59:2, 70
Isaiah 64:8, 76

J

James 1:5, 49
James 1:12, 163, 342
James 1:17a, 243
James 1:19-20, 10
James 1:22, 246, 276
James 2:25-26, 182
James 4:7, 138
James 4:8, 265
James 5:16a, 137
James 5:16b, 305
Jeremiah 7:6-7, 203
Jeremiah 10:6, 114
Jeremiah 17:9, 233
Jeremiah 17:14, 204
Job 12:12, 126
Job 20:5b, 25
Job 37:5, 356
Job 37:6a, 7a, 8

Job 37:14b, 296
John 1:1-4, 291
John 1:14, 42
John 3:3, 365
John 3:16, 168
John 3:18, 365
John 3:36, 281
John 4:13-14, 3
John 5:24, 271
John 6:12, 179
John 6:35, 307
John 8:12, 355
John 8:31b-32, 186
John 8:34, 171
John 10:14-15, 346
John 11:25-26a, 236
John 13:34, 55
John 14:1, 257
John 14:2-3, 278
John 14:6, 77, 348
John 14:9b, 350
John 14:11a, 350
John 15:5b, 21
John 15:7, 282
John 15:8, 139
John 15:10-11, 221
John 20:29, 146
John 20:31, 96
1 John 1:5b, 308
1 John 1:7, 308
1 John 1:9, 58, 219
1 John 2:1c-2, 274
1 John 2:17, 129
1 John 2:17b, 317
1 John 2:25, 283
1 John 3:1a, 217
1 John 3:5a, 107
1 John 3:18, 22, 333
1 John 4:11, 241
1 John 4:19, 45
1 John 4:21b, 241
1 John 5:1a, 270
1 John 5:14, 205
Joshua 4:24, 184
Joshua 22:5, 46
Joshua 24:14a, 230

L
Luke 1:37, 183
Luke 2:11, 360
Luke 2:30-31, 4
Luke 6:23a, 269
Luke 9:35, 189
Luke 9:62, 9

Luke 11:27-28, 85
Luke 12:8-9, 248
Luke 15:10, 110
Luke 19:10, 28, 339
Luke 22:27, 29

M
Malachi 3:10, 215
Mark 9:23b, 71
Mark 11:17b, 358
Mark 11:24, 299
Mark 16:15-16, 166
Matthew 3:2b, 109
Matthew 3:11c-12, 26
Matthew 3:17, 242
Matthew 4:17, 207
Matthew 4:19, 157
Matthew 5:5, 239
Matthew 5:6, 150
Matthew 5:13, 292
Matthew 6:8b, 352
Matthew 6:9-13, 304
Matthew 6:21, 321
Matthew 6:33, 174
Matthew 7:12a, 95
Matthew 9:12-13, 323
Matthew 9:35, 90
Matthew 9:37-38, 329
Matthew 10:30, 5
Matthew 11:28, 227
Matthew 16:24-26a, 353
Matthew 18:11, 33
Matthew 19:14, 161
Matthew 21:9b, 98
Matthew 21:22, 363
Matthew 22:37-38, 225
Matthew 22:39b, 268
Matthew 24:36, 249
Matthew 24:42, 249
Matthew 25:13, 92
Matthew 25:40, 300
Matthew 28:19, 326
Matthew 28:19-20, 63
Micah 5:2, 6

P
1 Peter 1:3-4, 105
1 Peter 1:13-16, 336
1 Peter 1:15, 39
1 Peter 1:18-19, 318
1 Peter 1:25a, 347
1 Peter 2:2-3, 164

1 Peter 2:24, 103
1 Peter 3:3-4, 178
1 Peter 4:10, 279
1 Peter 4:11c, 279
1 Peter 4:13, 124, 331
1 Peter 5:7, 260
1 Peter 5:9a, 192
2 Peter 1:3, 197
Philippians 1:27a, 83
Philippians 2:9-11, 143
Philippians 3:14, 117
Philippians 3:20-21, 132
Philippians 4:6, 188
Philippians 4:7, 285
Philippians 4:12b, 177
Philippians 4:12b-13, 295
Philippians 4:19, 37, 322
Proverbs 1:7a, 325
Proverbs 3:5-6, 111
Proverbs 3:9a, 170
Proverbs 4:23, 160
Proverbs 7:1-3, 23
Proverbs 9:10, 62
Proverbs 10:4, 69
Proverbs 10:6a, 17
Proverbs 11:16, 208
Proverbs 12:10, 128
Proverbs 16:3, 214
Proverbs 16:17, 136
Proverbs 17:17a, 238
Proverbs 17:22a, 12
Proverbs 20:7, 121
Proverbs 20:11, 266
Proverbs 20:28, 20
Proverbs 21:13, 224
Proverbs 22:6, 314
Proverbs 22:29a, 135
Proverbs 28:20a, 306
Proverbs 31:28, 134
Psalm 5:11, 148
Psalm 7:8b, 53
Psalm 13:6, 13
Psalm 15:1-3a, 245
Psalm 15:5b, 245
Psalm 19:9-10, 286
Psalm 19:14, 54
Psalm 24:1, 277
Psalm 24:4a, 5a, 14
Psalm 27:14, 267
Psalm 28:7, 316
Psalm 33:6, 50
Psalm 33:12a, 125
Psalm 34:14a, 181

Psalm 36:6b, 180
Psalm 40:5, 320
Psalm 47:2, 89
Psalm 47:7-8, 79
Psalm 50:11, 312
Psalm 51:7b, 235
Psalm 56:3-4, 144
Psalm 56:11a, 113
Psalm 61:4a, 120
Psalm 63:4-5, 84
Psalm 66:4, 80
Psalm 72:18, 127
Psalm 73:28a, 91
Psalm 74:16, 202
Psalm 74:17, 34
Psalm 77:11-12, 194
Psalm 77:13-15, 130
Psalm 78:3-4, 327
Psalm 86:12, 364
Psalm 90:17, 67
Psalm 95:1-2, 311
Psalm 96:1-3, 2
Psalm 100:5, 153
Psalm 103:2-5, 330
Psalm 104:24, 112, 176
Psalm 104:33-34, 335
Psalm 107:1, 11
Psalm 111:2-3, 196
Psalm 111:5, 87
Psalm 118:1, 234
Psalm 119:35, 159
Psalm 119:57, 152
Psalm 119:103, 303
Psalm 119:125, 263
Psalm 132:8, 140

Psalm 136:26, 99
Psalm 141:4a, 24
Psalm 143:5, 173
Psalm 145:13b, 262
Psalm 147:1, 200
Psalm 147:4, 131
Psalm 147:5a, 68
Psalm 148:1a, 211
Psalm 148:7, 108, 220
Psalm 148:7a, 193
Psalm 148:10a, 193
Psalm 149:3-4, 38

R

Revelation 3:5, 151
Revelation 7:15-17, 93
Revelation 22:17, 165
Romans 1:16, 287
Romans 3:10, 58
Romans 3:22-24, 18
Romans 5:1, 65
Romans 5:3-4, 244
Romans 5:8, 212
Romans 5:12, 154
Romans 5:18, 154
Romans 6:4, 104
Romans 6:12, 324
Romans 6:17-18, 32
Romans 6:23, 324
Romans 8:3c-4, 254
Romans 8:17, 149
Romans 8:28, 284
Romans 8:38-39, 201
Romans 10:13, 357
Romans 10:17, 272
Romans 11:20-21, 191

Romans 12:1, 315
Romans 12:1-2, 213
Romans 12:11, 349
Romans 13:1, 310
Romans 13:6-7, 106
Romans 14:17-18, 334
Romans 15:4, 240
Romans 15:7, 15
Romans 15:17, 156
Romans 16:20a, 78

S

1 Samuel 2:2, 319
1 Samuel 16:7b, 44

T

1 Thessalonians 4:16-18, 119
1 Thessalonians 5:12a, 343
1 Thessalonians 5:16, 122
1 Thessalonians 5:16-18, 332
2 Thessalonians 2:15-17, 7
2 Thessalonians 3:13b, 354
1 Timothy 2:5-6a, 88
1 Timothy 4:4-5, 47
1 Timothy 4:10b, 302
1 Timothy 6:12, 258
1 Timothy 6:17, 256
1 Timothy 6:18, 297
2 Timothy 3:16-17, 118, 123
Titus 2:11-13, 259
Titus 3:4-7, 155
Titus 3:5-7, 345

Curriculum Index

A

Aardvark, 349
Abbreviations, 7, 124
Addition, 169, 215
Adjectives, 27, 40, 228
Adverbs, 181
Africa, countries of, 144, 362
Agriculture. *See* Farming
Alcohol, effects of, 101
Alphabetizing, 14, 43, 81, 174
American Revolution, 16, 186
Amphibians, 262, 296
Analogies, 5
Animal classes, 112, 197
Animal names, 61, 86
Anteater, 349
Antonyms, 26, 31, 221
Art, 52, 67, 108, 162, 251
Asia, countries of, 213
Astronomy, 50, 131, 201, 202, 211
Automobile timeline, 109
Averages, 184

B

Ballet, 38
Baseball, rules of, 163
Basilisk lizard, 133
Basketball, rules of, 339
Bees, 257
Bible study: books in Bible, 123, 250, 301, 329; dictionary use, 126, 283; miracles of Jesus, 241; names for Jesus, 283; twelve disciples, 167
Bicycle safety, 136
Biography: Boone, D., 159; Braille, L., 4; Columbus, C., 288; Cook, Captain J., 307; Crockett, D., 230; Fleming, Sir. A., 154; Gallaudet, T., 270; Gillespie, D., 273; King, Jr., M. L., 15; Low, J. G., 72; Luther, M., 305; of musicians, 13; Parks, R., 337; of president, vice president, 20; St. Nicholas, 341; Tubman, H., 340; Whitney, E., 343; Wright brothers, 327
Biology: aardvark and anteater, 349; amphibians, 262, 296; animal classes, 112, 197; animal names, 61, 86; basilisk lizard, 133; bees, 257; birds, 37, 148, 248, 351; body parts, 218; bones, 313; brain, parts of, 185; cat family, 245; circulatory system, 44; deer family, 346; dinosaurs, 277; dog breeds, 272; ear, parts of, 271; endangered species, 172; eye, functioning of, 116; fish, 157; flowers, 174, 191; growth stages, 161; insects, 176; lungs, 218; mammals, 193; molds and fungi, 154, 289; muscles, kinds of, 236; ocean animals, 108; pandas, 354; pinnipeds, 82; plant, parts of, 139; reptiles, 296; respiration, 299; seed, parts of, 100; senses, 4, 155, 158; teeth, 69; trees, 53, 237, 267, 315, 347; vertebrates and invertebrates, 240; zoos, 180, 354

Birds, 37, 148, 248, 351
Birthstones, 140
Blueprint, drawing of, 278
Bones, 313
Book reports, 210
Boston Tea Party, 352
Boy Scouts, 39
Brain, parts of, 185

C

Calendars, 1, 68, 98
California Gold Rush, 231
Canadian provinces, 361
Careers, 12, 64, 138, 207, 226, 255
Cat family, 245
Check writing, 318
Chemistry, 170, 309
Christianity, symbols of, 103
Christmas celebrations, 336
Circles, 21, 46
Circulatory system, 44
Circumference, 21
Civics, 125, 310. *See also* History
Clocks, 73
Clothing styles, 261
Clouds, types of, 36
Color combination, 162
Color wheel, 52
Communication, changes in, 195
Compass, reading of, 152
Compound words, 88, 322
Computers, 23, 114, 275. *See also* Internet use
Conjunctions, 238
Constellations, 131
Contractions, 246
Cooking, 24, 25, 150, 298, 303, 360
Counting, 59, 92, 123, 189, 366

D

Dairy products, 164
Dance, 38
Days in month, 60
Decimals, 279
Deer family, 346
Dentistry, as career, 64
Dewey decimal system, 96
Dictionary, use of, 290
Dinosaurs, 277
Directions, giving of, 217
Dog breeds, 272
Drugs, effects of, 101

E

Ear, parts of, 271
Egypt, 32
Encyclopedia use. *See* Biography; Research topics
Endangered species, 172
Estimating, 22
Etiquette, 177
Europe, countries of, 77
Expanded notation, 323
Eye, functioning of, 116

F

Family history, 146, 168
Farming: agricultural products, 84, 141, 198, 317; in Biblical times, 9; careers in, 207; farm animals, 97, 265
Fasteners, 120
Field trip, to animal shelter, 128
Figurative language, in literature, 293
Fire safety rules, 282
Firefighting, careers in, 255
Fish, kinds of, 157
Five senses, 4, 155, 158
Flags of U.S., 166
Flash cards, 99
Flowers, 174, 191
Food groups, 57
Football, 28
Fractions, 115
Fungi, 154, 289

G

Geneology, 146, 168
Genres of literature, 308

Geography: Africa, 144, 362; Asia, 213; Bible lands, 6, 48; Canadian provinces, 361; compass reading, 152; continents, 130, 326; Egypt, 32; Europe, 77; imaginary lines on globe, 192, 306, 355; islands, 18, 307; landmark location, 91; lighthouse locations, 222; Middle East, 203; neighborhood map, 216; North America, 187; North Pole, 353; oceans, 200; rivers in U.S., 165; seas, 153; Sinai Peninsula, 32; state capitals, 117; states in U.S., 132; terms in, 10, 219, 320; tourist attractions, 8, 127, 276; zoo locations, 180
Gettysburg Address, 324
Girl Scouts, 72
Golfing, 19
Government, 125, 310
Grammar. *See* Language arts
Graphs, 304
Gravity, 89
Greetings, forms of, 122

H

"Have Thine Own Way, Lord," 76
Health: alcohol and drugs, 101; bicycle safety, 136; fire safety rules, 282; nutritional information, 47, 57, 83, 164; thermometer, reading of, 137
History: American Revolution, 16, 186; automobile timeline, 109; Boston Tea Party, 352; California Gold Rush, 231; of computer, 114; flags of U.S., 166; Gettysburg Address, 324; Pilgrims, 260, 325; presidents of U.S., 49; Statue of Lib-

erty, 302; transcontinental railroad, 281; wars with U.S. involvement, 149. *See also* Biography
Home Economics. *See* Cooking
Homeless people, 295
Homonyms, 78
Homophones, 145
Hyphen use, 199

I

Index, use of, 298
Insects, 176
Interjections, 147
Internet use, 8, 71, 176, 198, 207, 214
Islands, 18, 307

L

Language arts: abbreviations, 7, 124; addressing envelopes, 344, 359; adjectives, 27, 40, 228; adverbs, 181; alphabetizing, 14, 43, 81, 174; classifying, 223, 235; conjunctions, 238; contractions, 246; Dewey decimal system, 96; directions, giving of, 217; figurative language, 293; genres of literature, 308; greetings, 122; homonyms, 78; homophones, 145; hyphen use, 199; index use, 298; interjections, 147; magazines, 41, 314; newspapers, 285; nouns, 134, 204, 242, 266; phonics rules, 17, 118, 179, 225, 268; poetry, 80, 111, 293; possessives, 209; prepositional phrases, 206; pronouns, 183, 229; punctuation, 252, 254, 264; rhyming, 17, 75; road signs, 348; sentence types, 208; story analysis, 338; subject-verb agreement, 263; syllabication, 160; verbs,

182, 188, 205, 227, 263.
See also Research topics; Spelling; Vocabulary study; Writing
Lavender, growing of, 198
Law enforcement, careers in, 138, 255
Legal system, careers in, 226
Letter writing, 7, 135, 344, 359
Lighthouse locations, 222
Long division, 328
Lungs, 218

M

Magazines, 41, 314
Mammals, 193
Mathematics skills: addition, 169, 215; averages, 184; check writing, 318; circles, 21, 46; clocks, 73; conversion formula use, 178; counting, 59, 92, 123, 189, 366; days in month, 60; decimals, 279; estimating, 22; expanded notation, 323; flash cards, 99; fractions, 115; graphs, 304; long division, 328; measurement, 3, 24, 46, 65, 95, 156; metric system, 196; money, 106, 110, 113, 215; multiplication, 171, 190, 253, 284; number line, 363; numbers from 1 to 1,000, 358; ordinals, 119; percent, 143, 279; place value, 93, 194; polygons, 21; practicing math facts, 87; Roman numerals, 11; rounding numbers, 256; subtraction, 107, 215, 259; tally marks, 51; telling time, 291, 365; terms in, 184, 321
Measurement, 3, 24, 46, 65, 95, 156
Metric system, 196
Middle East countries, 203
Missionaries, 287

Molds, 154
Money, 106, 110, 113, 215
Moon phases, 211
Multiplication, 171, 190, 253, 284
Muscles, kinds of, 236
Music, 13, 56, 311, 335, 342

N

Newspapers, 285
Nouns, 134, 205, 242, 266
Number line, 363
Numbers from 1 to 1,000, 358
Nutrition, 47, 57, 164
Nuts, growing of, 84

O

Ocean animals, 108
Oceans, 200
Ordinals, 119
Organization skills, 14

P

Pandas, 354
Paramedic, career as, 255
Percent, 143, 279
Perimeter, 21
Pharmacy, career in, 12
Phonics, 17, 118, 179, 225, 268
Physical education. *See* Sports
Physician titles, 90
Pilgrims, 260, 325
Ping-Pong, rules of, 350
Pinnipeds, 82
Place value, 93, 194
Planets, 50
Plant parts, 139
Poetry, 80, 111, 293
Police officer, career as, 138
Polygons, 21
Possessives, 209
Prefixes, 70
Prepositional phrases, 206
Presidents, of U.S., 49
Pronouns, 183, 229
Publishing process, 62
Punctuation, 252, 254, 264

R

Radio communications vocabulary, 2
Railroad, transcontinental, 281
Rain forest location, 297
Reading skills, phonics, 17, 118, 179, 225, 268
Report writing. *See* Biography; Research topics; Writing
Reptiles, 296
Research topics: aardvark and anteater, 349; air quality, 299; Alaskan natives, 233; alcohol and drugs, 101; armed services, 316; basilisk lizard, 133; bird migration, 351; Boston Tea Party, 352; California Gold Rush, 231; Christmas celebrations, 336; dairy products, 164; drums, 335; endangered species, 172; extinct birds, 248; farm animals, 265; favorite author, 151; fires in American history, 282; flags of U.S., 166; Forefathers of Christianity, 357; homeless people, 295; honey, 257; insects, 176; inventions, 214; Kwanzaa principles, 362; lavender growing, 198; molds and fungi, 154; mushrooms, 289; Nobel Prize, 345; North Pole discovery, 353; ocean animals, 108; pandas, 354; paper making, 71; peanut, 334; penguins, 29; Pilgrims, 260, 325; religious groups in India, 239; Salvation Army, 142; "Star Spangled Banner, The," 63; Statue of Liberty, 302; sugar production, 286; tea making, 30; teddy

bear, 319; Thanksgiving celebrations, 332; transcontinental railroad, 281; transportation forms, 234; trees, 267; twelve disciples, 167; water purification, 243. *See also* Biography; Language arts

Respiration, 299
Revolutionary War, 16
Rhyming, 17, 75
Road signs, 348
Roman numerals, 11
Rounding numbers, 256

S

Salvation Army, history of, 142
Science: astronomy, 50, 131, 201, 202, 211; gem stones, 140; gravity, 89; periodic table of elements, 309; surface tension, 79; water forms, 170; water purification, 243; weather study, 34, 36, 68, 173, 232, 356; winter solstice, 355. *See also* Biology
Seed, parts of, 100
Sentences, kinds of, 208
Service organizations, 333
Sign language, 270
Sinai Peninsula, 32
Skeletal system, 313
Smell, sense of, 158
Soccer, rules of, 258
Social studies. *See* Civics; History
South America, countries of, 280
Spelling: Asian countries, 213; body parts, 74; days of week, 58; "eigh" pattern words, 268; European countries, 77; family words, 33; months of year, 58; names of president, vice president, 20; oceans, 200; ordinal numbers,

119; planets, 50; plurals, 55; prefixes, 70; silent "h", 121; South American countries, 280; suffixes, 85, 94, 102, 175, 179, 292; titles, 66; twelve disciples, 167. *See also* Language arts
Sports: baseball, 163; basketball, 339; football, 28; golfing, 19; Ping-Pong, 350; soccer, 258; tennis, 212
"Star Spangled Banner, The," history of, 63
State birds, 37
State capitals, 117
State trees, 315
States in U.S., 132
Statue of Liberty, 302
Story analysis, 338
Subject-verb agreement, 263
Subtraction, 107, 215, 259
Suffixes, 85, 94, 102, 175, 179, 292
Surface tension, 79
Syllabication, 160
Symphony orchestra, 342
Synonyms, 26, 31, 45, 54, 104, 105, 221

T

Table setting, 177
Taste, sense of, 155
Teeth, 69
Television broadcast, 364
Tennis, rules of, 212
Thermometer, reading of, 137
Thesaurus, use of, 54, 221, 331
Time, telling of, 291, 365
Time zones, 249
Timelines, 146, 186
Trees, 53, 237, 267, 315, 347

V

Verbs, 182, 188, 205, 227, 263
Vertebrates and invertebrates, 240

Vitamins, 83
Vocabulary study: analogies, 5; animal homes, 269; animal names, 61, 86, 148, 220; antonyms, 26, 31, 221; armor of soldiers, 35; astronomy terms, 201; body parts, 218; Christian symbols, 103; compound words, 88, 322; cooking, 25; dictionary use, 290; dinosaurs, 277; figurative language, 293; football, 28; geography, 10, 219, 320; golfing, 19; math terms, 184, 321; medical professions, 90; music, kinds of, 311; opposites, 330; poetic terms, 111; polygons, 21; prefixes, 70; publishing process, 62; radio communications, 2; soccer, 258; suffixes, 85, 94, 102, 175, 179, 292; synonyms, 26, 31, 45, 54, 104, 105, 221; teeth, 69; tennis, 212; theology terms, 274; thesaurus use, 54, 221, 331; trees, 347; weather terms, 232; weddings, 42. *See also* Language arts

W

Wars, with U.S. involvement, 149
Water, 170, 243
Weather study, 34, 36, 68, 173, 232, 356
Writing: advertisements, 128; autobiography, 337; book reports, 210; editing, 294; letters, 7, 135, 344, 359; outlines, 224; poetry, 80; television broadcast, 364. *See also* Language arts

Z

Zoos, 180, 354

The Author

Julie Lavender is the author of *Creative Sleepovers for Kids* (Prima Publishing, 2001) and numerous articles, lessons, devotions, and unit studies for *Homeschooling Today, ParentLife, Secret Place, Pathways to God,* and Group Publishing, Incorporated. Julie has her master's degree in early childhood education and taught public school for six years before becoming a stay-at-home mom. Julie is married to a medical entomologist for the U.S. Navy, and together they have four children. Julie and David have homeschooled Jeremy, Jenifer, Jeb Daniel, and Jessica for more than ten years and in six states.

Other Books of Interest

Prayers for Homeschool Moms
Michele Howe
$12.95 Hardcover
ISBN: 0–7879–6557–X

"Michele Howe has not left one stone unturned in this vast compilation of life stories and prayers from moms in the homeschool community. In *Prayers for Homeschool Moms,* Mrs. Howe guides us from the surface tensions of our lives into the inner sanctum of prayer and hope, reminding us that we are never alone."

Susan Card, author,
The Homeschool Journey

Prayers for Homeschool Moms provides emotional support for those who are balancing the multiple pressures of being a good mom, teacher, wife, and household manager—all from the heart of one seasoned homeschool mom to another. Michele Howe, a homeschool mom of fifteen years, provides practical advice through heartwarming true stories of other moms who have solved problems successfully in their own homeschool families. For the mom who is often overwhelmed by her circumstances, this ideal gift book provides welcome advice, comfort, and support through its "teaching" stories.

Kids Say the Best Things About God:
Devotions and Conversations for Families On the Go
Dandi Daley Mackall
$12.95 Hardcover
ISBN: 0–7879–6967–2

Families today are busy juggling work and play schedules, after school activities, meals, and friends. Many families yearn to strengthen their spiritual lives together. Dandi Mackall offers a two-part plan to pull families together at the start of each morning and at the end of each night. Each of these delightful devotionals, designed to appeal to children of all ages, combines a humorous quote, fun facts around a central theme, a Bible verse, and ideas for implementing that day's spiritual truth.

[Prices subject to change]

LaVergne, TN USA
08 June 2010
185398LV00004B/67/P

9 780787 968199